In the African-American Grain

In the African-American Grain

Call-and-Response in Twentieth-Century Black Fiction

JOHN F. CALLAHAN

University of Illinois Press
Urbana and Chicago

First Illinois paperback, 2001
© 1988, 2001 by the Board of Trustees
of the University of Illinois
Introduction to the Wesleyan Edition
© 1989 by John F. Callahan
All rights reserved
Manufactured in the United States of America
P 5 4 3 2 1
♾ This book is printed on acid-free paper.

Previously published with the subtitle *The Pursuit of
Voice in Twentieth-Century Black Fiction.*

Library of Congress Cataloging-in-Publication Data
Callahan, John F.
In the African-American grain : call-and-response in
twentieth-century black fiction / John F. Callahan.
p.   cm.
Includes bibliographic references and index.
ISBN 0-252-06982-X (pbk. : alk. paper)
1. American fiction—Afro-American authors—History   ·
and criticism. 2. Afro-Americans in literature. 3. American
fiction—20th century—History and criticism. I. Title.
PS153.N5C34   1988
813'.009'896073   87-5888

To RALPH ELLISON
on the *higher* frequencies

". . . and to that vision of
fraternity expressed by
Frederick D. and
Danny O'C."
February 1978

I could see him vividly, half-drunk on words and full of contempt and exaltation, pacing before the blackboard chalked with quotations from Joyce and Yeats and Sean O'Casey; thin, nervous, neat, pacing as though he walked a high wire of meaning upon which no one of us would ever dare venture. I could hear him: "Stephen's problem, like ours, was not actually one of creating the uncreated conscience of his race, but of creating the uncreated features of his face. Our task is that of making ourselves individuals. The conscience of a race is the gift of its individuals who see, evaluate, record. . . . We create the race by creating ourselves and then to our great astonishment we will have created something far more important: We will have created a culture."

—Ralph Ellison

Contents

Preface to
the Illinois Paperback

A few months ago, while in Texas, I stopped to see an old college class-mate I hadn't laid eyes on for decades. Beforehand, over e-mail—that awkward, contemporary meld of letter, telephone, and telegram whose whole seems less than the sum of its parts—he had offered contradic-tory images. His hair had gone white, he wrote. He weighed exactly the same as he had in college, but he told me that his jalopy of a body had sixty thousand miles on the odometer.

As I walked off the plane to meet him, I suddenly panicked. More than thirty-five years had intervened between my warm, insulated, in-violate memories of Fred at Holy Cross, leaping down stairs from the dining hall to the post office, all the while releasing bursts of staccato, mesmerizing words, and the present unmediated, hot glare of the Texas sun this Sunday morning in May of the year 2000. Feature by feature I tried to compose his face and failed. Seeing young, fearing old, mid-dle age missing from my imagination, I looked around and spotted a somewhat emaciated old man with white hair not far from the ramp. A quick, nearsighted glance yielded no other likely suspects.

"Hey, Fred," I strode up and put out my hand.

The old man's face went blank and, trembling slightly, he shuffled backward a step. Then and only then I saw that he bore no resemblance to my old friend beyond the frayed image dancing between my inner and outer eyes. Mortified, I apologized and walked on, eager to put some distance between me and my mistake. Then I noticed Fred, the real, unmistakable Fred. He had seen the whole thing and was chor-tling off to one side.

"I said I had white hair, not that I looked eighty-five or ninety years old," he told me.

He had changed very little; what had played tricks on me was only my befuddled expectations and less than keen eyesight.

So it is, perhaps, with the books one writes. They go out of sight but not out of mind as they go out of print and fade from view. "Them's years,"[1] Invisible Man's grandfather told him in a disturbing dream about the contents of his briefcase. And in the case of *In the African-American Grain*, after a decade's hiatus I did not know what to expect. Would I find the book a kinsman I would immediately recognize and gladly acknowledge? Or would I meet an unprepossessing stranger— a tedious, secondhand literary face I would turn away from in disappointment or even disavowal? Would I find that my book, whose composition was still alive and immediate in my mind, had become so dated as to be outdated?

As it turned out, rereading *In the African-American Grain* ten years after publication of the 1990 Wesleyan Edition, I found myself responding to its call more as a reader than an author. After all, for the past half dozen years I had been working through the late Ralph Ellison's papers, now deposited at the Library of Congress, and editing posthumous volumes of his essays and fiction, a task that culminated in the 1999 publication of *Juneteenth*. This drastic shift in scholarly focus provided critical distance from my study of call-and-response in twentieth-century black fiction and perhaps gave me a more nuanced perspective.

As I reconsider *In the African-American Grain* as published in 1988 and reissued in 1990, there is very little I would change, except perhaps to remove the hyphen from "African-American." The book strikes me as a true beginning to a needed line of inquiry into the multifaceted literary uses of the spoken word, the oral tradition. With the emergence, year by year, of more and more vernacular fiction by American writers of all backgrounds and all formal, technical persuasions, this scholarly subject only grows in importance. In the second place, I realize all the more vividly now that although call-and-response is a form specific to African American culture, writers belonging to other tributaries of the great river of American literature also make use of the participatory pattern at the heart of black culture. From Melville and Twain's calls to a discourse of democratic equality in *Moby-Dick* and *Huckleberry Finn* to the spoken and unspoken, ambiguous fraternal incantations driving novels as different as Faulkner's *Absalom, Absalom!*

and Silko's *Ceremony,* American writers have identified their readers as individuals and as "we the people."

∘ ∘ ∘

Writing *In the African-American Grain* back in the 1980s, I chose to concentrate on six exemplary—not only representative, but exemplary—African American works of fiction. Of course, as several reviewers pointed out, and as I knew at the time, many other writers could have been included, and not simply black writers. Yet there was (and is) a special case to be made for exploring call-and-response as a practice and motif in the fiction of numerous African American writers, past and present. Moreover, as the editors of *Call and Response: The Riverside Anthology of the African American Tradition* (1998) recognize, call-and-response becomes a persistent and protean pattern in almost every literary form practiced by black writers. Throughout the volume Patricia Liggins Hill and her fellow editors are sensitive to call-and-response both within individual works and in the overall oeuvres of particular writers. In a bold and fascinating move, they organized the anthology into a succession of calls and ensuing responses across genres and periods, oral and literary traditions. Their book is aware of and alert to the continuing reciprocity between oral and literary forms in African American culture from the early days to the beginning of the twenty-first century.[2]

Certainly, call-and-response as it developed and continues to evolve, preeminently but not exclusively among black writers, is an increasingly open and important field of study. In a review of *In the African-American Grain,* as salient now as when it was published in 1992, Robert Butler called for the book's "ideas [to be] applied to other seminal black texts such as Johnson's *The Autobiography of an Ex-Coloured Man* [1912], Wright's *Native Son* [1940], and Baldwin's *Go Tell It on the Mountain* [1953]." Butler rightly adds that "much could be learned by an investigation of how novels by Nella Larsen, Jessie Fauset, and Toni Morrison deal with the problem of voice. Then, too, it would be profitable to study the special handling of voice in the large and growing body of black experimental fiction. Specific works by Charles Johnson, John Edgar Wideman, Ishmael Reed, and Clarence Major offer fresh—and very different—insights on the search for authentic black voices."[3] And it should be said that other black American writers also reside along the frequencies of call-and-response. The late Leon Forrest put the pattern indelibly into his fiction; in 1988 he went so far as to add "new branches"[4] in the form of a call-and-response coda to his 1973 novel, *There Is a Tree More Ancient Than Eden.* And in Forrest's 1992 magnum opus, *Divine Days,* call-and-response fuses with the jazz riff to give his vernacular saga its bass line. Of contemporary writers, Albert Murray, Gayle Jones, Jamaica Kincaid, and Colson Whitehead have also put the voices of their characters and narrators through the prism of call-and-response in direct and indirect guises.

In the midst of this reawakening, it should not be surprising that Ernest Gaines, that indomitable Brer Tortoise of the tradition, should have cut a new path down the old road. Gaines, whose work from the 1960s though the 1980s adapts oral performance from storytelling and the black church to the page, creates another literary variation of call-and-response in his 1993 novel, *A Lesson before Dying.* Throughout this story of many voices, black and white, Jefferson, the barely literate young black man unjustly convicted of murder and sentenced to die in the electric chair, expresses himself in halting, piecemeal speech. But just before his execution, in brave acknowledgment of the man he is becoming, with excruciating effort Jefferson writes down his thoughts and feelings in a dairy. There, in appreciation for the teacher who has worked with him and become his friend, he signifies who he is in an eloquent black vernacular that must be heard to be read. A far more unlikely character than Miss Jane Pittman in Gaines's eponymous novel, *The Autobiography of Miss Jane Pittman,* Jefferson, by telling "who he's for," extends the transforming reach of oral and written call-and-response patterns. With his creation of Jefferson, Gaines goes beyond even the fault line of American social hierarchy occupied by Celie in Alice Walker's novel *The Color Purple.*

African American writers use the call-and-response tradition as a bass line in their pursuit of voice, and their work is also a call to other American writers seeking their own voices. That shared pursuit of voice, as Ralph Ellison has insisted in urgent, democratic terms, is nothing less than each and every writer's attempt to account for the American experience. Although *In the African-American Grain* focused on twentieth-century black fiction, other writers like Melville, Twain, Davis, Chopin, and Faulkner were present "on the lower frequencies." It now seems palpable and inevitable that future explorations of the influence of the oral tradition—traditions, really—will consider brown, red, white, and yellow writers as well as black. Why shouldn't studies of the oral tradition and the evolving literary variations of call-and-response also discuss the relationship among the diverse fictions of Sherman Alexi, Rudolfo Anaya, Saul Bellow, Louise Erdrich, Gish Jen, Scott Momaday, Tillie Olsen, Leslie Silko, Amy Tan, and Helena Viramontes, for example—not forgetting, by the way, the role of the spoken word and participatory, conversational form in turn-of-the-century novels such as Bellow's *Ravelstein* (2000), Stanley Crouch's *Don't the Moon Look Lonesome* (2000), and Philip Roth's *Human Stain* (2000)?

In the twenty-first century there is no going back; this is fast becoming more and more a nation of color, literally as well as metaphorically. And yet there is a cautionary note. If we are not scrupulous and careful, *E pluribus unum* could become too unearned and glib a metaphor for American culture. It is too easy (and too false), as Al Gore noted in his thoughtful remarks on race and the body politic, for "a member of the majority [to] say, 'Let's just transcend this distinction,' without any apparent appreciation for what the distinction means in the life of the person you're trying to communicate with." In the then vice president's mind, transformation on racial matters is "a two-step process. You have to first establish absolute and genuine mutual respect for difference. And that respect for difference has to include both an appreciation for the unique suffering that has come about because of the difference and the unique gifts and contributions that have come about because of the difference. Then and only then, in Gore's view, are Americans able truly "to embrace all the elements that we have in common in the human spirit."[5]

So it is perhaps with the study of American literature and its many-hued writers, characters, and readers. In this regard the progression suggested by *In the African-American Grain* involves critical and moral responsibilities as well as rights. The book's movement from the "who *you* for" of its introduction to the "who *we* for" of its conclusion is a possible harbinger of the mingling to come both in literature and in literary scholarship. Future studies will cross color lines. Although often drawn in our time in order to identify, respect, and embrace long-neglected or scorned voices and traditions, these lines can also somewhat dam up and isolate naturally free-flowing tributaries. As a consequence, the immense potential momentum of American literature's mighty Mississippi may be diminished. Like Ernest Gaines's Miss Jane Pittman, writers know that water will run free whether human beings like it or not. The charge to scholars is that they, too, like the writers they interpret, forge respectful, rigorous connections where they find them. Across the vast territory of American literature, ritual and improvisation flow together over the common ground of speech and performance, and the African American oral tradition is an essential bedrock of that ground.

o o o

On a frequency both higher and lower, personal and professional, I confess to a shock of delayed recognition. *In the African-American Grain* was the farthest thing from my mind during the more than three years that I worked to edit a book out of the many manuscripts and fragments belonging to Ralph Ellison's forty-years-in-the-making, unfinished second novel. Along the way I almost forgot that I had dedicated *In the African-American Grain* to Ellison, relegating that fact to the underground of my consciousness. At least I thought I had, as I was attempting to discern—not create, but discern—a work of art within what Ellison once called, referring to early drafts of *Invisible Man*, a "seemingly intractable body of material."[6] In the end it was impossible not to conclude that Ellison—who had boldly aimed at an epic novel charting the immense, uneasily settled moral and racial territory of America—had not managed to thread his way out of his self-designed labyrinth. Nevertheless, a central, gripping narrative began to stand out in clear relief from the maze of manuscripts, for Ellison had settled on the heart of his story. It is the story of Alonzo Hickman, jazzman turned minister, and his relationship from birth to death with Bliss, the little boy who looks white, talks and is raised black, runs off passing for white, winds up as the race-baiting Senator Sunraider, and dies from wounds suffered at the hands of an assassin who is his unacknowledged, part-black, part-white, part-red son.

Coming to rest on the story, I realized that, as much or more than anything else, the dimensions of call-and-response in Ellison's prose and his technique had given the tortured kinship between Hickman and Bliss a magical, original power. The center of *Juneteenth*, of course, is the antiphonal exchanges of the resurrection service on Juneteenth night, climaxed by the response of the boy preacher, Bliss, to Reverend Hickman's call. Only later on do we, as readers, discover the fullness of call-and-response in the lives of Hickman and Bliss/Sunraider. In the assassination scene, however, Ellison reunites the two men by enacting the pattern of call-and-response in that national church of idealism and cynicism, the U.S. Senate. Formerly, the senator betrayed the sacred purpose of call-and-response. Profaning the pattern, he issued false calls designed to serve only his ruthless ambition. Perversely, he even "does" Hickman as he puts down his people in a speech on the senate floor moments before his assassination. But suddenly, reeling from the impact of several bullets, Senator Sunraider loses control and inadvertently peels away the rind of his identity, exposing the vulnerable heart beneath. "'Lord,' he heard," his standard idiom giving way to the African American vernacular he thought he had left behind, "'LAWD, WHY HAST THOU . . .'" To his astonishment, the senator recognizes Hickman's voice responding from the gallery above him: "*For Thou hast forsaken . . . me.*'"[7] At the hospital Senator Adam Sunraider calls for Hickman, and only Hickman, to be brought to his bedside. There, for the duration of the narrative, the two men reenact the past in the present moment and the present in the past through antiphonal exchanges of stunning variety and complexity.

"Sometimes," Ellison explained in an introductory note to "Night-Talk," published in 1969, Hickman and Bliss/Sunraider "actually converse, sometimes the dialogue is illusory and occurs in the isolation of their individual minds, but through it all it is antiphonal in form and an anguished attempt to arrive at the true shape and substance of a sundered past and its meaning."[8] When the stakes are those of life and death—literally for Senator Sunraider, figuratively for Hickman and "that vanished tribe" he represents, "the American Negroes,"[9] as well as for the nation—call-and-response lends its transforming power to the action. In the mind, between the voices of long-estranged kinfolk of experience and culture, and on the page, the old African American pattern of call-and-response revivifies the promise of liberation given that first Juneteenth in 1865 and renewed ever since in life and art.

Finally, I am reminded that, while at work on his second novel, Ellison wrote of the "troubling suspicion," shared in different ways by all Americans, "that whatever else the true American is, he is also somehow black."[10] Upon the reissue, once more, of *In the African-American Grain,* I'd like to think that in some measure this book prepared the way for the editing of Ellison's *Juneteenth*. Certainly it alerted me to the essential meaning and the endless literary possibilities of call-and-response. I hope, too, that in its new printing it exemplifies some of the unpredictability and indivisibility of American life, literature, and personality.

John F. Callahan
October 2000

NOTES

1. Ralph Ellison, *Invisible Man* (New York: Random House, 1952; Vintage International Edition, 1982), p. 26.

2. *The Riverside Anthology* takes an expansive, experimental approach to the African American literary tradition. Unfortunately, the volume is marred by an occasional tendentious, even ad hominem headnote.

3. Robert J. Butler, "Answering the Call," *African American Review* 26, no. 4 (Winter 1992), 685.

4. Leon Forrest's inscription in the author's copy of the 1988 edition of *There Is a Tree More Ancient Than Eden*.

5. Albert Gore Jr., quoted by Nicholas Lemann, "The Political Scene: Gore without a Script," *The New Yorker,* July 31, 2000, pp. 63, 62.

6. Ellison's statement to the National Book Award Foundation, 1959, container 61, Ellison Papers, Library of Congress, Washington, D.C.

7. Ralph Ellison, *Juneteenth,* ed. John F. Callahan (New York: Random House, 1999), p. 26.

8. Ralph Ellison, Note to "Night Talk," *Quarterly Review of Literature* 16, nos. 3–4 (1969), 317.

9. Ellison, *Juneteenth,* p. vii (dedication).

10. Ralph Ellison, *The Collected Essays of Ralph Ellison,* ed. John F. Callahan (New York: Random House/The Modern Library, 1995), p. 583.

Introduction to
the Wesleyan Edition

Back in New Haven the summer after *In the African-American Grain* was published, I looked up Roy Fitch, my old boss in the mail room at Security Insurance. Although I had been to New Haven many times in the intervening years, I had not sought him out. More than once I had thought to, yet each time I drew back, afraid I'd find him gone or, worse, discover that we had become strangers. Perhaps too, after all that Roy had given me, I felt a little ashamed to return empty-handed. But now I had something to give this man I had not seen for twenty-five years, who nevertheless found his way into the autobiographical tale I told at the beginning of my book.

So I surprised Roy one morning in front of the building he looks after on Church Street, not far from the plebeian end of the New Haven green at Church and Chapel. As we crossed the street, I recognized familiar turns of phrase spoken like blues refrains in the rising octaves of his voice. Trying to keep in step with his slow, stooped, but from time to time deceptively accelerating walk, I was moved by his patient pride, his quiet energy and dignity—as always, held in reserve. I felt again his sense of who he was and where he came from. Across the street we had coffee in a place of upscale design and surpassingly egalitarian plastic, where you could get croissants with unsalted butter, bagels in sundry flavors, and even a jelly doughnut—I was back in New Haven after all.

"Not too long after you left, Johnny, I started teaching black history," Roy Fitch told me. "One of the first courses in New Haven.

"I went to Africa in 1970," he said after a while in that blackened

Yankee drawl of his. "But that's another story," he chuckled gently as he stirred more cream into his coffee.

Half telling that story, Roy warmed up. Before long he was jamming in the easy, comfortable, familiar yet deceptive rhythm I remembered. The bite was there, too, on the beat every time. Then, as I began to anticipate and count on it, without warning, like a veteran pitcher changing speeds—Eddie Lopat, maybe, or Satch Paige—Roy abandoned the beat for a syncopated rhythm. During the long break of his solo, he told a story from the old days I had never heard before.

"You remember that Executive Vice President at Security, Johnny? The one with the loud voice who'd yell at the people that worked for him and yell louder if the other executives were in hearing distance. Always showin off." I remembered all right. I remembered a bastard with a pot-bellied voice; he'd caught me dallying with his secretary more than once as I picked up the afternoon mail.

"Shortly after the boss hired him," Roy continued, "I saw him eyin me when we'd speak. 'Roy,' he said one day when he had me cornered, 'Roy, where you from?'

"'New Haven,' I told him. He kept lookin at me screwin up his eyes like I was a treed possum. I just looked back at him. I'm telling you he had eyes like a hunter without a permit.

"'No, I mean where you from, Roy?'

"I knew what he wanted, Johnny, and it wasn't his business, but he wouldn't quit. Every time he saw me he'd screw up his eyes like he had a ratchet upside his head. Ask the same question all over again like I hadn't heard him the first or second time. He didn't want me to have the satisfaction of knowin he was mad, so the madder he got, the slower and more patient he made his voice.

"I knew it was his way of telling me he was from the deep South, but that he wasn't a cracker. But I'm tellin you, he could control his voice some but not his complexion. His face, his neck, got redder and redder."

Roy's hands closed around his coffee cup.

"Like most crackers in those days, Johnny, he thought any black person up here's got to be from Mississippi. Made him feel more at home, like he belonged. Anyway, it got so every damn day he'd ask me: 'Roy, where you from?' He'd go that far and no more. Finally, he asked me in front of some visitors from Georgia he was trying to impress, 'Roy, where you from?' I didn't pay them no mind. I looked all the way through his mean little pig eyes and told him: 'Mr. So-and-So, I'm from New Haven. My parents were born in New Haven. My people before them came to New Haven in the early 1800s, before Mississippi was a state.'"

As Roy spoke, I saw how blue his eyes were—sheepishly I realized I had forgotten and called them brown in my book. But they were light blue—much lighter than mine as they caught the morning light. "What happened?" I asked after blinking a couple of times.

"Nothing," he said. "Not then. He walked off, that's all." He chuckled again, and the wide open, defiant, come-get-me-if-you-can timbre of the sound reminded me of another man, and in my mind's ear Roy's tenor laugh suddenly mingled with the rolling thunder of Ralph Ellison's baritone. He went on to tell me that several months later the executive's wife had approached him at a company party. "Roy," she said, "Art tells me you're from New Haven."

"She took as much pleasure in that as I did, Johnny. Like we'd been in cahoots the whole time, and I'd never laid eyes on her before." Roy stopped.

"Hell," I responded after Roy's story began to sink in, "my father's parents didn't come to New Haven from Ireland until the turn of the century. And my mother's people not too much earlier than that."

"That's right, Johnny," he said. "You weren't here until after the Civil War."

After that, Roy cruised back to the beat of our original conversation, so smoothly you'd almost never know he'd broken rhythm while telling the story. He didn't follow up by telling any story of ancestors shielding runaway slaves or going South in union blue as soldiers in the Grand Army of the Republic, though I was sure some had done both. And he didn't tell me how funny the first wave of Irish looked to his great-grandparents. He let all that lie. He opened and closed the book I'd given him, overlooking my inscription—deliberately, I thought. He stood up, thanked me for the coffee, and said he'd be in touch. Then he went his way, back to the tiny office inside the glass door of the building he watched over, and I went mine.

Months later, while I was teaching "My Kinsman, Major Molineaux," I found that I was utterly focused on a line I'd all but overlooked before. "May not one man have several voices, Robin, as well as two complexions?" Hawthorne's young man from the provinces is asked by a new acquaintance among the variously disguised rebellious citizens of the town. That's it, I thought. That's the reason I've been uneasy about "the pursuit of voice" as the subtitle for *In the African-American Grain*.

At first, I had been pleased with my phrase's echo of the Declaration of Independence, particularly since the new nation's first narrative was preeminently both a critical and an imaginative act of rhetoric. But even before the book was published, and without knowing why, I regretted not using call-and-response. Gradually I realized that although "pursuit of voice" expresses the individual's inalienable right (and need) to discover his or her unique voice, it does not evoke the lovely, dangerous, vulnerable, mysterious, sometimes magical mingling implied and inspired by call-and-response. Recalling Roy Fitch's story, and his masterful use of narrative technique as self-definition, I decided that for the paperback edition, I'd have the satisfaction of a title that tells where my book is from.

In the African-American Grain traces *some* of the variations and adaptations of the call-and-response pattern worked out in twentieth century black fiction. In their approaches to fiction, the different writers whose work I discuss exemplify the continuing struggle to imagine and realize a truly inclusive and vernacular democratic culture in this country. For black American writers, the pursuit of voice has been an arduous, distinct challenge and a task bound up with the tradition of call-and-response. The writers I have written about (and many others for that matter) sought, as William Carlos Williams did in *In the American Grain*, "to rename the things seen"—and also the things heard. Perhaps for most writers "things seen" often come to consciousness because of what's been heard or overheard. Yet because of their proximity to a living oral tradition and because of the respect given to word of mouth by African-American culture, black writers are particularly well equipped to adapt to fiction some of the nuances of performance essential in storytelling. In both oral and literary traditions, complexities of audience were bound up first with survival and then with life-and-death matters of power. These circumstances led black storytellers and writers to a heightened awareness of rhetorical occasion. Consequently, for reasons of craft, culture, and social urgency, black writers tend to imbue their fiction with the multifaceted, improvisational, participatory, transforming strategies of call-and-response.

At some point, literary criticism, like fiction, comes to be a complex act of personal and cultural autobiography. However well veiled by abstract rhetoric or tightly analytical argument, the themes critics pursue are the themes of their lives, the stuff of their identities. Rereading *In the African-American Grain*, I am struck by the extent to which the book tracks a double progression—of successive writers' attempts to bend the patterns and assumptions of call-and-response to their untold, unwritten, unvoiced stories, and of my urge to mingle the autobiographical implications of call-and-response with its usefulness to literary criticism. Like Roy Fitch's story, each of these progressions relies on a continuous narrative beat, from which the individual voice departs and to which it returns, sometimes returning so changed that those who listen are changed too.

After the opening call of "Who You For?" and throughout the chapters on individual writers, I tried for a mingling of voices, tried to identify sufficient common ground to prepare readers to engage the closing question: "Who We For?" And who knows?—to paraphrase Invisible Man's closing, and at the same time open-(ing) question: if the book is accessible enough, suggestive enough, familiar and unfamiliar enough, it might call you who read it to test your voices on the mingled frequencies of American culture.

John F. Callahan
August 1989

Acknowledgments

I am grateful to Lewis and Clark College for sabbatical leave and faculty research support, and to President Leon Botstein and the faculty of Bard College for appointment as a Bard Center Fellow during some of the time it took to write this book. A number of other people have my thanks and appreciation: my brother, Brian Callahan, who proofed the manuscript at a crucial time; Sharon Barnes, my good angel on the word processor, and G. J. Barker-Benfield, a.k.a. Ben, who read and commented on the entire manuscript as if it were his own. And mostly, I am grateful to Sherman Paul. He read a not so early draft and told the truth. "Still very much in the rough," he said, and stayed with me all the way. He read the manuscript again, chapter by chapter as I revised, and his responses often called me back to more authentic lines of argument and voice.

Others, too, are present in this book: My mother, Margaret Dinnean Callahan, and my late father, for whom I am named, passed on a love of stories and the ancestors who told them. But, first and last, I want to acknowledge my daughters, Eve and Sasha, and my wife, Susan, storytellers singly and together, for bearing with me and bearing me up during the more than five years it took to write this book.

Author's Note

Black, Negro, Afro-American, African-American: these terms recall a unique historical condition and experience; namely, the capture of Africans in their homelands and their subsequent enslavement in the New World. Though these words have different connotations and tonalities, each expresses something of the complex mixture of bloodlines and cultures that followed from American slavery. Each appears in this book but primarily, I use African-American to signify both African descent and the African contribution to American culture.

Originally, however, the book was called *In the Afro-American Grain*. In a 1985 conversation Alice Walker suggested I change Afro-American to African-American. At first I resisted because I preferred the sound of Afro-American and perhaps because I thought that term would be acceptable to everyone. But as I reconsidered, I came to believe that as a safe and somewhat vague term, Afro-American might lessen the impact of what I had to say about call-and-response as a narrative pattern adapted from an oral tradition with strong roots in African as well as American culture. I also wanted a term that would imply the connection between art and politics, specifically between literary acts of citizenship and the struggle for freedom and nationhood on the continents of America and Africa.

So now, appropriate to "the strange phosphorus" of American life explored in *In the American Grain*, my title is inspired by two American writers of different yet reciprocal sensibilities: William Carlos Williams and Alice Walker.

In the African-American Grain

CHAPTER 1

Who You For?: Voice and the African-American Fiction of Democratic Identity

1

Stories were the skins on the potatoes and voices the brine on the corned beef when I was a boy growing up in New Haven. I heard and loved, then for a while mocked and resisted this "book of the people" — W. B. Yeats's paradoxical phrase for the flow of culture from the spoken to the written word — but I always absorbed it. Now I remember the words and images, the rhythms and voices of its storytelling with feelings of wonder and kinship.

In June of 1962, a few months before my grandfather died, President Kennedy came to New Haven to receive an honorary degree — the best of both worlds, he said, a Harvard education and a Yale degree. I was in college at the time, and I did not share my family's enthusiasm for John Kennedy. My resistance acted out an American variation of the war between the Irish. Rebellious, skeptical, ungenerous, I saw my father's allegiance to Jack Kennedy as a symbolic response to the Yankees who advanced in the Connecticut bureaucracy and held him back, though his qualifications were better than theirs. So we were told and so I believed because I loved my father even in those days when I bent my energies to escape what I regarded as the Irish-Catholic ghetto of his life and mind.

"You're not interested in Kennedy," my father told me the morning of JFK's arrival. "Don't go downtown. I want you to take Pop-Pop over to the corner so he can see the president when the car goes by." "Okay," I said, and uncharitably imagined my father downtown outside the restraining ropes craning his neck to catch a glimpse of his sweet Jack. I felt contemptuous of my father because he didn't have savvy or connections enough to get a ticket to the Yale commencement. Besides, I was uncomfortable at the prospect of having to steer a run-down old man, my grandfather, out to the curb to see President Kennedy when his motorcade drove up the street from the New Haven airport, less than a mile from our house. I imagined neighbors in every house parting their curtains to stare at me as if I were the Callahan responsible for bringing the pig into the parlor.

I liked my grandfather, but on this day the quality of kinship was strained. Barney O'Callaghan was eighty-six or seven. He had lost the O' and the g, some would say the breath of the old country, to an immigration officer somewhere between Ellis Island and New Haven harbor while I, I am ashamed to admit now, entertained fantasies of Anglicizing my name to Call. Until he died, my grandfather remained something of a stranger in America. He came from the Irish midlands before the turn of the century, some said with a small price on his head, and in New Haven worked the trolley cars for forty years. As he told it, on snowy nights, exposed on open-air platforms, he presented an easy target for snowballs when he drove his trolley through the Yale campus, for decades alien country for the Irish. Now he had cataracts and a painful, humiliating fatal disease whispered about but unrevealed to his grandchildren. His was a slow, toiling walk, and once we got across the street I wondered how his veiled eyes would see anything more than a quick blur from the presidential limousine. Under my breath I cursed my father's benevolence—at my expense, I thought bitterly.

While the two of us waited, my grandfather was uncharacteristically quiet, so much so that I began to wish for one of his stories.But he said nothing, and I began to hear in my mind's ear, more vividly than the details of the stories, the rhythms of his speech and the melancholy shifts of his voice. I became a little boy again waiting for the color to increase in his face and his words as his breath grew warm with whiskey poured from bottles he'd hidden from his tee-totaling, lace-curtain Irish wife. Sunday mornings we'd sit alone in the corner of a high-ceiling Victorian parlor whose sliding wooden doors he kept shut. We had an alliance in those days, and somehow I knew I reminded my grandfather not of my father but of himself when he was a boy in Ireland. I knew, too, that whatever his tricks, his Irish coldness and parsimony, my grandfather loved me. He didn't need to tell me. I saw it in his eyes even then beginning to be filmed with cataracts, heard it in his sighing brogue, absorbed it from the images he conjured and colored, the stories he told of troubles in Ireland and hard years in this country.

Now as my grandfather leaned hard against me on the streetcorner, I forgot my resistance and looked at him. I began to be moved by his face, the hooked nose like one of the birds in the *Book of Kells*, the lines like crooked furrows on the small homestead back in County Cavan, the million tiny wrinkles quickening as if to make up for the twinkle now all but gone from his eyes. I decided I owed this old man something. The least I could do was get him a good look at President John Fitzgerald Kennedy.

Flashing red lights and the high notes of a siren startled me. As the motorcade approached, I took my grandfather's arm and led him to the spot where the limousines would turn the corner. The escort car went by. Kennedy's car was next, and I put my arm tightly around my grandfather's shoulder to press him forward. I pointed carefully at the imaginary spot where his eyes would get the best view of Kennedy who, I thought with secret exaltation, was going to pass no more than two or three feet from where we stood. I saw him all right. He looked tanned, thoughtful, and suddenly very Irish as his expression changed into an ironic and fraternal smile that grasped the scene before him. Who knows, I thought, maybe images flickered before his eyes of times past when he'd made the rounds of his South Boston Congressional district with his own grandfather, Honey Fitz.

"See him? Did you see him?" I demanded of my grandfather who had turned his head toward me. "Didn't you see him?" I asked again, impatient because I was pretty sure my grandfather had been looking at me while Kennedy was riding by. All of a sudden, impatient himself, my grandfather knocked away my pointing finger. Then he looked at me for a long, quiet moment. He moved his face into mine, eyes a murky yellow from age and the sun. "I never thought, Jack," he told me, "when I came to this country, I'd see the day an Irish-Catholic would be president." He shook his head. "I never thought it." Without another word he tugged on my arm and nudged me up the street as if I were his seeing-eye shillelagh.

God-damn, I thought. I bring this guy out here to see Kennedy when he doesn't need to see him at all. What he needs is to tell his story. And that June morning the cunning Irishman, who'd used me to get a drink and used drink to loosen his tongue those Sunday mornings long ago, used Jack Kennedy to tell his story and used his fading voice to make me take another look at Kennedy and maybe myself.

My grandfather's voice opened the living book of the past. The stories told by him and by my mother's Aunt Lizzie—Hoo-Hoo was the name I gave her—were meant to stick to the ribs of my mind, to do double duty as nourishment and instruction. When at sixteen in 1957, I went to work as a mailboy in the old New Haven Bank on Chapel Street, I began to see and hear the truth of this spoken "book of the people" the hard way. The stories attuned me to what I was hearing in the bank about Micks and Negroes—they didn't say Negroes. I began to understand that what was happening had roots in the past and to remember vividly things I'd dismissed as the sentimental stuffed animals of childhood. I was learning that despite my wish that things be otherwise, there were choices to be made, allegiances to be declared—complex allegiances. From my present vantage point I see that back in the New Haven Bank I was beginning to believe that the written word held its purpose and its power most eloquently when those who used it remembered and built off its sources in the spoken word.

"Well," I overheard a bank officer say about me soon after I'd been hired, "if the little funny Mick doesn't work out, we can always bring in a Nigger." He was on the phone looking out the window, his long legs stretched over a corner of his desk. He chuckled until he saw me standing there and then showed no embarrassment, only annoyance that his Italian secretary had broken protocol by letting me into the office without his okay.

Before I knew it, some debris from my first day at parochial school floated to the surface of my mind. As an out-of-the-parish kid at St. Francis in Fair Haven, a formerly Irish enclave turned heavily Italian, I underwent initiation in the schoolyard at the hands of several tough, streetwise Italians. Smaller than my eight years and vaguely afraid of a beating, I was reassured by a seemingly good-natured question. "Do you know the definition of an Irishman?" the biggest of the Italians asked. "No," I bit, "what?" "A Nigger turned inside-out," they shouted in unison then pummeled me harmlessly but humiliatingly, and stole my Yankee baseball hat. "Dimag is ours," a kid called the Mouth yelled in parting, his voice sharp and remorseless as the crack of ball on bat when Joe DiMaggio hit one of his vicious line drives.

Now at sixteen, scared speechless that my dreams of going away to Holy Cross, my father's college, were about to evaporate along with this job as a mailboy, I was puzzled by the bank vice-president's reference to a hypothetical and symbolic but at that moment very real African-American. Flustered, I remembered my mother's father — Jeremiah Dinnean, a big-boned, reddish, six-foot-four farmer turned tough Irish cop — telling a relative who was going to vote for Dwight Eisenhower over Adlai Stevenson in 1952: "I'd sooner vote for a Nigger than vote the Republican ticket." Earlier, when I was two or three, my mother, tied down with another baby, had attached me to the clothesline with a harness, but Grandpa Dinnean raised so much hell that I was freed. He was a carpenter, too, and raised vegetables, to me a giant of a man, whom I loved and feared. By 1952, when I was eleven, he was nearly eighty and his hands shook so much he let me lick the foam from the outside of his glass of beer. But when I piped up that day in 1952 and said, "Do you mean Levi Jackson?" he paid no attention. Back in the bank I wondered why the vice-president associated my alleged bumbling — I'd been set up by an elderly Yankee afraid that I was after his job — with Negroes. What did he mean, bring in a Nigger? What about Levi Jackson? I thought, but did not say. I was too scared, and so instinctively I composed a mask to hide my feelings of anger and bewilderment. But as I tried to contain the chaos around me, images of Levi Jackson ran wild across the broken field of my mind.

Almost ten years before that sixteen-year-old's day at the bank, Levi Jackson broke my little boy's heart, not once but twice in six months. He was a hell of a football player for Yale and captain of the 1949 team. But, you see, my father had gone to Holy Cross along with many other Irish-Catholics from New Haven, and in their

5

continuing battle with the Yankees, they longed for "the Cross" to come in and beat Yale. Chances slim to none in football, but basketball favored Holy Cross, especially in 1950, the year of All-American Bob Cousy.

That October my father did not take me to Yale Bowl, but I listened to the broadcast too excited to sit down when, the score tied 7-7 in the fourth quarter, Holy Cross made a first down on Yale's one yard line. For three downs Yale held, and on fourth down Levi Jackson clinched the goal line stand. Maybe he batted down a pass, maybe he made the tackle, I don't remember, but I do remember his name riding over the static that filled our small kitchen. Then Yale went 99 yards for the winning touchdown. I say Yale, but I remember Levi Jackson running 99 yards on the first play from scrimmage. That's wrong; when I checked recently, I found that on the drive Jackson ran for 24 and 68 yards. Curiously, the *Yale Daily News* praised some big fullback who, returning from an injury, scored the winning touchdown. But I still hear the name of Levi Jackson, the only black man on the field, who, for me, singlehandedly beat my team.

"Don't worry," my father told me the following March, when I asked if Levi Jackson played on the basketball team, "he won't help Yale tonight. Not against Cousy." Once inside the Payne Whitney Gymnasium, we settled down on the visitors' side, surrounded by people wearing purple armbands, holding purple pennants, and stamping their feet to the beat of a huge purple drum. For weeks Holy Cross had been ranked first in the country, and sure enough the game began reassuringly. Ten minutes into the half, Holy Cross was ahead 20-12. Then I heard hoots of laughter and saw a chunky black man hustle out on the court. "This isn't the Yale Bowl," one of the Holy Cross rooters shouted at Levi Jackson. "You gotta bounce the ball and think. Not just grin and run."

Defiantly, two or three times Levi Jackson dribbled unmolested almost to the foul line and threw in unorthodox, improvised running one-handed push shots. Another time he stole the ball from the magician Cousy and fed a teammate for a breakaway basket. Yale trailed only 33-31 at the half.[1] Jackson returned in the second half, maybe scoring his third basket, maybe not, but I know he got in Cousy's hair. He wasn't in the game at the end when Cousy was called for traveling and a guy named Pocock scored a couple of baskets to give Yale the win, 66-62. On the way out I realized I'd left my pennant back where we'd been sitting. Tears were coming down by the time I retrieved the purple banner now rumpled with a grimy footprint casting a shadow over the archaic gothic lettering that spelled out Holy Cross. Looking at the ground to hide my face, I was too embarrassed to hold my father's hand, but I heard the voices of stragglers. None of the Yalies mentioned Levi Jackson, and though the disappointed Holy Cross fans didn't use his name, the words they spoke referred to him. "He won't be back," they said. "Yeah, if they let him graduate." My father now had me by the hand. "Next year they got no shines."

I thought of my father shining my shoes Saturday nights for Sunday mass and of old black men at the railroad station snapping their rags with a crack to signal that they were done with the shine and that the man next in line should lift his right shoe on the polished iron rail on top of the beaten-up wooden box full of shoeshine paraphernalia. "Oh, that's a way of talking," my father told me when I asked him what shines had to do with the basketball game. "Besides," he said, "Jackson didn't do much damage. Cousy was tired, and they got a couple of bad calls at the end." Maybe so, I thought, and didn't talk back. But in my little boy's mind Levi Jackson had once more performed heroically the anti-hero's role in an athletic morality play that cut my little world further down to size.

These flash fires of memory fueled my desire to blindside the bank officer by speaking Levi Jackson's name. I knew damn well that this immaculately groomed Yankee who sat smugly disposing of Micks and Niggers had probably stood to cheer in Yale Bowl, all mussed up, as Levi Jackson rallied Yale past Holy Cross and other teams that mattered more, though he and his bunch would have found it humiliating to lose to Jesuit Holy Cross. Levi Jackson had been quick, crafty, and strong; skillful, useful, and smart—traits Pop-Pop and Hoo-Hoo had drummed into me as handy for survival and, along with luck, essential to success in the big world. And now into the trivial mix of whether to fire a part-time mailboy, the vice-president lumped Irish and African-Americans as a contemptible, expendable lower caste. Wishing for Levi Jackson's help on this treacherous field of combat and knowing I would not find him or his like anywhere in the New Haven Bank, I kept quiet. I had a name to speak but so far no voice, no form, and no audience for my unfolding story.

For one thing, I had little or no context beyond my immediate experience. My fate linked to African-Americans by that Yankee bank officer, I became more alert and sympathetic to black Americans my own age and younger who, though cursed, spat upon, and beaten, put their lives and voices on the line to uphold the law of the land and integrate public schools in the South. But I did not know of the longstanding Irish/African-American connection in this country. And I knew little or nothing about the complex, ambiguous record of Irish-Americans on the matter of race.

I did not know that while a teenage slave in Baltimore, Frederick Douglass was told by a couple of Irish dockhands that "it was a pity so fine a fellow should be a slave for life." Moved by young man Douglass, the two Irish offered him rebellious radical advice. "They went so far as to tell me that I ought to run away, and go to the North; that I should find friends there, and that I should then be as free as anybody." Neither did I know that from the North Douglass had gone to Ireland during the famine of 1845-46 and was welcomed and called "the Black O'Connell of the United States"[2] by "the Liberator," Daniel O'Connell. I did not know that while in Ireland this same Douglass came across a music whose wild, mournful, melancholy sounds and "same *wailing notes*"[3] reminded him of the sorrow songs of his struggling people. I did not know that before the Civil War, as Douglass told the disheartening tale in 1853, "The Irish people, warm-hearted, generous, and sympathizing with the oppressed everywhere, when they stand upon their own green island, are instantly taught, on arriving in this Christian country, to hate and despise the colored people. They are taught to believe that we eat the bread which of right belongs to them."[4]

I did not know that only ten days after many Irish-Americans fought valiantly at Gettysburg for the Union Army, others, crazed at the prospect of leaving jobs and families to fight, they were told, for black freedom, exploded into the streets of New York in the brutal Draft Riots of 1863. For three days predominantly Irish mobs went on a rampage, beating, looting, and lynching throughout the Negro section of the city, not resting until they had attacked and burned down the Colored Orphans Asylum. And neither did I know of the counterpoise exerted by other Irish-Americans. The police chief, a man named John Kennedy, was nearly killed leading his men, mostly Irish-Americans, against the mobs. And Al Smith's father, a fireman, risked his life to save more than a few black lives. He knew, as would his son, the governor and presidential candidate, and as President John Kennedy would come to know during the civil rights struggle of the 1960s, that on these shores African-Americans were his countrymen as much as the Irish. The black Irish: a metaphor to conjure with in this republic—and not wholly a metaphor. For there were Moors in Ireland before the English kings, and in this country more than a few African-Americans are also Irish-Americans, and Irish-Americans also African-Americans.

Going through college I worked for two black men at Security Insurance. Of different breeds, together they taught me a great deal about the hard work of becoming a man. The president's chauffeur answered to Bill Jackson, but his name he revealed as the summer wore on was William X. H. Jackson. "X is for the unknown; my daddy gave me that name when I was five years old," he said well before he went to hear Malcolm X speak in Hartford. He wouldn't tell me much of what Malcolm said; he both trusted and did not trust me too much for that, but his pride and passion told me something more was in the wind than the orgy of hate the white press associated with Malcolm's political preaching. Bill Jackson's improvising energy and the unpredictable range of his voice made me envy and seek kinship with the stoicism and fluidity through which this man kept the spirit flowing in his stories.

"You just a kid wid words," Jackson told me one day. "Listen! I'm tellin' you what I know." When I went back to college I wrote a story about him called "What I Know." But I didn't know much, and I wrote less than I knew. I left out the important things: his prolonged silent challenge to me after, culpable and unculpable, I'd hollered, "Hey, Bill, you black bastard!"; the protection he gave me from a custodian who thought us both lesser breeds; his insistence on treating me and the president's son as equals; and, not least, his trickster's way of teaching me how to drive a clutch car by jumping out of the company jeep in noontime traffic on one side of the New Haven Green and ordering me to pick him up on the other. William

X. H. Jackson told and taught me many things I wouldn't have learned otherwise, things essential to my evolving voice and story.

Leroy E. Fitch was another of the very few men I knew in old New Haven. Everyone at Security called him Roy; he'd have preferred Mr. Fitch, but under no circumstances did he want these people messing around with Leroy. In-house, Roy Fitch was head of the mailroom. Outside, he was thirty-second, verging on thirty-third degree in the Prince Hall Masonic lodge. I didn't get to know him until I got kicked out of Holy Cross for a year and was kept on to help that ornery custodian I mentioned before, but by now Bill Jackson was gone and I had no protection.

Why Leroy Fitch rescued me I still don't completely understand. He was of the old school; he called his father a letter carrier, never a mailman. He and Bill Jackson were civil, but Bill would no more have mentioned Malcolm X to Roy than Roy would have confided in Bill about Prince Hall affairs. Besides, Roy Fitch had a bone to pick with me. I was still a Yankee fan and during the 1960 World Series I made a comment to the telephone operator in front of Roy about Vern Law being the only white man on the Pittsburgh Pirates team. (I'd picked up that expression from a friend of mine—Tom Cooke, an Irish-Catholic Yalie with some pretensions to WASP idiom and sensibility, though to be fair I better add that he also introduced me to jazz and the blues. He'd roll up in front of my house in his father's green Chevy, honk the horn, and, against my father's wishes, I'd join him to find he'd want me to hear some Charlie Parker or Leadbelly coming over the radio from New York.) By the time I realized what I'd said, Roy had left the switchboard. And that bone never did get picked; once or twice when I was about to bring it up, his light blue eyes shot off a warning flare: "You poached once, fella," they told me. "Now leave it. Don't climb no mountain on my back." So I had to deal with what I'd said inside my own voice, and I learned that going about my business was harder and more painful than the quick fix of an apology.

Months later I was surprised when Roy Fitch asked that I be transferred to the mailroom. He knew I'd worked in a mailroom before, and he'd been watching me. He saw that I did my work quickly and stayed visible enough to deflect attention from the daily hour or two when I'd sneak off to the basement to write. He never surprised me there; he was too smart, but he knew my tricks. In the mailroom he broke me into his system. Leroy Fitch opened, sorted, and distributed mail faster and more efficiently than anyone I've ever seen before or since. And he camouflaged his speed and skill in a way reminiscent of Levi Jackson's fakes and feints on the football field and basketball court. Soon, satisfied his hunch was right and I could be trusted, he initiated me into a ritual of double coverage. If I kept pace with him in the morning and hustled on afternoon pickups, the hours between ten and three belonged to us, all the more he pointed out because most of the department heads passed by on their way in and on their way out and so they had firsthand evidence that before they arrived and after they went home, we were sweating to get their mail done.

The deal was this: I covered for Roy while he went on the bank run and took care of other business. When he returned, I could disappear. He also showed me how to conceal a yellow pad in a pile of mail so deftly that I could fool anyone who wandered into the mailroom during off hours. He did other things, too. One Saturday morning I staggered into the mailroom, reeling from a party the night before. "Gin," he said shaking his head. "Johnny," he told me after I sheepishly helped him get through the mail, "I'm going to teach you about Scotch before you go back to school." And he did. He took me to saloons with long gilt-edged mirrors and to dives with bars across the small square window in the door—anywhere they had Ambassador 25 or another suitably aged Scotch we went.

Down South other things were happening then and in subsequent summers when I returned to work for Roy. In Mississippi Klansmen murdered Medgar Evers, and Roy Fitch, a quiet, politically conservative man who had family in North Carolina and who feared and hated the South with a northerner's defensive superiority, talked about it in an angry voice. "Just when things were happening down there," he said. "Looks like they'll still stop some things, Johnny." About a week later the company brought in an efficiency expert, a red, bone-and-gristle, rag-and-bone shop man named Kelly. An "Irish cracker," he called himself. "Plenty of us down there," he told me one day and kept on talking because he was so proud of his Georgia drawl. Now, as I see and hear him in memory, Kelly recalls another Irishman, the Fenian, John Mitchel who "on reaching this country, from his exile and bondage," uttered "a wish for a 'slave plantation, well stocked with slaves.' "[5] For my part I stayed out of Kelly's way hoping he'd pursue bigger targets than the mailroom.

He quickly found us, though, and made Roy's operation the thin end of the wedge he intended to drive through the company's work force. Even apart from Kelly's cracker chauvinism, he and Roy took an instant, intense, constitutional dislike to each other. At first I tried to intervene in the guise of the bumbling stage Irishman. But Roy told me to knock it off. "We do the job," he told me. "That smart ass cracker better stay out of my way." A couple of times I praised Roy to Kelly, but he just winked and put his arm around my shoulder as if to tell me I didn't know any better and to reassure me that my job was safe. And Roy mocked my warning, "Don't let him sweet-talk you, hear?"

Late one afternoon when Roy came downstairs, mail piled three stories high in his arms, Kelly was waiting, hands on his hips like the boss of a work gang. "C'mere boy, let me show you something new," he said pointing at the Pitney-Bowes postage meter. Now Roy had been with the company since his discharge from the Army after World War II, and sometimes he feigned being hard-of-hearing from the war, but on this day he looked at Kelly, at me, at him again. Then he threw the mail in Kelly's direction, turned on his heel with military bearing, and marched upstairs. There, I heard later from the president's secretary as well as from Roy, he walked straight into the president's office, interrupting a meeting. "Ain't nobody gonna call me a damn boy. And that's no threat, just how things are." That's all I know except that neither Kelly's feet nor his voice carried as far as Roy Fitch's mailroom again. Best of all, Mr. Fitch had done the trick his way, with a spur of the moment performance calculated to release both the moral and strategic power of the spoken word. Asking no favors, he called others to respond to the small crises of daily life with what Alice Walker has termed "simple justice."[6] Like a savvy jockey, he reined in his voice until the homestretch when he broke free with a few well-chosen words and galloped across the finish line ahead of the field. Roy Fitch accepted responsibility for the consequences of being a black man and a citizen, but I fear that Irish-Americans have given too little moral answer to Kelly's breed in the nation. What would have happened, I wondered later, if I had challenged Kelly and told him there were no boys in Roy Fitch's mailroom, or, if, on the national scene, President Kennedy had gone South in that summer of 1963 after the murder of Medgar Evers and declared in a variation of his "Ich bin ein Berliner" speech: I am a black Mississippean?

In the intervening years the African/Irish-American connection has persisted in the private and public, intellectual and political guises of my life and consciousness. Writing my dissertation after the tough year of 1968, I was confronted with a riddle of history and moral imagination in F. Scott Fitzgerald's *Tender Is the Night*. I went in vain to many sources before the poet Michael Harper sent me to *The Souls of Black Folk* by W. E. B. Du Bois and to Ralph Ellison's little known essays, "Society, Morality, and the Novel" and "Tell It Like It Is, Baby." There I found the connections—"In the beginning was not only the word but the contradiction of the word"[7]— between the color line and the nation's moral and historical predicament I had been feeling in the marrow of my bones. To invoke Frederick Douglass again, the perspectives of Ellison and Du Bois became a pass freeing me to write what I wanted to write in a voice of my own.

A year later I challenged Congresswoman Edith Green in the Democratic primary. I was a newcomer and a nobody. I ran to call attention to what I considered Congresswoman Green's dangerous reversals on civil rights and the war in Vietnam. March 1970 was not a propitious time; even George McGovern was declaring that the economy was the real issue. The Multnomah County Democratic chairman was a black man and Irish, too, way back. Bill McCoy had migrated to Oregon from east Texas during World War II when the shipyards needed workers, and he told me a sinister tale of the 1948 Vanport flood and the subsequent disappearance and departure from Oregon of several thousand African-American citizens. When I ran, McCoy supported me, quietly, almost privately at first, but after the nuns at Providence Hospital (where he directed the Foster Grandparents Program) told him one of Edith's men had been snooping around the hospital asking questions about his activities and reminding the mother superior how much the program depended on Congressional appropriations, Bill McCoy got his black Irish up and publicly endorsed me at a breakfast well covered by television, newspaper, and radio reporters.

Bill McCoy and I got nothing from that campaign but 20 percent of the vote and what Ellison's storyteller, old Jim Trueblood, calls "a heapa satisfaction."[8] McCoy was damned if he'd let his young candidate, however scared and inexperienced, represent the issues he jeopardized his livelihood for in anything less than his best voice. "You better learn to breathe, boy," McCoy told me after I'd lost one audience by speaking rapidly, self-consciously, unrhythmically. "Now that's *your* voice," he told me late in the campaign after I'd spoken to a labor meeting about some of what I've written here on my discovery of America. I learned to use my voice, I now suspect, only when I understood that telling my story, and so making it up as I went along, was simultaneously an act of personal and social responsibility.

Memories fuse the past with the present moment of identity. As I look back I find the voices of Bill Jackson, Roy Fitch, and Bill McCoy in cahoots with my grandfather and my Great-Aunt Lizzie. All used storytelling to advance a common eclectic democratic identity. Because of them, I came to sense in fits and starts that the pursuit of voice is bound up with the struggle for freedom and that both test the still evolving, revolutionary idea of citizenship in America.

2

In twentieth-century African-American fiction the pursuit of narrative often becomes the pursuit of voice. And by voice I mean the writer's attempt to conjure the spoken word into symbolic existence on the page. Because they are close to an oral culture — "*It has been longer than that, further removed in time,* I told myself, and yet I knew that it hadn't been"[9] — black writers bring a dimension of immediacy to the struggle with the written word. They adapt call-and-response to fiction from the participatory forms of oral culture. Writers as different as Charles Chesnutt, Jean Toomer, Zora Neale Hurston, Ralph Ellison, Ernest Gaines, and Alice Walker realize what Robert Alter calls "the idea of the voice — voice arising from a living breathing body, enjoying a kind of uncanny afterlife in the writer's rhythms, images, diction, syntax, all the fine inter-connections of his language."[10] And there is also a sacred political purpose involved in many African-American writers' use of voice: the pursuit of freedom, equality, and diversity as American first principles. As part of what Charles Chesnutt called the "literature of necessity,"[11] black fiction often responds to and projects a fluid, improvisational context beyond the writer's verbal personality. Through their commitment to the oral tradition's pattern of call-and-response, African-American writers have long sought "to restore the words to a source, a human situation involving speech, character, personality, and destiny construed as having a personal form."[12] Their fiction of voice at once looks back to the culture of community among African peoples and African-American slaves and forward to that diverse democratic culture of individuals aspired to in this nation's motto: *e pluribus unum.*

In tribal Africa, according to Roger Abrahams's testifying words, "the vitality of the storytelling lies in two characteristic elements: first, the seizure of the role of narrator and the maintaining of it in the face of ongoing critical commentary; second, the constant au-dience commentary and periodic introduction of call-and-response songs." African storytellers, like their cultural descendants of all races in America, turn to their advantage dissenting as well as assenting voices in the audience. "In their African setting these tales are called upon not just to deliver a specific message but to initiate talk about that message." Those listening are responsible to the community for carrying on the work of interpretation begun by storytellers as they tell their tales. A catalytic process, African oral storytelling expresses the flux of social and natural reality through its open form. "For as the Mandingo say at the beginning of a story: 'A really unique story has no end.' " It follows that "achieving a sense of closure, of strong and definitive conclusion, is a condition regarded as neither possible nor desirable." Neither is the action confined to moments of per-formance, for storytelling exerts power over the life of the community in the form of continuing dialogue after the audience's initial response to the storyteller's call. Contrasting African tales transcribed on the page with the same tales told in performance, Abrahams testifies that "the spoken word can actually create bonds and bring about personal or social transformation."[13] This push for change in and beyond the immediate responsive community of listeners was uttered and heard with new urgency in the oral culture of African-American slaves.

Call-and-response is both a fundamental, perhaps even universal oral mode and a distinctively African and African-American form of discourse in speech and story, sermons and songs. It is also especially well suited to the vernacular culture of an experimental democratic society. As it evolves in black American oral tradition, the call-and-response pattern registers the changing relationship between the individual musician or storyteller and the community.[14] Lawrence Levine traces variations in the pattern through the forms of black music in America. At first, "the overriding antiphonal structure of the spirituals placed the individual in continual dialogue with his community, allowing him at one and the same time to preserve his voice as a distinct entity and to blend it with those of his fellows." Over time, the circumstances of slave life led to recognition of change, contingency, and possibility not just in nature but in the historical and moral universe of African-American experience. The songs and stories of slave culture respond to change with variations on existing patterns of call-and-response. In the blues, for instance, after and perhaps before Emancipation, call-and-response becomes more individual and interior in the sense that "it was the singer who responded to himself or herself either verbally or on an accompanying instrument."[15] Like oral storytellers and subsequent modern writers, as performers, blues singers improvise variations on existing songs and thereby confirm and intensify bonds of kinship and experience with their listeners. Bearing witness to love's pleasure and pain, and passion's terrific compulsions, to natural disasters like floods, whose devastating effects were compounded by Jim Crow, and to unjust social conditions, the blues, like the tales, assume shared experience on the part of musician and audience and set the juices of those listening flowing with their own stories. "I'm gonna spread the news all around," Leadbelly sings in "Bourgeois Blues," referring to racial hypocrisy in the "home of the brave and land of the free," and he expects his listeners also to carry the word in endlessly individual, improvisatory variations.

In African and, importantly, in African-American oral culture, call-and-response was a pattern and a practice functionally bound up with daily life. But in literary works the relationship between writer and reader is necessarily more remote, if not imaginary, so African-American writers use the act of voice as a metaphor for the process of change. Alert to the participatory quality of oral story-telling, black writers imbue their fiction with the improvisatory energy and testamental ritual of the oral tradition. In their hands call-and-response evolves into a resilient literary device that persuades readers to become symbolic and then perhaps actual participants in the task of image-making, of storytelling. As a narrative technique adapted from the forms of music and storytelling, call-and-response opens up a potential relationship between writer and reader analogous to the human situation that exists between performers and their audience.

From the beginning, the inferior official status imposed on African-Americans in American life complicated the dynamics of audience. Often, African-Americans spoke and wrote expressly as agents of change. They sought to persuade a white audience that theirs was a sufficiently compelling story in American terms to warrant the nation's compliance with its values and first principles. In such a context, the possibilities of true self-assertive voice sometimes seemed greater with the written than the spoken word. "You have seen how a man was made a slave," Frederick Douglass writes, addressing his audience directly; "now you shall see how a slave became a man."[16] As a writer, Douglass combines factual detail with interpretation in the manner of oral storytelling. But paradoxically, as a *speaker* for the Massachusetts antislavery society, Douglass had to fight for the right to an individual voice. In order to control Douglass's relationship with his audiences, his white superiors tried to define his identity as a performer and circumscribe his freedom to improvise. In *My Bondage and My Freedom* (1855), he writes of how white abolitionists presented him as a speaker more than ten years earlier: "I was generally introduced as a *'chattel'* — a *'thing'* — a piece of southern *'property'* — the chairman assuring the audience that *it* could speak." The white abolitionists allowed this static, de-humanized slaveholder's fiction of Douglass to govern their conception of his oral testimony.

" 'Give us the facts,' said Collins, 'we will take care of the philosophy.' 'Tell your story, Frederick,' would whisper my then revered friend, William Lloyd Garrison." But Douglass craves the freedom and fluidity of improvisation, because he knows that telling your story can bring together fact, fiction, and interpretation in the same complex act of performance. "My simple narrative," he testifies, "was an old story to me; and to go through with it night after night, was a task altogether too mechanical for my nature." Instead, he pursues that organic American vernacular expression urged and practiced by Ralph Waldo Emerson in his lectures and essays. "I was growing, and needed room," he tells us. To become a citizen he becomes a writer and by authoring the story of his quest for voice and self, he reshapes the identity expected of him as a speaker. Douglass considers power over the word, spoken and written, essential to his identity as an individual and a free man. "And still," he concludes his subsequent written response to the limited, false call of his sponsors, "I must speak just the word that seemed to *me* the word to be spoken *by* me."[17] And so as an orator *and* as a writer Douglass changes the context in which he delivered the word by addressing audiences as a free agent, not as anyone's employee, by writing three successive versions of his unfolding story, and by publishing the *North Star* in response to Garrison's *Liberator.*[18]

Douglass's experience points up the need for African-American writers to replace others' fictions about their voices and stories with their own, and a corresponding need to reach out to an inclusive democratic audience as Herman Melville and Mark Twain do through Ishmael's and Huck's direct conversational calls to readers at the beginning of *Moby-Dick* and *Huck Finn,* and as Rebecca Harding Davis does in *Life in the Iron Mills.* The written word and the form of fiction offer a spacious, yet to be inhabited landscape. "The writer's audience is always a fiction," Walter Ong notes in *Orality and Literacy* and goes on to express a corollary proposition: "the reader must also fictionalize the writer." Observing that "the reader is normally absent when the writer writes and the writer is normally absent when the reader reads, whereas in oral communication speaker and hearer are present to one another," Ong later dares the following paradoxical assertion: "Nor is orality ever completely eradicable; reading a text oralizes it."[19] You read with your ear as well as your eye, Ong implies, and so affirms every reader's submerged connection with an oral tradition. Ong's postulate converges with Douglass's revoicing, revising rejuvenation of the word and the context of the word, and with subsequent African-American writers' preoccupation with compatibilities between the eloquence of speech and that of the vernacular written word. Committed to a "literature of necessity" by virtue of their *and the nation's* distinct predicament, African-American writers seize the opportunity to regard their reading audience as both characters and citizens. This particular fiction enables black writers to imagine white Americans becoming more open to African-American personality and experience as readers than most were as citizens. In the end this repeated act of fictionalizing is a liberating patriotic act, for it allows the writer to call on the reader to become simultaneously an individual and, indivisibly, a member of the potential national community. American identity becomes a fluid estate: not only are blacks true Americans but "the true American," as Ralph Ellison notes, "is also somehow black."[20]

The contemporary African-American writer, James Alan McPherson, sketches out the lineaments of this fictional American reader by way of *characterizing* the lawyer-novelist Albion Tourgee's brief to the Supreme Court in *Plessy v. Ferguson.* "What he was proposing in 1896," McPherson writes eighty years later, "was that each United States citizen would attempt to approximate the ideals of the nation, be on at least conversant terms with all its diversity, carry the mainstream of the culture inside himself. As an American, by trying to wear these clothes he would be a synthesis of high and low, black and white, city and country, provincial and universal. If he could live with these contradictions he would be simply a representative American."[21] Tourgee's idea of the citizen informs McPherson's idea of character, and in many of their fictions black writers imagine American identity as a condition subject to a collaborative improvisatory national tradition of call-and-response. This idea and practice of an extended democratic fiction presumes a society that, despite its hypocrisies, its contradictions and injustices, remains emergent and experimental, open and responsive to new voices, new stories. It assumes the presence of voice and the potentiality of stories within everyone and rejects the view that literature or storytelling is the gift of the few. Within this framework each citizen is a potential character and every character has the rights and responsibilities of citizenship. Characters in this fiction of necessity share with readers and writers that mutual accountability essential to democratic identity.

The African-American fiction of voice proposes a new American version of the common context and shared experience relied on by the call-and-response pattern of oral culture. Against the grain of a society where both orality and literacy are menaced, African-American writers use the oral tradition to project values of community and citizenship. Perhaps this is why Alice Walker, when asked to talk about what she "considered the major difference between the literature written by black and white Americans," responds by saying that "it is not the difference between them that interests me, but, rather, the way black writers and white writers seem to me to be writing one immense story—the same story, for the most part—with different parts of this immense story coming from a multitude of different perspectives." One story flows from many stories, *e pluribus unum* again, and Walker's response, like McPherson's and Ellison's, calls readers to listen to other diverse individual voices as a primary act in the discovery of their own voices and the generation of a single continuing story. Yet Walker notices an important difference between black and white American writers. The latter, she says, making the same point Ellison has made about many twentieth-century American novels, "tended to end their books and their characters' lives as if there were no better existence for which to struggle." But "black writers seem always involved in a moral and/or physical struggle, the result of which is expected to be some kind of larger freedom."[22] Even as they are attenuated in narrative fiction, the variations on African-American call-and-response speak for change and keep faith with the promise and possibility of American language and experience.

To know and use your voice you need to hear and read and interpret other voices, other stories. The act of voice counts on someone else listening and preparing to respond. In fiction voice is a metaphor and call-and-response a symbolic pattern. No matter how keen a writer's ear, how eloquent his voice, on the page voice is not speech but the imagination of speech. The eye calls the ear to attention. Voice and its accompanying African-American call-and-response variations intensify the possibilities in and beyond the acts of writing and reading. Specifically, call-and-response awakens a number of dormant relationships: between different writers; different readers; different texts; different characters in the same text; a writer and his characters; and always between a writer and his fictionalized and actual readers and between those same readers and the writer. Symbolically present in the literary genre of fiction, these variations of call-and-response summon us to read and hear and, potentially, contribute to the still unfolding "immense story" in our lives and voices beyond the solitary, private act of reading. And these African-American writers are disarmingly honest and direct about the scale of the task. Theirs is the necessity common to all writers to test their fiction-making power against the demands of discipline, craft, and form. Yet they also write stories to connect and reconnect generations of Americans—African-Americans, yes, and preeminently, but all others too, Irish-Americans like me, for instance—with those past and present oral traditions behind our evolving spoken and written voices.

3

Who you for?

Twice in Ernest J. Gaines's *The Autobiography of Miss Jane Pittman*, that question interrupts the action. First, in 1865:

"Who y'all for?" he said.
"We ain't for nobody," I said. "We free as you."

Then, in 1962:

"Now, there will be multitudes," that long head boy said.
I was getting fed up with that boy. "Boy, who you for?" I asked him.
"Joe and Lena Butcher," he said.
"They teach you to talk like that?" I said.
"Ma'am?"
I just looked at him.
"That's retrick," he said.
"Well, I can do without your retrick here," I said. "If you can't say nothing sensible, don't say nothing."[23]

Who you for? Asked by a stranger, young Jane Pittman "could see was nothing but white trash," the question riles because at last she has no master and no mistress. In the sense of ownership she is free and belongs to no one. But when, at 108 or 109, Jane Pittman asks the civil rights worker who he's for, her call poses deeper questions of identity and allegiance. Not who owns or controls you, but who are you? Who are your people, your family, your community? What are your traditions, your history, your values? And why don't your words come more spontaneously and palpably from the grain of your experience? Why do you settle for a synthetic voice? Jane calls the young man boy because his voice lacks relatedness to life's actualities. Tradition and kinship, she has learned the hard way, are not fixed, guaranteed conditions or inalienable rights; they depend on rigorous, dangerous acts of discovery and creation. Leadership, too, she knows, is bound up with the eloquent flow of language from individual to individual as they prepare for action as a people.

Jane Pittman and the others in the quarters husband the oral tradition as an agency essential to their struggle for freedom and justice. To Jane's storyteller's ears the long head boy does not use but is used by his imposed, artificial, high-faluting, snap your fingers and you'll change the world words. Because she hears in the tones of his voice that he is a home boy in bondage to an alien idiom, an arrogant language, Jane holds him strictly accountable for his falsely responsive speech. In her view, the long head boy's *retrick* betrays (tricks) the people he mistakenly, prematurely seeks to lead. Say something "sensible" or "don't say nothing," she tells him, and unable or unwilling to risk authentic speech and maybe tell his story, for the time being he makes the cowardly choice. Unready, he says nothing and refuses the pursuit of voice and identity.

Let that long head boy stand for the critic who, sometimes without knowing it, intrudes on literature's authentic primary voices in a synthetic, vicarious voice. And let Jane Pittman be the writer whose mnemonic, participatory voice calls critics and readers alike to participate in the telling of our "one immense story." Who you for? is properly the anthem of every citizen, of writer, reader, and critic alike. It is a call to self, to voice, to community, to nationhood. And, who knows, maybe by telling you a little of who I'm for, I am better able to tell you what I'm for.

NOTES

1. *Yale Daily News*, vol. 71, Sept. 14, 1949–May 19, 1950; the stories in question appeared in issues for Oct. 22, 1949, and Mar. 9, 1950.

2. Frederick Douglass, *The Life and Times of Frederick Douglass* (1892; rpt., London: Collier-Macmillan, 1967), pp. 92, 237.

3. Frederick Douglass, *My Bondage and My Freedom* (1855; rpt., New York: Dover, 1969), p. 98.

4. Ibid., p. 454.

5. *The Life and Times of Frederick Douglass*, p. 258.

6. Alice Walker, *In Search of Our Mothers' Gardens* (San Diego: Harcourt Brace Jovanovich, 1983), p. 322.

7. Ralph Ellison, "Society, Morality, and the Novel," in *Going to the Territory* (New York: Random House, 1986), p. 243.

8. Ralph Ellison, *Invisible Man* (1952; rpt., with author's introduction, New York: Random House, 1982), p. 47.

9. Ibid., p. 206.

10. Robert Alter, "Literary Criticism, from A to Z," *The New Republic*, July 25, 1981, p. 35.

11. Charles Chesnutt, quoted in Sylvia Lyons Render's *Charles W. Chesnutt* (Boston: Twayne Publishers, 1980), p. 82.

12. Denis Donoghue, *Ferocious Alphabets* (Boston: Little Brown, 1981), p. 99.

13. Roger D. Abrahams, *African Folktales: Selected and Retold by Roger D. Abrahams* (New York: Pantheon, 1983), pp. 14, 9, 14, 15, 1-2. African fiction, too, communicates the values of participatory oral culture. In *Forest of a Thousand Daemons*, for example, the Yoruban novelist, D. O. Fagunwa, turns both the act of storytelling and the act of written narrative into vehicles for the expansion of audience. The ancient storyteller and hunter, Akara-ogun, tells the narrator to write down his story; then, as he tells it, the audience expands to include first the narrator's family and friends and then all the people of the city. This inspires the narrator to frame his written version of the tale with an imaginary performance that merges music, dancing, and feasting with storytelling in the participatory manner of African culture.

14. Unlike the improvisational intent behind the African and African-American principle of call-and-response, the eighteenth-century Puritan

practice of "lining out" prodded unlearned congregations *not* to vary the text of a hymn's verses. On the improvisational aspects of call-and-response, see among other sources, Roger D. Abrahams's companion collections, *African Folktales* and *Afro-American Folktales,* and his perceptive and useful introductions to each volume. For this dialogic facet of Native American poetry, song, and story, particularly the relationship between performer and audience, see Dennis Tedlock's *The Spoken Word and the Work of Interpretation* (Philadelphia: University of Pennsylvania Press, 1983). In this connection I am grateful to Milton R. Stern for querying the possible connection between "lining out" and call-and-response, and for his generous suggestions in response to successive drafts of this chapter. Roger Abrahams, too, made helpful comments about my discussion of narrative and story-telling voices in this chapter and in Chapter 2.

15. Lawrence W. Levine, *Black Culture and Black Consciousness* (New York: Oxford University Press, 1977), pp. 33, 221.

16. Frederick Douglass, *Narrative of the Life of Frederick Douglass, An American Slave* (1845; rpt., New York: Signet, 1968), p. 77.

17. Douglass, *My Bondage and My Freedom,* pp. 360, 61, 62.

18. Frederick Douglass is by no means the only African-American who had to fight for his voice nor is his case the most extreme. Sojourner Truth was initially denied the right to speak at all at the 1853 Akron women's rights convention lest her ungainly presence and earthy black idiom offend southern white women. In response, Truth improvised her eloquent "A'n't I a Woman" speech.

19. Walter J. Ong, *Orality and Literacy: The Technology of the Word* (New York: Methuen, 1983), pp. 102, 171, 175.

20. Ellison, *Going to the Territory,* p. 111.

21. James Alan McPherson, "On Becoming an American Writer," *Atlantic* 242, no. 6 (Dec. 1978), 57.

22. Walker, *In Search of Our Mothers' Gardens,* p. 5. For Ellison's comments, see *Going to the Territory,* pp. 252-74, 317-20.

23. Ernest J. Gaines, *The Autobiography of Miss Jane Pittman* (New York: Dial, 1971), pp. 31, 228.

CHAPTER 2

The Spoken in the Written Word: African-American Tales and the Middle Passage from *Uncle Remus: His Songs and Sayings* to *The Conjure Woman*

1

During and after slavery African-American culture performed a double function. Its musicians and storytellers developed songs and stories that evoked the distinct quality and meaning of black life. But the black oral tradition also affirmed the centrality of African-American experience for American society. Its music and tales testified to an indomitable will able to overcome the brutalities of slavery and project possibilities of citizenship based on democratic equality. The cultural tension between an African past and an American present and future led to the conscious practice of what W. E. B. Du Bois called the psychology of "double-consciousness." "One ever feels his twoness," Du Bois wrote in 1903, refusing to sacrifice his sense of the truth, "—an American, a Negro; two souls, two thoughts, two unreconciled strivings; two warring ideals in one dark body, whose dogged strength alone keeps it from being torn asunder." As individuals who considered themselves citizens, black Americans experienced "this strife—this longing to attain self-conscious manhood [and womanhood], to merge [their] double self into a better and truer self."[1] Paradoxically, they learned to "wear the mask"[2] in their pursuit of wholeness. They learned to say yes when they meant no and no when they meant yes in forms resilient and eloquent enough to advance the cause of freedom. And they survived and thrived as a people by combining the trickster's wit and irony with the patriot's love and loyalty.

As a form that emerged from a fluid, improvisatory tradition, the African-American tale helped forge a simultaneous sense of racial solidarity and American identity. Usually, the tales were told to exclusively African-American audiences. These storytelling performances created a community of speech, interpretation, and response among the slaves and, later on, among freedmen and -women. Ironically, the dehumanizing conditions of slavery, its prohibitions against literacy, against African language and ritual, reinforced the communal values of the oral tradition. Variations on the old African animal stories and the new American tales of Jack the slave and his master fed what Sterling Brown calls the "abiding deep well of Negro folk experience."[3] At the same time there was a progressive, to-be-continued feeling about many of the tales, which opened the potential for action implied by the call-and-response pattern.

But the hostile slave environment generated a strategic consideration. It would have been dangerous and self-destructive to allow white masters and overseers with capricious, often absolute power to hear subversive stories either directly or, secondhand, from slave informers. Even tales about conflicts worked out responsibly by blacks might have raised doubts even in gullible white minds about the subservient comic masks worn by many slave leaders. All the same whites were aware of the vitality and exuberance of slave speech. To prevent the wrong knowledge and information from reaching whites, the slave storytellers crafted for the tales a style of understatement, a rhetoric of indirection and double meaning. As strongly metaphoric, ironic fictions, the tales are self-authenticating; they shun the testimonials that frame the endlessly vouched-for slave narratives.

Perhaps this careful storytelling craft led some early twentieth-century scholars to overlook the importance of individual performance and improvisation to the oral tradition. "In true folk tales," folklorist Arthur Huff Fauset claimed, "the storyteller himself was inconsequential; he did not figure at all." Consequently, according to Fauset, "the stories take on an impersonal character, more or less lacking in artistic embellishments."[4] About oral storytelling Fauset is wrong. As performers, storytellers overlay their particular style, energy, and interpretation on the essentials of a tale. They collaborate and compete, as preachers, blues singers, and jazz musicians do, over nuances of meaning. There is abundant testimony on the importance of timing, the improvised image or detail, the mimicry of bird calls, animal noises, and different human voices. Moreover, from the many versions of classic tales like "Tar Baby," it is clear that oral storytellers were also fiction-makers who reconstructed, interpreted, and altered the stories they learned from their predecessors. For many storytellers impersonality followed from the complexity of personality. "He [she] has met life's conditions but never accepted them,"[5] Sterling Brown declared about the archetypal heroes of Negro history and legend, like John Henry or Frederick Douglass or Harriet Tubman. And his characterization identifies impersonality as a personal response both to the general human condition and the specific historical scheme of things faced by black Americans. Among storytellers stoicism led to a metaphorical style that was pithy, stark, and pared down, while a sense of struggle grounded the most outrageous lies and actions in elemental reality.[6] In the African-American grain, stories were told in unceasing collaboration between the storyteller and his audience, the black community. Call-and-response was so fundamental to the form and meaning of the tales that anyone, black or white, allowed into the circle was bound to become a participant as well as a witness.

Long before the Civil War, fragments of African-American culture found their way into the expanding vernacular repertoire of American music and speech. And as northern states abolished slavery at the end of the eighteenth century and the beginning of the nineteenth, free blacks and escaped slaves shared their songs and stories with their white countrymen to advance the cause of freedom. You find this impulse throughout the slave narratives, expressed most tellingly, perhaps, in Frederick Douglass's 1845 *Narrative*. Douglass acquainted his mostly white readers with African-American culture and folklore with the shrewdness of a slave storyteller and the self-conscious honesty of a young writer discovering his identity through his craft. He withholds the details of his escape on the underground railroad as a matter of strategy and principle. But he confesses to a gradual understanding of the narrative function of slave music and thereby invites his readers to become interpreters and, therefore, symbolic participants in slave culture. According to Douglass, the slaves expressed their viewpoint on slavery immediately and, over-poweringly in the *tones* of their songs. "I did not when a slave," he writes, "understand the deep meaning of those rude and apparently incoherent songs. I was myself within the circle; so that I neither saw nor heard as those without might see and hear. *They told a tale* of woe which was then altogether beyond my feeble comprehension; they were tones loud, long, and deep; they breathed the prayer and complaint of souls boiling over with the bitterest anguish. Every tone was a testimony against slavery."[7] Long after he heard them per-formed, Douglass discovers the songs as tales and in the narrative present they inspire him to a reciprocal, simultaneous act of story-telling and intepretation.[8] Douglass's account makes the point that slaves were not born to interpretation. Craftily, they mastered the skills required to decode their dangerous world and recode it in their own image. Finally, the tears rolling down Douglass's cheeks while he is "writing these lines" extend the immediacy of call-and-response to his subsequent acts of writing and reading.

Douglass's command of both oral and written narrative foreshad-ows the cultural shift after the Civil War when the tales were written down, framed, and became absorbed into American literary history. By no means did oral performances cease; African-Americans con-tinued to work out a distinct, exclusive relationship with each other within the circle of oral culture. Yet on the printed page the tales converged with a point in national experience when the drive for literacy among black citizens intensified despite the ebbing tide of Reconstruction. Namely, as political freedom receded in the late nineteenth century, culture sustained the African-American dream of citizenship. The tales' metamorphosis into literary narratives near the end of the century was bound up with a struggle over African-American personality. For the tales were not simply spoken to col-lectors, written down verbatim, and put into books. To some extent, transcription occurred but it largely followed from Joel Chandler Harris's use of the tales to advance a particular myth (and ideology) about southern history and Negro personality. Once Harris pressed the tales into service on the Jim Crow side of the reopened civil war, black writers, led by Charles Chesnutt, undertook rescue missions in their rebellion against white supremacy. On both sides of the color line the oral stories became touchstones for modern fiction's complex variations of frame and form.

As they begin to write fiction, African-Americans use the oral tradition to interpret the past and influence the conditions, relationships, and possibilities of the American present. Both the idea and practice of an African-American literary tradition assumed an inclusive audience. Always, there remained the goal of transforming national consciousness to prepare for the extension of democratic principles and possibilities to black Americans. This meant winning over a predominantly white audience while remaining true to the sensibilities of black culture and experience. Chesnutt is explicit: "The object of my writings," he reflects in 1880 before Harris's *Uncle Remus: His Songs and Sayings* appeared, "would not be so much the elevation of the colored people as the elevation of the whites."[9] Chesnutt intended his fiction to restore to consciousness American first principles. Recognizing that for a while the most telling contact between the races might come vicariously, black Americans like Chesnutt concentrated on writing and reading, individual acts that sought connections on the basis of a common citizenship. So it is that fiction joins an autobiographical and polemical nineteenth-century tradition that linked persuasion with enactment, eloquence with action.[10] Chesnutt's fiction of necessity addresses an inclusive double audience, and in this sense, too, narrative is both a critical and an imaginative act. Like the oral tradition, this view of fiction implies that the story is unfinished, continuing, evolving, endlessly unfolding new patterns, and that reader and writer are responsible to each other as citizens.

The tales' passage from the spoken to the written word was not simple or self-contained but complex and contextual. The first skirmish involved Joel Chandler Harris's Uncle Remus versions of the animal tales, for they raised some fundamental questions. Was the essential integrity of speech and action preserved? How authentic was the Harris/Remus presentation of African-American personality? Here the essential characteristics of narrative come into focus. Who tells the stories? To whom? With what resiliency and complexity of performance? And what is Uncle Remus's attitude toward the past and toward his position in postbellum American society?

Unquestionably, Joel Chandler Harris and Charles Chesnutt are catalytic writers, but each maps the territory in a radically different way. Harris keeps faith with the language but not with the form and spirit of the tales as performed by slave and free black storytellers. Chesnutt improvises freely upon existing stories and conjures new tales profoundly faithful to the essentials of slave culture. Together, the work of Harris and Chesnutt has "a heap of signifying wrapped up in it."[11] Unsurprisingly, in the framing and telling of their fictions, later black writers often respond to the voice and form that emerge in Harris and are challenged and reconstructed by the tales of Chesnutt.

2

Joel Chandler Harris did not come out of nowhere. He is a historical character of the late nineteenth-century American South just as his Uncle Remus remains a mythical figure from that time and place. Each reflects the social values of white supremacy and the literary values of the Plantation School then in vogue nationally as well as in the South. Born in 1848, Harris was the illegitimate son of Mary Harris and an Irish day laborer who deserted her. In 1861 young Harris left home "to learn the printer's trade on the only newspaper ever published on a plantation, Joseph Turner's *The Countryman,* printed at 'Turnwold,' nine miles from Eatonton in Putnam County [Georgia]."[12] On the plantation during the Civil War, Harris was admitted into the circle of children, black and white, slave and free, for whom the slave storytellers George Terrell and "Old" Harbert performed the African-American animal tales.[13] So Harris's earliest experience with oral storytelling was anomalous, and his subsequent narrative frame is even more so, for it consists of only Uncle Remus and the seven-year-old grandson of Remus's former owners in the roles of performer and audience. But in folk culture adults told tales to adults with slave children gradually initiated into the storytelling ceremony.

Harris began his writing life as a columnist and editorial writer for the *Atlanta Constitution.* His editor was Henry C. Grady, who emerged in the 1880s as a national spokesman for southern industrial development. In his influential essay, "The New South," Grady advised southerners and northerners to put business above politics; until his death in 1889 he worked to strengthen the alliance between northern capitalists and the reconstituted old guard of the South.[14] Meanwhile the so-called Redemption of the white South was eliminating the gains of Reconstruction. Throughout the "New South" the state by state disenfranchisement of Negroes occurred in the 1880s and 1890s, culminating in the Supreme Court's proclamation of separate but equal as the law of the land in *Plessy v. Fergusson* in 1896. Harris's relation to this is palpable but not simple. As a journalist, Robert Bone notes, Harris "was an active propagandist in the cause of white supremacy, and as a literary man, a leading proponent of the plantation myth."[15] As a folklorist, his material was the subversive, violent, volatile stuff of the African-American animal tales. Nonetheless, Harris's adaptations of the tales and his invention of Uncle Remus and the little white boy are faithful to his personal and public identity as a figure of the white southern establishment. In effect, his narrative voice and his frame act as a literary white picket fence around the black folktales. Moreover, Harris's selection is much narrower than the true range of black folktales. But this may be due to the fact that he probably never heard the tales of John or Jack the slave and old master as much as to the fact that they contradict his myth of the South. During slavery these tales of irreverent, often outrageous, impudent behavior and resistance to the codes and customs of slavery were told within the slave community, and long after Emancipation African-American storytellers seldom told these stories to whites.

Even Negroes, if strangers to a place, were severely tested before local storytellers told subversive tales in their presence. In *Mules and Men* (1935) Zora Neale Hurston explains African-Americans' "feather-bed resistance" to white folks. "You see," she wrote to her then mostly white audience, "we are a polite people and we do not say to our questioner, 'Get out of here!' We smile and tell him or her something that satisfies the white person because, knowing so little about us, he doesn't know what he is missing." Born and bred in the black town of Eatonville, Florida, Hurston went to New York and, then in the 1920s, back to Florida to collect folklore. When she arrived in unfamiliar Polk County with its freewheeling mill camp life and explosive jooks, she found local folks suspicious of her clothes,

her city ways, and her Chevrolet. Not surprisingly, her initial mask
of bootlegger's moll failed to gain her entry to the intimate local
circle of storytelling. To develop a familiar ease with the men—
whose "laugh has a hundred meanings"[16]—Hurston sang on the
table, danced, drank coon dick, cussed back, and told stories. To
become a member of the audience she had to become a performer,
and the local storytellers responded to her performances by telling
her all manner of tales—stories about John outwitting Massa and
sometimes, as in "Ah'll Beatcher Makin' Money," getting his master
killed. These slave tales are not simple fictions of unlikely slave
triumphs. They are full of folk wit and wisdom, and also some of
the hyperbole of the tall tale, a tradition whose bravado both belies
and confirms the slaves' defensive position. John does not always
best his master, but his tales reinforce the virtues of courage, discipline, and craft—"shit, grit, and mother-wit."[17] Sometimes, too,
these tales warn slave audiences against overconfidence and hubris.
They tell of slaves outwitting each other instead of the master or
mistress. And the tales' resolution of competing claims illustrates the
ambiguous contextual power of language. The outwitting might tell
the outwitted: "I didn't say I'd cussed him to his face," or "I never
said she was *in* the drawers." The playful aggression reinforces a
deadly serious point about vigilance. Before and after slavery, the
conditions of race required both a subtle grasp of context and a
command of the points of contact and departure between the word
and worldly realities. To thrive, African-Americans first had to shore
up their survival space with the protective camouflage of a double-
conscious culture.

Like Hurston, Harris told tales to get tales. By telling tales like
"Tar Baby" in an authentic black dialect, he moved black railroad
workers to tell stories in front of him.[18] But he heard tales it was
safe for black storytellers to tell him—tales that evoked memories
of the animal stories he had heard as a boy from George Terrell.
Years later, his daughter-in-law, Julia Collier Harris, told about his
handling of original material. "I have found," she observed, "several
fragments of tales scrawled in almost undecipherable characters, on
scraps of paper and signed 'Jim' or 'Buck.' One outline sent from
Senoia, Georgia in 1881, I give as characteristic of the form in which
many of the legends came to their compiler:

Mr Harris I have one tale of Uncle Remus that I have not seen in print yet. Bro Rabbit at Mis Meadows and Bro Bare went to Bro Rabbit house and eat up his children and set his house on fire and make like the children all burnt up but Bro Rabbit saw his track he knowed Bro Bare was the man so one day Bro Rabbit saw Bro Bare in the woods with his ax hunting a bee tree after Bro Rabbit spon howdy he tell Bro Bare he know where a bee tree was and he would go an show and help him cut it down they went and cut it an Bro Rabbit drove in the glut while Bro Bare push his head in the hole Bro Rabbit nock out the glut and cut him hickry. Mr. Harris you have the tale now give it wit. I never had room to give you all you can finish it.

"This outline," Mrs. Harris concludes, "was elaborated and shaped into the story, 'The End of Mr. Bear.' "[19]

The anonymous oral storyteller writes down more of the tale's essentials than Harris does in "The End of Mr. Bear." He arranges the tale's bones sparely, impersonally, unself-consciously except for mention of Harris's wit, and even this seems a matter of decorum and convention—an unlettered storyteller paying homage to a famous man of letters. But Remus's embellishments on his audience's, the little boy's situation, blunt much of the folktale's stark cruel force. Remus moralizes about "swell-head folks like dat 'oman w'at come en tell yo' ma 'bout you chunkin' at her chilluns, w'ich yo ma make Mars John strop you" (*UR*, p. 134), but this narrative bridge trivializes the action of the tale. Uncle Remus also omits the terrible cause of the revenge Br'er Rabbit takes on Br'er Bear—the eating of Br'er Rabbit's children—whereas surely the slave storytellers and listeners were acting out, in symbolic form, the community's urge to avenge the buying and selling, whipping and working to death of its children by master and overseer. But Harris's Br'er Rabbit is more mischievous than avenging, so much so that the Remus tale reeks of pointless cruelty committed by children. In the pithier, tougher folk version cruel, unnatural acts lead to avenging acts of torture, and there is a natural justice and a causality about this sequence. Harris's unknown corrspondent leaves the tale's bleaching bones to refract their light at the reader, whereas Harris foregrounds Uncle Remus's context, personality, and point of view.[20]

Throughout *Uncle Remus: His Songs and Sayings* Harris seeks to have the issue of form both ways. At no point does he turn the narrative over to Remus for longer than it takes the old man to tell and embellish a tale or two, and his third-person, standard English voice encircles both Remus's dialect and the little boy's vernacular. Consequently, Harris's ventriloquism diminishes the folk voice and banishes any sense of communal African-American relationships from some of the most expressive and essential tales in the canon.

Consider Harris's "The Wonderful Tar-Baby Story" alongside the unframed, oral version. The original African-American tale is terrifically terse and opens up a whole new world as if returning to a time when, in Zora Neale Hurston's words, animals and people "were walking the earth like natural men way back in the days when God himself was on the ground and men could talk with him."[21] And the folk version also comments on the social and political world.[22] The story tells how the community handles one of its own who shirks responsibility and selfishly, foolishly, expects to benefit first and fully from the efforts of others. The animals, who build the well at Br'er Rabbit's suggestion, meet and "study a plan to git Brother Rabbit." The political process continues when, finding Br'er Rabbit stuck to the tar baby, the animals pass a resolution "to burn him up." Some of the satire aims at the persistence of vengeful punishment by the community—sometimes through the democratic process as Tocqueville warned—as well as at the hands of avenging individuals. Presently, cruelty overcomes the immediate commonsensical political task when the animals forget what they know about Br'er Rabbit's habitat and sadistically seek pleasure from the method of his execution. They fall for his feigned cries of horror at the prospect of the briar patch and defeat their purpose of ridding the community of a slothful troublemaker. This is a wonderful piece of folk wit, for what is the briar patch but a figure for the milieu of slavery? Except for a lapse into malicious cruelty, how could the other animals forget Br'er Rabbit's familiarity with his (and, symbolically, their) environment? So the tale warns that identification with cruel, capricious power— the sort often exercised by master and overseer and sometimes by slaves on each other—can cost you your wits.

In Harris's Uncle Remus version the controversy becomes primarily personal, the contest wholly between Br'er Fox and Br'er Rabbit. And Br'er Fox's object is not retribution but a good meal.

Br'er Rabbit gets into trouble by meddling "'some'rs whar you got no bizness,' sez Br'er Fox, sezee" (*UR*, p. 63). Br'er Fox is right: Br'er Rabbit overreaches when he challenges something that cannot harm him if he leaves it alone. In both versions Br'er Rabbit recovers in time to outwit those determined to kill him because he knows the other animals better than they know him or themselves—exactly the position slaves needed to occupy with their masters.

In the Uncle Remus version Br'er Fox moralizes so insufferably and self-righteously, the audience's sympathies swing completely to Br'er Rabbit. Harris's narrative intervention strengthens the reader's identification with Br'er Rabbit because Remus breaks off the story with Rabbit stuck and at the mercy of the Fox. In effect, Harris's contrived suspension of the dramatic context discloses Br'er Rabbit's escape. Not so the unframed, folk version. There, the reader and the listening community identify initially with the other animals' resentment and grievance against Br'er Rabbit. After all, it was his idea to build the well. Then he pretends to be sick, but as soon as the well is finished, he sneaks out for water—a thief in the night. So he deserves punishment—a good stiff comeuppance. But soon you resist the animals' gratuitous cruelty because a savvy community ought to turn wit to its advantage as the African-American community has done with its tricksters during and after slavery. In its unframed form the Tar Baby tale explores the allegiances, conflicts, and responsibilities between the individual and the group. As a reader who lives on both sides of the line, my sympathy and antipathy, identification and detachment swing back and forth. And that's the point. The unframed folktale does not lead its audience to any final judgment. Br'er Rabbit needs the community and the community needs him, and the tale points to the need for "antagonistic cooperation"[23] between the two forces. Life goes on and along with it the likelihood that combat between the witty, idiosyncratic, irresponsible, ingenious, irrepressible individual and the community will continue to find expression in God knows what rich, outrageous, unexpected, stubbornly particular, contingent ways.

In his 1880 introduction Harris calls the tales "myth-stories" and "valuable contributions to myth-literature" (*UR*, pp. 46, 40). Both his essayist's rhetoric and his literary frame affirm what

Sterling Brown has characterized as the contented slave stereotype.[24] For although Harris ostensibly turns over the performance of the tales to Uncle Remus and the little white boy, their oral context is a confined and confining rhetorical space. And between the immediate dramatic occasion and the reader Harris's third-person authorial voice insinuates a particular vision of race relations and southern history. Specifically, Harris's third-person statements and images uphold a myth of unbroken Negro loyalty to master and mistress before and after the Civil War. That mythical loyalty includes Negro complicity with the view that the old, aristocratically based social and political order was somehow fitting and proper, natural and just.

Wittingly or not, writers respond to tradition, and Harris knows that his work favors the interpretation of southern life and Negro character and consciousness worked out by apologists for slavery before and after the Civil War. He needs a bridge between African-American folkfore and his fellow whites and seizes on the authenticity of black dialect. Remus's speech, he insists, "is wholly different from that of the Hon. Pompey Smash and his literary descendents, and different also from the intolerable *misrepresentations of the minstrel stage*" (*UR*, p. 39, my italics). Harris is doubly canny here. First, he admires both the tales he compiles and their expressive, original language. (He could, Harris told Walter Hines Page, "if necessary, think in Negro dialect" [*UR*, p. 16].) Second, if he is faithful to black folk English, his audience will be more likely to credit *what* he says than if he uses the caricatured language of minstrelsy. Smoothly and shrewdly he seeks the reader's complicity in exchange for his exquisite verbal hospitality. With southern charm he indulges, then patronizes his audience, ever so gently asking permission to speak for us. In fact, he counts on silent assent; his feelings would be hurt, his solicitude and courtesy betrayed, if we responded with the least dissenting word. For Harris has a point to make about Uncle Remus's relations with the white folks he serves, first as a slave and then as a "free" retainer allowed to stay on the plantation at the pleasure of its owners. His narrative frame advances the position that the South was well on its way toward "practical reconstruction" after the failure of the official political Reconstruction imposed by the federal government—a line that surfaced fifty years later with literary vehemence in the Fugitives' collection of essays, *I'll Take My Stand.*

Accordingly, Harris projects a mythical oral tradition in which relations between the races are restored to harmony after the upheaval of the Civil War and its violent aftermath.

> If the reader not familiar with plantation life will imagine that the myth-stories of Uncle Remus are told night after night to a little boy by an old Negro who appears to be venerable enough to have lived during the period which he describes — who has nothing but pleasant memories of the discipline of slavery — and who has all the prejudices of caste and pride of family that were the natural results of the system; if the reader can imagine all this, he will find little difficulty in appreciating and sympathizing with the air of affectionate superiority which Uncle Remus assumes as he proceeds to unfold the mysteries of plantation lore to a little child who is the product of that practical reconstruction which has been going on to some extent since the war in spite of the politicians. (*UR*, pp. 46-47)

This is an extraordinary sentence. Its roundabout but unswerving rhetorical course flows with all the sweep and deceptively innocent, subtly dangerous power of the Mississippi as that river figures in similar accounts of the imaginary harmony of class, caste, and race claimed on behalf of the vanished (and in Harris's time not so vanished) world of the old South.

Using a disingenuously hypothetical syntax, Harris fords the tortuous streams of African-American history and personality at several apparently convenient points. Uncle Remus, he observes, tentatively in our name, has "nothing but pleasant memories of the discipline of slavery." Now you might turn up a former slave or two who held these views, but Harris tries to create an archetype, so his assertion raises questions about history's claim upon the generalizing, rhetorical power of fiction and myth. Harris advances the myth of the Plantation School by virtue of the personal qualities *he* confers on Uncle Remus. As Harris imagines him, Remus is in circumstances a peasant, in bearing and opinions something of an aristocrat. His superiority follows from his loyalty and allegiance to the institution of slavery, and perhaps from a measure of white blood, while his kindness comes from his experience as a slave. Harris enacts his case through the fiction of an old former slave passing on the lore and values of the antebellum South to the young white scion of slaveholders. When Harris speaks of "practical reconstruction," he tacitly affirms, for his purposes, the power of oral culture. He implies that Uncle Remus's relationship with the little white boy is archetypal and was repeated in countless variations at that time in the South. Presumably, too, the boy's kinship with Remus insulates him from the racial poison spread, according to Harris's genteel myth, only by disreputables like the Fevres whom Remus implies are white trash in the immediate neighborhood. The storytelling practiced by Harris's Uncle Remus has little to do with the forms of African-American oral culture or with the political perspective of Negro Americans after the Civil War. When Harris elevates culture above politics, he insulates his myth of the South from the southern politics of his time, from the politics of terror and disenfranchisement and the emerging social and political rituals of lynching and the race riot. He does not acknowledge or understand that African-American oral culture, with its pattern of call-and-response, was deeply committed to a politics of radical change.

Imaginatively, with his rhetoric of myth Harris seeks to transform his personal history as well as the history of the South. His frame revises those boyhood occasions when he heard Uncle George Terrell tell tales in the slave quarters of Turnwold plantation. Specifically, he moves an imaginary past into the present moment and has the tales told to one little white boy (perhaps his fantasy self), whereas in the 1860s Terrell told stories to a community of children, black and white, slave and free. Harris's Uncle Remus frame expresses a longing for personal and psychological legitimacy and security. Taking cues again from Julia Collier Harris's biography, not to mention the subversive power of African-American folk culture, I surmise that Harris, a literally illegitimate, half-shanty Irish outsider occupying middle ground between black slave children and the white Turner children, came to feel at home at the hearth of George Terrell. Maybe this experience compelled him to invent a personal narrative frame compatible with the particular fiction of southern history and Negro personality he wished could be the reality of his region and its present and future generations. This configuration puts the tales, as told by Uncle Remus, at odds with the complex oral culture from which the slave tales issued and from which flows the African-American stream of American literary tradition.

3

Once Joel Chandler Harris invented Uncle Remus and adapted black folk storytelling to popular literary narrative, there was no going back. As framed by Harris and told by Uncle Remus, the tales seemed to confirm the nation's limited, false view of African-American history and personality. Harris's call, however distorted, cried out for an African-American response. Indeed, at the time Harris composed his static myth of the Negro and the old (and new) South, Charles Chesnutt was formulating literature's role in the process of historical change. "The Negro's part," Chesnutt wrote in his journal in 1880, "is to prepare himself for recognition and equality; and it is the province of literature to open the way for him to get it—to accustom the public mind to the idea; to lead people on, imperceptibly, unconsciously, step by step, to the desired state of feeling."[25] Light enough to pass, Chesnutt affirmed his African-American identity, and in Cleveland, where he earned the highest score on the bar exam but worked for years as a legal stenographer, he wrote "The Goophered Grapevine" (1887), the first of his Uncle Julius tales.

Encouraged by white southern writers like George Washington Cable and the lawyer-novelist, Albion Tourgee, Chesnutt collected seven of these tales in *The Conjure Woman* (1899). After a brief success *The Conjure Woman* was neglected—perplexingly, because from the vantage points of form and voice (personality) it is an essential innovative contribution to African-American fiction. Chesnutt unfolds the tales in a complex double narrative frame. A white narrator frames in florid, legalistic prose stories told to him and his wife in dialect by a black oral storyteller, Uncle Julius McAdoo. These conjure tales counter Harris's uses of the animal tales and the often viciously sentimental plantation legends of Thomas Nelson Page and other literary proponents of the comic myth of slavery as a generally benevolent if somewhat peculiar institution.

Coming to *The Conjure Woman* from Harris's *Uncle Remus: His Songs and Sayings*, I am struck by the open and closed form of these respective narratives. In Harris, personality is static. Nothing happens to change Uncle Remus in character or outlook. He remains entirely consistent with Harris's initial ventriloquist's portrait. He is kind and grandfatherly. He knows how a boy should handle his mother and how he should avoid disreputable, trashy neighbors of a caste supposedly abhorrent to both slaves and masters. He also displays the whims of advancing age: petulance, silence, real and feigned lapses of memory. And the unquestioning, uncritical allegiance and adulation of his single audience dulls Remus's improvisatory reflexes. But this is emphatically not the case with Chesnutt's two narrators. In contrast to the formulaic, mechanical relationship between Uncle Remus and the little boy, the voices of Chesnutt's narrators, John and Uncle Julius, contend dynamically on the field of narrative. Chesnutt's frame keeps their personalities unfolding and not merely reiterative; subtly and, in the case of John, unwillingly, each becomes responsive in unanticipated ways because of his experience with the other. Unlike Remus and the little white boy, John and Uncle Julius are each performer and audience; they engage in a variation of call-and-response.

As collections, *The Conjure Woman* and *Uncle Remus: His Songs and Sayings* have in common several crucial elements of taletelling. Both retell stories from the past in a contemporary context, and both counterpoint dialect with a formal, sententious standard English. But Harris introduces and periodically interrupts Uncle Remus in a third-person voice, whereas Chesnutt hands responsibility for the narrative frame over to John, and within it Uncle Julius performs his acts of storytelling. Chesnutt respects fiction's artifice, and his form forces narrator and storyteller to battle for the audience's allegiance. In *The Conjure Woman* Uncle Julius uses tales and the occasion of storytelling to tell the truth about slavery and to overcome an apparent disadvantage of race and class, for his mastery of oral expression and tradition gives him certain advantages over John.

Most of all, Chesnutt enacts the fiction of a pluralistic American reading public by creating a double audience for Julius McAdoo's tales. John and his wife, Annie, represent different facets of human personality and of American social reality in the period after the Civil War. Their responses suggest a tension between contrary impulses of the individual human heart often repeated in the contest

between head and heart, will and sympathy in the tales of Nathaniel
Hawthorne. John is an eighteenth-century man who wants his truth—
whether in fact, in history, or in fiction—measured and laid out
according to exact specifications and premises. And his simple, superficial empiricism is more than a way of thought; it becomes a
way of life, a way of response. But Annie is open to realities beyond
her direct or indirect observation. She tests what she hears against
her feelings and imagination. She understands that there is a mystery
to things and that Julius possesses the storyteller's power to reveal
what lies behind the surface of nature and human behavior. She is
a responsive listener and through her responses to Julius's tales encourages readers to bring the commonplace and mysterious, known
and unknown, into forthright relationship. Dramatically, Annie is
the fulcrum, the swing vote, and the two men, John and Julius,
contend for her allegiance, with Julius aware that she exercises
indirect power over the household and that she has the exemplary
power to change her husband's mind. Officially, according to background and position, she is of her husband's party. But as a woman,
she keeps in touch with a range of sympathies and possibilities far
wider than John's self-centered world of discrete, practical details.

Yet John is not simply a closed, rational mind. His skepticism is
a function of how he thinks he should act, a paradoxically passive
response to his society's norms of behavior. He migrates from Ohio
to North Carolina for his wife's health and his business interests.
Once there, he obeys the conventional male reflexes of power and
southern custom in his dealings with Julius, a former slave who still
lives on the quarters of the abandoned, rundown, old plantation.
Julius is an African-American whose ingratiating manner paradoxically belies and enhances his craft as a storyteller and his identity
as an individual. Gradually, his stories and the occasions they respond
to exert a cumulative influence on John. John is swayed, often in
submerged ways, by the mutual power of Julius's storytelling and
his personality. At stake is the nature of craft. Julius's strategy allows
his adversary maneuvering room. For instance, after John buys the
old McAdoo place for its scuppernong vineyard despite Julius's tale
of goophered grapevines, he hires Julius. His words express his need
to save face, to rationalize. "I believe, however," John tells not Julius
but his readers, "that the wages I paid for his services as a coachman,

for I gave him employment in that capacity, were more than an equivalent for anything he lost by the sale of the vineyard."[26] His words also reveal a Yankee shrewdness. After all, he discovered Julius savoring the grapes, so although Julius's tale of conjuration—of grapes and a slave bewitched—does not persuade John to take Julius's advice against buying the vineyard, the tale does move him to hire Julius as a coachman, an occupation that, during and after slavery, often put the African-American in the double role of spy and advisor. Here Chesnutt acknowledges the contradictions driving even the best relations between black and white Americans in his time. For John has things both ways. He scoffs at the mystery and metaphor of conjuring and dismisses Julius's biting indictment of slavery as biased, fanciful, and overdrawn. Yet though he condescends to Julius, at a deeper level he affirms the old man's usefulness and wisdom. For, as he writes, he knows that without Julius the restored vineyard would not be "often referred to by the local press as a striking illustration of the opportunities open to Northern capital in the development of Southern industries" (*CW*, p. 34).

Despite John's doubts about the tales he hears, he recognizes Julius as a historian of this plantation and the Pateville locale. From Julius, he learns things about the people and the place essential to living there and doing business that he could not figure out on his own. His doubts about Julius's tales confirm his disregard for and perhaps fear of the insolubles in human experience. Nevertheless, he heaps praise on Julius as a storyteller. In "The Marked Tree," John includes Julius in the class of world masters. "I suspected Julius at times of a large degree of poetic license—he took the crude legends and vague superstitions of the neighborhood and embodied them in stories as complete, in their way, as the Sagas of Iceland or the primitive tales of ancient Greece." Presently, John hedges, but the qualification is Chesnutt's way of calling readers to acknowledge Julius's achievement. "Had Julius lived in a happier age for men of his complexion the world might have had a black Aesop or Grimm or Hoffman—as it still may have, for who knows whether our civilization has yet more than cut its milk teeth, or humanity has even really begun to walk erect?"[27] In the first place, between John's moralizing about the past and the future stands the actual achievement of Julius's storytelling. Second, according to Herodotus, Aesop was a slave, probably of African origin or descent. Finally, in his own time and place Julius is a citizen of good heart and will who adapts African and African-American techniques of call-and-response to his story-telling before an uninitiated white audience—as if declaring that after the Civil War all of his countrymen and women are necessarily members of the same tribe.[28] As one who surrounds Julius's tales with a discourse close to legal writing, John should understand that the tales have more than an oral duration. For his part, Chesnutt, acting on his inner necessity to write fiction, places the spoken tale and its white audience's responses in a continuing, inclusive, pluralistic literary tradition.

4

Throughout *The Conjure Woman* Julius's individual tales pivot on the act and metaphor of conjuration. At the heart of the conjurer's art, like the storyteller's and the fiction writer's, is the power to turn one thing into another, to change the things of the earth and, as a consequence, alter relationships in the mind of the listener and reader. A conjurer possesses special powers. Using the juices, herbs, and powders of Nature, he steps outside ordinary ideas of cause and effect. But the conjurer's agency depends on craft as well as imagination; like the art of fiction, conjuring derives its power from thorough, indeed scholarly knowledge and the application of precise techniques and skills to the natural world.

Like the storyteller and the writer, the conjurer discloses reality's possibilities. Aunt Peggy and the others in *The Conjure Woman* bring an old African tribal art to bear on the environment of slavery. Through his tales and his participation in the work of interpretation Julius undermines his white listeners' [and Chesnutt's white readers'] static view of slavery. For one thing Aunt Peggy and the conjure man of the tales are free Negroes. They dare to cross conventional lines between slavery and freedom, black and white relationships. Both slaves and masters are rightly wary of antagonizing conjurers. People of each race, though more often slaves, consult conjurers, obey their rules, and pay for services rendered.

Here, Chesnutt intends a tie between the mobility and independence free Negroes enjoyed even in the midst of North Carolina plantations and the power to change the environment. Chesnutt's passion for history compels him to mix elements from the animal tales with those of more realistic folktales, the tales of John the slave, for instance. He uses tales not as an escape from history into myth but as one of history's unofficial sources—what Ellison calls that "stream of history which is still as tightly connected with folklore and the oral tradition as official history is connected with the tall tale."[29] And the debate among Julius, John, and Annie about the past raises questions about the prevailing social order in the dramatic narrative present of the 1880s. In "The Dumb Witness," John displays a classic nineteenth-century view of racial hierarchy. Referring to the "low morality of inferior races," he claims that "our own race excels them all, when it wishes, because it lends to evil purposes a higher intelligence and a wider experience than inferior races can command."[30] But the craft of Uncle Julius and the skills of his characters refute John's patronizing, backhanded claim for Caucasian "higher intelligence and wider experience." As a storyteller who both instructs and entertains, Julius revises the terms of discussion about race and personality. *The Conjure Woman* places the strongest *individual* levers of power in the hands of black conjurers and the strongest *institutional* levers in the hands of white masters. On this level, too, the battle is joined in the present between John and Julius, and won by Julius, often because he improvises an effective answer to John's negative response to the tale just told.

Julius never forces his tales on John or Annie. In every case one or both of them asks him for a story. Because of his venerable, low-key, understated, unthreatening but always savvy voice, his tales persuasively indict slavery and affirm the principle of human equality Chesnutt sought to advance in his fiction.[31] Julius's continuing presence around the plantation makes him centrally important to the narrator and his wife. At first, Julius obeys the conventional rules. He is respectful, speaks when spoken to. But his is the stance of a man who knows who he is and, though inquiring by nature, is less interested in these new northern white folks than they are in him. For them, he is a guide to an unfamiliar place and a people more legendary than actual to many northerners. He is inseparable from the natural, moral, historical landscape. And he possesses such a storehouse of tales that, whatever the present controversy, he can choose a story to advance his point of view and his specific objective. The connections between the tales Julius tells and his life in the present underline the complexity of his storyteller's craft and his progressive resolve to help create a community of both black and white citizens. Will he continue to have free access to the vineyard? Will he be able to use the lumber from a crumbling old kitchen for his new church? Will he persuade John to rehire his grandson? Less self-interestedly, will he be able to ease Annie's melancholy, and can he stop time long enough for her young sister to work through her lover's quarrel with young Malcolm Murchison? These issues are small matters, and alongside the life and death action of the tales, they seem almost trivial. Julius knows this and makes the apparent disjunction serve a double purpose. The dialogic form of his return to the present both lessens the immediate tragic tension of the tale just told and intensifies what has been heard by allowing its after-effects to reverberate in the listeners' minds as if to prepare a space in which Julius can serve as interpreter of past and present.

As a collection, the tales express the diversity and complexity of African-American life during slavery. "The Conjurer's Revenge" and "The Grey Wolf's Ha'nt," for instance, turn wholly upon relations among blacks, with free Negroes avenging themselves upon slaves not by virtue of justice but through the power of conjuration exercised amorally. The other five tales are closely bound up with the influence of slavery on the basic conditions of human life. In them conjuring counters slavery's institutional power to fray or break the ties of human kinship. In this sense, Julius's tales locate the offical and unofficial forces at work during slavery.

At first, Chesnutt mutes his irony and appears simply to initiate an educated but provincial northerner in the ways of the South. In a rambling, satisfied voice John begins "The Goophered Grapevine" by tracing his and his wife's migration to North Carolina. A cousin sponsors him, and John feels so acutely the tourist's false familiarity that he regards Julius McAdoo as a curiosity, an old man sitting on a log with a hatful of grapes. Embarrassed, Julius grasps that these two strange Yankees jeopardize his poacher's privileged position. Introducing John and Annie to African-American storytelling, Julius, wearing a mask that evokes the minstrel manner along with folk speech and folk values, unfolds a tragic tale. He tries to persuade

John not to buy the vineyard, knowing that even if he fails, he will have made a good impression for future dealings with an important new white man.

In Julius's tale of "The Goophered Grapevine" the natural and human orders are violated by the master's greed. To prevent his slaves from eating grapes and diminishing slightly his profits, Mars Dugal hires Aunt Peggy to charm the vineyard. Like Julius's role as storyteller, Aunt Peggy's position as conjure woman is complex, though unambiguous. (Although she conjures for whites as well as blacks, she insists on cash payment from whites, while the slaves' offerings are usually pilfered from the master's smokehouse or chicken yard.) After conjuring the vineyard and telling one of the slaves that "a nigger w'at eat dem grapes 'ud be sho ter die inside'n twel' mont's" (*CW*, p. 16), Peggy, at the overseer's request, immunizes a new fieldhand from the conjured grapes he has eaten by mistake. Henry, the new slave, is a good worker so Aunt Peggy does Mars Dugal a favor, too.

The tale turns on nuances of relationship. Once conjured, Henry's vitality, like the grapevine's, waxes and wanes according to changes in the seasons and also according to the vicissitudes of Mars Dugal's management. Unmindful of Henry's wishes, Mars Dugal hoodwinks other men who, like him, seek to profit from slavery's human traffic. For five years he sells Henry in the spring and buys him back for a pittance during the dead of winter. As long as Mars Dugal plays his grotesque tricks within the natural cycle to which Aunt Peggy has attached Henry's life, the natural order continues to function. But eventually Mars Dugal, outgambled and half-bewitched by a fast-talking Yankee, hires this confidence man to increase scientifically the yield on his scuppernongs. The charlatan's intervention disrupts the fragile balance between natural and moral forces restored by Aunt Peggy's conjuring.

"The Goophered Grapevine" is about the sources, uses, and consequences of power. Aunt Peggy's comes from a knowledge of living things, yet her individual power is subject to the larger institutional force of slavery. When the grapes wither and die, Henry dies, too, because his well-being depends on relationships in the world around him. Rounding out his tale, Julius testifies eloquently to the mysterious yet verifiable pattern of connection and causality in nature and consciousness.

> All dis time de goopher wuz a-wukkin'. When de vimes sta'ted ter wither, Henry 'mence' ter complain er his rheumatiz; en when de leaves begin ter dry up, his ha'r 'mence' ter drap out. When de vimes fresh' up a bit, Henry 'd git peart ag'in, en when de vimes wither' ag'in, Henry 'd git ole ag'in, en des kep' gittin' mo' en mo' fitten fer nuffin; he des pined away, en pined away, en fine'ly tuk ter his cabin; en when de big vime whar he got de sap ter 'n'int his head withered en turned yaller an died, Henry died too,— des went out sorter like a cannel. (*CW*, pp. 31-32)

Julius's account is also an exemplary tale for the present circumstance. After all, John, also a Yankee, eventually buys the vineyard and hires Julius to take advantage of his knowledge and lore, his presence as a genius of the place. He learns from Mars Dugal's experience that it is to his advantage to live tolerantly with "his mild suspicion that our colored assistants do not suffer from want of grapes during the season" (*CW*, p. 34). He learns from Julius that this practice is part of the pact, the needful relationship between those who work the vineyard and the grapes, and that it is in the best interest of the owner to respect this relationship. Presumably, too, John learns about agriculture from Julius who, in the absence of an owner controlling the vineyard, was content to take only a "respectable revenue" from the grapes. So, because of the tale and Julius's sneaky, comic, understated manner of performance, the use of power undergoes a subtle change. As coachman and counselor, Julius now has an official and unofficial relationship with John and Annie. Contrary to John's view that Julius "seemed to lose sight of his auditors, and to be living over again in monologue his life on the old plantation" (*CW*, p. 13), the old storyteller is shrewdly, deceptively, and constantly aware of his audience. His performer's guile and craft enable him to enlarge John's narrow scheme to include a simultaneously moral and historical frame of reference and rhetoric.

In response and as introduction to "Po' Sandy," the next story, John testifies to the diverse and wide range of tales in Julius's repertoire. "Some," he says, "are quaintly humorous, others wildly extravagant, revealing the Oriental cast of the Negro's imagination; while others poured freely into the sympathetic ear of a Northern-bred woman, disclose many a tragic incident of the darker side of slavery" (*CW,* pp. 40-41). John's comments are primarily self-revealing. The differences between him and Annie are differences of sensibility, and Chesnutt makes gender a figure for sensibility. "Northern-bred," both hear the same tales, but as a master storyteller and performer, Julius quickly senses that Annie's sympathy runs deeper than her husband's. Even *after* he has heard "Po' Sandy" and other tales and begun to write them down, John limits the full power of the tales to disclose "many a tragic incident of the darker side of slavery" to Annie. His response seems both a concession and a revelation of his lingering compulsion to view slavery in terms of a balanced moral equation. Yet his comments prepare the responsive reader to listen carefully to the forthcoming voices of Julius and Annie. Julius is finely sensitive to the sensibility called for by this story, for his essential purpose is to compel his audience to see and feel and understand the sinister values behind the institution of slavery. No doubt he knows about the coming split in the Sandy Run Colored Baptist Church, knows the old schoolhouse could provide his faction with a meeting place. But he is not about to play the minstrel with a story so expressive of his people's unalterable tragic past. Here and elsewhere, John misunderstands the complementary relationship between performance and entertainment; he tends to stereotype Julius and ignore the serious and profound uses to which Julius puts his comic gifts.

In this tale Sandy and Tenie (and also Sandy's first wife) are victims of the capricious ownership—the buying and selling and swapping—of human beings. That power knows no limits to its abuse. To keep her husband Sandy near her, Tenie turns him into a tree.

> "Shill I turn you ter a wolf?" sez Tenie.
> "No, eve'ybody's skeered er a wolf, en I doan want nobody ter be skeered er me."
> "Shill I turn you ter a mawkin'-bird?"
> "No, a hawk mought ketch me. I wanter be turnt inter sump'n w'at'll stay in one place."
> "I kin turn you ter a tree," sez Tenie. "You won't hab no mouf ner years, but I kin turn you back oncet in a w'ile, so you kin git sump'n ter eat, en hear w'at's a gwine on." (*CW,* pp. 46-47)

Within the prison of slavery, Tenie and Sandy sustain the essentials of their love and life. But Tenie is shipped off to nurse one of the master's relatives. While she is away, Sandy is cut down and, in another transformation, sawed into lumber for Mrs. Marrabo's new kitchen. Desirous "ter 'splain ter 'im dat she had n' went off a-purpose, en lef' 'im ter be chop' down en sawed up" (CW, p. 54), Tenie is tied up like a crazy woman by the mill hands, and excruciatingly watches Sandy die.

Julius ends the tale with a dying fall. Folks say, he tells John and Annie, that any remaining lumber from the tree that was Sandy "is gwine ter be ha'nted tel de las' piece er plank is rotted en crumble' inter dus' " (CW, p. 60). Annie, the woman, understands instantly and completely. " 'What a system it was,' she exclaimed, under the sorrowful spell of the tale, 'under which such things were possible!' " (CW, p. 60). True to form, John's narrow, literal mind misconstrues Annie's reference to such things. "Are you seriously considering the possibility of a man's being turned into a tree?" (CW, p. 60). She demurs, seeming to yield to his intimidation, then murmurs with, as John describes her, "a dim look in her fine eyes, 'Poor Tenie!' " (CW, p. 61). Writing down the exchange, John undercuts his position during the time of Julius's actual storytelling, as if admitting that Julius's sense of tact and timing—his complex sense of performance—has nudged him toward a more compassionate historical awareness.

A week or two after Annie decides against using any of the old lumber for her new kitchen, Julius asks her if his Baptist faction "might not hold their meetings in the old schoolhouse for the present" (CW, p. 62). John's irritation, he freely acknowledges, stems partly from the fact that he has just received a bill for the new lumber, and partly from Annie's admission that she has donated money toward the new church. Despite this, and perhaps in irrepressible admiration for Julius's consummate performing skill, John reveals how Julius disposed of even his last meanly literal question. " 'Oh,' replied Annie, 'Uncle Julius says that ghosts never disturb religious worship, but that if Sandy's spirit *should* happen to stray into meeting by mistake, no doubt the preaching would do it good' " (CW, p. 63). Julius has been the articulate voice for Sandy and his ghost, and his message, intended for John through Annie, is that his storytelling has already put John through some beneficial changes. If that is the case, maybe the preacher's testifying will have similar salutary effects on the mind of a restless ghost. Julius's mischievous words, conveyed to John by Annie, reinforce his storyteller's whammy over John in their call-and-response combat. Their contention continues, but here Julius and John may begin to anticipate an eventual fraternal outcome to the contest.

In "Mars Jeems's Nightmare" the conjuring of Aunt Peggy *in* the tale and Uncle Julius *with* the tale leads to changes in values and to subsequent actions in the past and present. But John introduces the tale by affirming the view of the African-American held by the Plantation School. Julius, he tells us, "had attached himself to the old plantation, of which he seemed to consider himself an appurtenance." Writing *ex cathedra*, he concludes that "we found him useful in many ways and entertaining in others, and my wife and I, took quite a fancy to him" (*CW*, p. 65). John's mask of genteel condescension veils the intensity of the conflict about to unfold. John hires Julius's grandson "mainly to please the old man." Irritated by his own spurious, sentimental generosity, he soon sours on the young man and calls him lazy, careless, and "trifling" — about the worst things he could say about a young Negro male. Julius responds by putting on his minstrel's mask. "I knows he ain' much account, en dey ain' much 'pen'ence ter be put on 'im. But I wuz hopin' dat you mought make some 'lowance fuh a' ign'ant young nigger, suh, en gib 'im one mo' chance" (*CW*, p. 67). But John reasserts his identity as a practical northerner and rejects Julius's appeal to paternalistic southern ritual. According to his deserts a "fair trial" is sufficient. He fires the grandson, and Julius addresses the issue from behind his storyteller's veil.[32]

Knowing that his most important listener is no longer John but Annie, Julius conjures with the tale as his goopher. He waits for a suitable occasion and finds it in a man furiously beating his horse. " 'A man w'at 'buses his hoss is gwine ter be ha'd on de folks w'at wuks fer 'em,' " remarks Julius, and he tantalizes John and Annie with dark hints about the offensive gentleman's grandfather and his bad dream "way back yander, long yeahs befo' de wah" (*CW*, p. 70). John calls for more, and Julius responds with a tale. Mars Jeems McLean's "niggers wuz bleedzed ter slabe fum daylight ter da'k, w'iles yuther folks's did n' hafter wuk 'cep'n' fum sun ter sun" (*CW*, p. 71).

To Julius, with his memories of slavery's abuses, differences of degree were bad enough. But in Jeems's case, some of the differences were in kind, as when, unsuccessful in love because his fiancee interprets his cruelty to slaves as a sign of his true character, he forbids love and courting among his slaves. Defied by one pair of lovers, he sells the woman and orders forty lashes for her man, Solomon. Solomon promptly enlists Aunt Peggy's aid. For two pecks of corn, she prepares a goopher, which sends away Mars Jeems and paradoxically leaves his slaves at the mercy of an overseer who is even harsher than Jeems. But soon Jeems returns in the form of a recalcitrant, amnesiac slave and for his insolence is mercilessly hounded but not broken. Transformed back into a white man by Aunt Peggy, Jeems turns his values and policies inside out. He pretends to enjoy his overseer's account of cruelty toward the unidentified slave, then, suddenly, capriciously fires him. The slaves love again and prosper, and Jeems's former sweetheart, hearing about his changed character, restores him to her affections. But Julius's concluding images of happy days on the plantation are received sarcastically by John. " 'And they all lived happy ever after,' I said, as the old man reached a full stop. 'Yes, suh,' he said, interpreting my remarks as a question, 'dey did' " (*CW*, p. 99). Julius, always a master of timing, seizes the role of interpreter. " 'Dis yer tale goes ter show,' concluded Julius sententiously, 'dat w'te folks w'at is is so ha'd en stric', en doan make no 'lowance fer po' ign'ant niggers w'at ain' had no chanst ter l'arn, is li'ble ter hab bad dreams, ter say de leas', en dat dem w'at is kin' en good ter po' people is sho' ter prosper en git 'long in de worl' " (*CW*, p. 100).

Julius revises the myth of the contented slave in favor of an attitude closer to that dream of American possibility proposed by the Declaration of Independence. Perhaps feeling pressured, John, too, retreats to first principles and accuses Julius of making up the tale. Julius's response bears witness to the complexity of the oral tradition: "My mammy tol' me dat tale w'en I wa'n't mo' d'n knee-high ter a *hopper-grass*' " (*CW*, p. 101, my italics). By invoking his ancestor and by replacing grasshopper with hopper-grass, Julius affirms both the tale's longevity and his own improvisatory power. But John still

51

does not grasp that tales as told, embellished, and retold have a function in daily life. In this case Julius embellishes a tale whose outcome upholds values central to the tradition held sacred by John and, particularly, his wife. Treat those less well off badly and you will have bad dreams and worse. Treat them better than you need to, and they and you will prosper.

Once again, Chesnutt advances his theme of change through small actions in the present. In John's absence, Annie hires back Julius's grandson. When John returns, he is quietly furious, yet the glimpse he now gives of the grandson is another persuasive reversal of stereotypes. "I saw a familiar figure carrying a bucket of water to the barn" (*CW*, p. 101), he notes, and this image of the young man performing his duties replaces John's earlier portrait of shiftlessness and hopelessness. Julius, the storyteller and trickster, uses a tale to change both his grandson and his boss for the better.

In "Sis Becky's Pickaninny" Julius's storytelling addresses Annie's psychological and spiritual depression and restores her to health. After two years in North Carolina, she becomes "the victim of a settled melancholy, attended with vague forebodings of impending misfortune" (*CW*, p. 132). When Julius shows up and silently fingers his rabbit's foot as a sign of concern, John seizes eagerly on his presence. But he soon ridicules the old man, and his sententious little speech against superstition is Chesnutt's signal that the rabbit's foot will have metaphorical power both within the tale and its narrative frame.

> "Julius," I observed, half to him and half to my wife, "your people will never rise in the world until they throw off these childish superstitions and learn to live by the light of reason and common sense. How absurd to imagine that the fore-foot of a poor dead rabbit, with which he timorously felt his way along through a life surrounded by snares and pitfalls, beset by enemies on every hand, can promote happiness or success, or ward off failure or misfortune!" (*CW*, pp. 134-35)

Julius counters with a slapstick, almost minstrel response: "De fo'-foot ain't got no power. It has ter be de hin'-foot" (*CW*, p. 135). Julius's outrageous, wonderful riff mocks John's refusal to admit mysterious, rationally unaccountable phenomena into his scheme of reality, and calls satiric attention to John's reference to the rabbit's hard, hapless life, apparently without the slightest awareness of the trickster's role performed by Br'er Rabbit in African-American folklore.[33] Then, too, Julius's refutation of John's syllogistic logic, reminiscent of Jim's demolition of Huck's flawed argument about language in *Huck Finn*, establishes his power on John's ground. Julius's stubborn discrimination between effectual and ineffectual rabbit's feet also reinforces his power as storyteller, for his craft confers on everyday objects a form and meaning they have not had before for his audience. In the end, after he tells the tale and Annie responds sympathetically, he loans her his rabbit's foot because she has traveled outside her depression and entered imaginatively a historical world where grief and trouble more intense and terrible than hers are suffered and overcome.

Recall the profoundly historical simile of the old spiritual: "Sometimes I feel like a motherless child/A long ways from home." Everything about Julius's tale and its strategy of conjuring suggests that in the hands of slaves and for that matter in the hands of abolitionist forces in the North, ordinary weapons like "reason and common sense" were powerless to reverse the personal cruelty and tragedy that accompanied slavery. The tale's action examines the assumptions and institutional power of slavery. Sis Becky's master wants another master's horse. To get it he exchanges her but not her baby son. Colonel Pendleton's self-justifying, cowardly idea of kindness leads him to lie to Sis Becky about where she is going and for how long. Aunt Peggy's conjuring succeeds because through it the health of both woman and horse appears to decline, so that out of self-interest the two plantation owners disingenuously negotiate the return of each other's property. Here and in other Chesnutt tales a struggle goes on between property and the more fluid pursuit of happiness as primary human rights. "Sis Becky's Pickaninny" projects an advance on the condition of happiness characterized in "Mars Jeems's Nightmare." Even when the spell of conjuring ends, the boy Mose retains the ability to sing like a mockingbird. He sings for white folks, improves his mother's life with the proceeds, and after becoming a successful blacksmith, buys her freedom, then his own. Freedom remains the objective and the last best expression of the pursuit of happiness. And conjuring, an example of transformation at a cost — Aunt Peggy always insists on payment — provides a catalyst for change.

Back in the present, as if demonstrating her worthiness of Julius's rabbit's foot, Annie responds to John's mockery of the tale's literal level. "Those are mere ornamental details and not at all essential," she tells him. "The story is true to nature, and might have happened half a hundred times, and no doubt did happen, in those horrid days before the war" (*CW,* p. 159). She understands and succinctly expresses the form and meaning of the slave tales as told and performed by Julius in variations on what has been handed down to him. When John characteristically ignores Annie's case and asks Julius about the relevance of the rabbit's foot, Julius calls on Annie to be his interpreter. Her responses to the spell of the tale make her restoration to health and vitality a continuing condition. As a sign of friendship and appreciation, Julius loans her his rabbit's foot, a symbolic object he swears he "wouldn' sell, no indeed, suh, I wouldn' " (*CW,* p. 136). His gesture, together with his tale and Annie's whole-souled response, affirms the pursuit of happiness as an inalienable right that ought to be available to every citizen, black and white, male and female, a right more essential than property.

Lest the act and metaphor of conjuring seem too easy, Chesnutt closes out *The Conjure Woman* with "Hot-Foot Hannibal," a comic tale that turns tragic because the lovers who retain Aunt Peggy fail to learn the lesson of craft essential to their efforts to displace Hannibal from his position as the house slave favored to have Chloe by the master and mistress. Chloe and Jeff concentrate so entirely on each other they forget Aunt Peggy's instruction to return " 'dis baby doll' " and her warning that "it's monst'us powerful goopher, en is liable ter make mo' trouble ef you leabe it layin' roun' " (*CW,* p. 208). Perhaps the lovers assume that trouble can never be their lot. But they are wrong. Hannibal, banished from the big house to the fields, and still afflicted because of the lovers' negligence, guesses that Chloe and Jeff are responsible for his sudden change in estate. Guilefully and cruelly, he plays on Chloe's jealousy to set in motion another reversal of fortune. Conjuring, then, is a catalyst for possibility, but most attractive possibilities have a quotient of danger and may boomerang if discipline and craft are not observed.

Certainly, in the present, craft is a necessary condition for Julius if he is to help heal the lovers' quarrel between Annie's sister, Mabel, and young Malcolm Murchison. From John we learn that the "match thus rudely broken off" is in his self-interest as "another link binding [him] to the kindly Southern people among whom [he] had not long before taken up residence" (*CW*, p. 197). But the potentiality for action belongs to Julius. He suggests the long way on a drive but draws back when Annie insists on the short way. To argue with her would violate good form. Besides, to fight and lose might close out his options. Instead, Julius keeps his distance and his discipline, though in his tale he recounts that Mars Dugal "would 'a' had old Aun' Peggy whip' long ago, on'y *Aunt Peggy wuz a free 'oman, en he wuz 'feared she'd cunjuh him*" (*CW*, p. 219, my italics). Julius is content with this oblique reference to power's actual and potential checks and balances.

In cahoots with a recalcitrant mare, Uncle Julius tells an appropriate tale and so persuades Annie to take the lead and the long road. In the end the lovers seize the opportunity Julius has offered and work out a reconciliation. They marry and offer him a position. Skillfully, Chesnutt has Julius turn it down as a way of undermining John's smug, suspicious comment "that a most excellent understanding existed between [Julius] and Murchison after the reconciliation." But Chesnutt does something else, too. He allows John to record Julius's decision. "For some reason or other, however," he writes, "he preferred to remain with us" (*CW*, p. 229). And why not? In life and in performance Julius finds his moveable frame, his foil, his opportunity to use form and convention to advance his interests, his values, and the well-being of the whole community of black and white citizens in generous progression. Yet John mutes his tone as if he, too, now knows these things, accepts them, and acknowledges that somehow he and Julius have become kin. And this kinship is palpably a consequence of craft, for in *The Conjure Woman* acts of voice lead to connections between contesting narrative personalities and points of view. Through storytelling Julius conjures the past, and by engagement with his audience he clarifies and in small ways changes the present situation. His performances may have changed John sufficiently that Julius need no longer resort to tricks in their relationship. To put it another way, John seems to have been conjured and to have accepted his transformation on a permanent basis. Because of John's grudging, gradual respect for Julius's craft, his attitude toward the former slave changes from arrogant paternalism to co-operation and perhaps even a preliminary acknowledgment of that democratic equality for which Chesnutt stands.

5

Recall the last words of *The Conjure Woman:* "The mare, I might add, was never known to balk again" (*CW,* p. 229). John's voice now joins Julius's in affirming the continuing power of conjuring and storytelling. And the mare, in John's possession but Julius's care, is a figure for the potential effects of storytelling. In the last tale, Julius first caused the mare to balk, then released her from a momentarily useful, fixed position into one of motion and freedom from restraint, of fluidity and possibility. The mare's release corresponds to Chesnutt's liberation of African-American tales, their black story-teller, white audience and white narrator, too, from the literary stereotypes of Joel Chandler Harris and the southern Plantation School.[34] On this point Chesnutt is specific. Two years after publication of *The Conjure Woman,* he declared his allegiance to a *"literature of necessity."* "The writings of Harris and Page and others of that ilk," he explained to Booker T. Washington, "have furnished my chief incentive to write something upon the other side of the very vital question."[35] That question was, as Ralph Ellison wrote some sixty years later in "The World and the Jug," "the Negro struggle for freedom." Like Ellison, who told Irving Howe that "my reply to your essay is in itself a small though necessary action" in that struggle,[36] and like Douglass before him, Chesnutt understood that literary freedom was bound up with the larger struggle. He understood, too, that the urgent relationship between storyteller and audience, between the word and the world needed imaginative expression in fiction.

Ellison once observed that *Huck Finn* was "a collaboration between a white American novelist of good heart, of democratic vision . . . and white readers, primarily." Chesnutt's form and Uncle Julius's story-telling voice allowed all Americans to become more truly "grounded" in the "reality of Negro American personality"[37] than exposure to Twain's Jim made possible. Chesnutt wrote for all his countrymen.

In its time *The Conjure Woman* invited white Americans also of "good heart, of democratic vision," to join the African-American audience. Confident he had mastered his craft, Chesnutt predicted his approach to fiction and folklore would "win out in the long run, so far as I am personally concerned, and will help the cause, which is vastly more important."[38] As a writer Chesnutt helped the cause so much that *The Conjure Woman* continues to challenge writers to discover their own form and voices, and tell their own stories inspired by the tales of folklore and the oral tradition. And the cause remains the double craft of fiction and democracy.

NOTES

1. W. E. B. Du Bois, *The Souls of Black Folk: Essays and Sketches* (1903; rpt., with an introduction by Saunders Redding, New York: Fawcett Publications, 1961), pp. 16, 17.

2. Paul Lawrence Dunbar, *The Complete Poems of Paul Lawrence Dunbar* (New York: Dodd, Mead, 1965), p. 112.

3. A favorite phrase of Brown's. His pioneering criticism is still essential on the importance of the oral tradition and its forms to African-American and American literary history. See *Negro Poetry and Drama* (1937), *The Negro in American Fiction* (1937), and *The Negro Caravan* (1941), particularly the latter's pithy, invaluable introductory essays on folk materials and folk forms. In his blues-ballads (see *The Collected Poems of Sterling A. Brown* [1980]) Brown brings the spoken word and folk forms of African-American oral tradition to new life on the page.

4. Arthur Huff Fauset, "American Folk Literature," in *The New Negro*, ed. Alain Locke (1925; rpt., New York: Atheneum, 1968), p. 240. Fauset's discussion contains useful comments on the Uncle Remus tales of Joel Chandler Harris as "not folk tales, but adaptations."

5. Sterling A. Brown in remarks made on the occasion of his 80th birthday at Brown University, Providence, R.I., May 1, 1981.

6. See Lawrence W. Levine's important chapter on African-American tales, "The Meaning of Slave Tales," in his *Black Culture and Black Consciousness* (New York: Oxford University Press, 1977), pp. 81-135.

7. Frederick Douglass, *Narrative of the Life of Frederick Douglass, An American Slave* (1845; rpt., New York: Signet, l968), p. 31, my italics.

8. See Robert B. Stepto's discussion of Douglass's narrative strategies in "Storytelling in Early Afro-American Fiction: Frederick Douglass's 'The Heroic Slave,'" *Georgia Review* 36, no. 12 (Summer 1982), 355-68.

9. Charles W. Chesnutt, as quoted by Sylvia Lyons Render in her introduction to *The Short Fiction of Charles W. Chesnutt* (Washington, D.C.: Howard University Press, 1974), p. 9. Render's discussion of Chesnutt's commitment to democratic equality and his ideas about the relationship between fiction and American democracy is especially valuable.

10. Until Chesnutt's time there were few attempts at fiction. Instead, black American writers won large reading audiences with slave narratives, autobiographies, speeches, essays, and public letters by Benjamin Banneker, David Walker, Henry Highland Garnet, Frederick Douglass, Harriet Jacobs, Moses Roper, and others.

11. Ralph Ellison, *Invisible Man* (1952; rpt., with author's introduction, New York: Random House, 1982), p. 293.

12. Robert Hemenway, introduction to Joel Chandler Harris's *Uncle Remus: His Songs and Sayings* (New York: Penguin Books, 1982), p. 12. This volume will be cited hereafter as *UR*. Also see Harris's account of his years at Turnwold in *On the Plantation* in which he recounts, as Hemenway notes, "that he befriended a runaway slave shortly after arriving, an act of kindness that caused Turnwold's black citizens to treat him with special respect" (p. 12). Hemenway's essay is perceptive about Harris's relations with blacks, about the genesis of Uncle Remus, and, not least, about Harris's sense of history and milieu. Roger D. Abrahams's unpublished manuscript, "Joe Harris and the Exploding Pumpkin," uses Harris's "white imitation of a black imitation of an Irishman" to suggest black tricksters' use of the Irish-American numskull stories.

13. See Hemenway's introduction to *UR*, p. 12. By coincidence, Eatonton is Alice Walker's hometown, and she watched as Harris, Uncle Remus, and Br'er Rabbit became an enormously popular and profitable tourist attraction. "There's even an iron rabbit on the courthouse lawn," she told me several years ago, "but no statue and no mention whatever of George Terrell."

14. Henry C. Grady, "The New South," *Orations and Speeches* (Norwood: Norwood Press, 1910), pp. 7-22. On Grady's use of race as an argument for "home rule" and "local autonomy," see Lawrence J. Friedman, *The White Savage: Racial Fantasies in the Postbellum South* (Englewood Cliffs: Prentice-Hall, 1970), pp. 41, 43-44.

15. Robert Bone, *Down Home: A History of Afro-American Short Fiction* (New York: G. P. Putman's Sons, 1975), pp. 19-20. See also Bone's discussion of Charles Chesnutt's debunking of the Southern pastoral ideal in his short fiction, ibid., pp. 74-93.

16. *Zora Neale Hurston, Mules and Men* (Philadelphia: J. B. Lippincott, 1935), pp. 4, 67.

17. Ellison, *Invisible Man*, p. 134.

18. "Curiously enough," Harris recounts, "I have found few Negroes who will acknowledge to a stranger that they know anything of these legends; and yet to relate one of the stories is the surest road to their confidence and esteem. In this way, and in this way only, I have been enabled to collect and verify the folk-lore included in this volume" (*UR*, p. 45).

19. Julia Collier Harris, *The Life and Letters of Joel Chandler Harris* (Boston: Houghton Mifflin, 1918), pp. 147-48. In this connection see also Hemenway's introduction to UR, pp. 17-18, in particular his notation of Harris's aside that "a couple of the storytellers 'if their language and their gestures could have been taken down, would have put Uncle Remus to shame.'" I should also note that Mrs. Harris dates receipt of this tale as 1881; since "The End of Mr. Bear" appeared in the first edition of *Uncle Remus: His Songs and Sayings* in November 1880, presumably she has confused the date.

20. In other tales like "Miss Cow Falls a Victim to Mr. Rabbit," Harris's variation on "Br'er Rabbit and Sis Cow," Uncle Remus's embellishments are ornamental rather than substantive. And in "Why the Alligator's Back Is Rough," Harris's narrator foreshortens but does not seriously alter the saltier, common version, "Why Br'er Gator's Hide Is So Horny." Nonetheless, Harris's Uncle Remus variations on some of the most important and archetypal African-American tales raise perplexing critical questions. The matter of cultural authenticity recalls confusions about authorial voice and identity and, therefore, about slave experience that grew out of the *narrative relationship* between some former slaves and the white abolitionists who served as their amanuenses. In this connection see Robert B. Stepto's convincing discussion on the authenticating devices of slave narrative and also his emphasis on "the quest for freedom and literacy" in chapter 1 of *From Behind the Veil: A Study of Afro-American Narrative* (Urbana: University of Illinois Press, 1979), pp. 3-31. Also see William L. Andrews's *To Tell a Free Story: The First Century of Afro-American Autobiography* (Urbana: University of Illinois Press, 1986).

21. Hurston, *Mules and Men*, p. 5.

22. This folk version of "Tar Baby" is found in *The Book of Negro Folklore*, ed. Langston Hughes and Arna Bontemps (New York: Dodd, Mead, 1958), pp. 1-2. On the versions of "Tar Baby," see Roger D. Abrahams's discussion of William Owens's "first journalistic notice of Afro-American tales in the United States." "Ironically," Abrahams writes, noting Harris's concern for authenticity, "Owens's version of this encounter was closer to the way in which the tale is commonly told in Africa than was Harris's rendition." *Afro-American Folktales* (New York: Pantheon, 1985), p. 16.

23. Ralph Ellison, *Shadow and Act* (New York: Random House, 1964), p. 143. Interpretations of "Tar Baby" abound. For two intriguing, complex responses to the tale see *Shadow and Act*, p. 147, and Hemenway, *UR*, pp. 26-7.

24. See Sterling Brown's essential discussion of this and other stereotypes of Negro personality in "A Century of Negro Portraiture in American Literature," *Massachusetts Review* 7, no. 1 (Winter, 1966), pp. 73-96; and in *The Negro in American Fiction* (New York: Arno Press, 1969). In the April 1932 issue of *Opportunity* Brown also has a perceptive essay on the contradictions present in Harris's attitude toward the Negro throughout his life and work.

25. Chesnutt as quoted by Render in her introduction to *The Short Fiction of Chesnutt*, p. 9.

26. Charles W. Chesnutt, *The Conjure Woman* (1899; rpt., Ann Arbor: University of Michigan Press, 1969), p. 35. This volume will be cited hereafter as *CW*.

27. *Short Fiction of Chesnutt*, p. 144. Render's collection includes Uncle Julius tales not in *The Conjure Woman;* it is to be hoped that all of these stories will be collected one day in a separate volume comprising Chesnutt's cycle of Uncle Julius tales, tales that inventively mix features of both the animal cycle and the cycle of John (or Jack) the slave.

28. See Roger D. Abrahams's discussion of storytelling and performance in his preface to *African Folktales: Selected and Retold by Roger D. Abrahams* (New York: Pantheon, 1983), pp. xv-xvi.

29. Ralph Ellison, "The Uses of History in Fiction," *Southern Literary Journal* 1, no. 2 (1969), 69. And I would note Chesnutt's connection to the American tradition of yarns and yarn-spinning, for it is not only in the black oral tradition that stories are "lies." Mark Twain was a master of the functional tall story. Huck Finn survives by making up stories on the spur of the moment. Paradoxically, his stories are "lies" whose realism wards off danger and allows him to persist in his anomalous friendship with Jim; recall the tall tale about smallpox that he tells the slavecatchers to keep them away from the raft. Huck, too, is a trickster whose power derives from quick-witted, finely responsive storytelling.

30. *Short Fiction of Chesnutt*, p. 157.

31. Chesnutt's letters to Booker T. Washington provide abundant evidence of his commitment in principle and practice to full citizenship for American Negroes. In a letter to Washington dated Jan. 1, 1908, Chesnutt wrote: "The importance of the ballot is to me a paramount element of citizenship"; in the same letter he criticizes Washington, whom he respected and worked with closely, for posing a false choice between "voting and

eating." This letter is in the Chesnutt collection at Fisk University, Nashville, Tenn., and is quoted by Sylvia Lyons Render in *Charles W. Chesnutt* (Boston: Twayne Publishers, 1980), p. 44.

For a different reading of *The Conjure Woman* and the meaning of its individual tales as well as a less positive view of Uncle Julius as storyteller and character, see Michael G. Cooke's *Afro-American Literature in the Twentieth Century: The Achievement of Intimacy* (New Haven: Yale University Press, 1984), pp. 54-61. Cooke notes what he calls "the compromised materialism and sentimentality of Chesnutt's work" (p. 61). Specifically, he argues that Julius's "very lack of sympathy with or overt concern for the victims of his tales becomes a testimony to the harm that slavery does; he is dull, numb to the suffering of others, and all taken up with his own immediate material needs, because slavery has not made room for him to grow and refine himself as a human being" (p. 57).

32. Contrast Uncle Julius's shrewd, double-conscious, trickster's manipulation of the lazy Negro stereotype with Uncle Remus's wholehearted acceptance of the same stereotype in Harris's "A Story of the War." 'Dey er too lazy ter wuk,' he was saying, 'en dey specks hones' fokes fer ter stan' up en s'port um. I'm gwine down ter Putmon County whar Mars Jeems is—dat's w'at I'm agwine ter do' (*UR*, p. 179).

33. Chesnutt no doubt recalls that the rabbit's foot given Frederick Douglass by Sandy played a role in Douglass's ability to resist Covey the overseer. Like Douglass, Chesnutt makes the rabbit's foot a complex figure for the agency of African-American culture.

34. Perhaps John, the white narrator whom Julius outwits and wins over, stands for northern public opinion-makers, that group of influential men Henry C. Grady, Thomas Nelson Page, Joel Chandler Harris, and others of "that ilk" wooed forcefully on behalf of the "New South," and that Chesnutt approached with the milk and honey—the wit—of fiction.

35. Render, *Charles W. Chesnutt*, p. 82, my italics.

36. Ellison, *Shadow and Act*, p. 142.

37. Ellison, "Uses of History in Fiction," p. 89. In "Huck, Jim, and American Racial Discourse," *Mark Twain Journal* 22, no. 2 (Fall 1984), 4-12, David L. Smith argues that Twain possessed sufficient moral imagination to realize what it means to be treated as an inferior in American society.

38. Render, *Charles W. Chesnutt*, p. 82.

CHAPTER 3

"By de Singin' uh de Song": The Search for Reciprocal Voice in *Cane*

1

In *The Conjure Woman* Charles W. Chesnutt adapted African-American call-and-response to a radically different cultural situation. Uncle Julius performs for a white audience, and his stories challenge his listeners' values and in small, important ways exert a salutary, subversive influence on their lives. Chesnutt's critical distance allows Uncle Julius to manipulate the color line between black dialect and standard English. Nevertheless, neither Chesnutt's black storyteller nor his white narrator crosses over into the other's verbal territory. It remained for later writers to take down the imaginary fence between the spoken and the written word, between the act of storytelling and the act of narrative. Writers like Jean Toomer and Zora Neale Hurston sought lyrical voices composed of many strains; like Herman Melville and Mark Twain they embraced the American vernacular as a bridge between folk speech and literary language.

Listening to the soul of black American experience expressed in song, Jean Toomer discovered how to conjure a world more vivid and compelling than the moment by moment passage of ordinary reality. He adapted call-and-response to the inner dialogue between his voice and the folk voices he heard in rural Georgia. "The visit to Georgia last fall," he wrote Waldo Frank in 1922, "was the starting point of almost everything of worth that I have done. I heard folk songs come from the lips of Negro peasants. I saw the rich dusk beauty that I had heard many false accents about, and of which, till then, I was somewhat skeptical. And a deep part of my nature, a part that I had repressed, sprang suddenly into life and responded to them."[1] In the South Toomer felt kinship between slavery's ancestral past and his struggle to be an artist. His reaction to the slave songs recalls Frederick Douglass's pre–Civil War belief that "the mere *hearing* of those songs would do more to impress truly spiritual-minded men and women with the soul-crushing and death-dealing character of slavery than the *reading* of whole volumes of its mere physical cruelties."[2] For Toomer the songs mediate between him and his audience, and his voice is resonant with the spirituals and the old blues, waning but still nourished and nourishing in the back country of Georgia.

Throughout *Cane* Toomer relies on a voice and frame more musical than rhetorical. As he told Claude Barnett a few months before *Cane*'s publication, while in Georgia he "peeped behind the veil" of his family's Washington, D.C., lace-curtain Negro gentility at the earthy, dusky souls of southern black folk. "And my deepest impulse to literature (on the side of the material) is the direct result of what I saw. Insofar as the old folk songs, syncopated rhythms, the rich sweet taste of dark-skinned life, insofar as these are Negro, I am, body and soul, Negroid."[3] For a time Toomer's individuality flowed from his participation in the life of the community, expressed most distinctly in music. Toomer imbued *Cane* with his intimate, individual being and what Barbara Bowen calls "the drama of finding authority through communal voice."[4] In story after story folk songs surge out of the landscape as companions to Toomer's passionate solo voice. Sometimes a song calls forth his voice. The songs also contribute to *Cane*'s form as a collage, which receives its grieving, rejuvenating, lyrical energy from the call-and-response pattern prominent in oral culture. "Caroling softly souls of slavery,"[5] Toomer writes in "Song of the Son," and his refrain, arising from the people's song, confirms his newfound ability to speak as one of them.

The old folk songs inspired Toomer to identify with the ancestral past of slavery. Like many writers of African-American descent, Toomer's reconsideration of slavery was essential to his pursuit of individual identity and a distinct voice. "Slavery," observed Eugene Holmes, "once a shame and a stigma, became for [Toomer] a spiritual process of growth and transfiguration and the tortuous underground groping of one generation, the maturing and high blossoming of the next. He found in the lives of these Georgians and their forbears a sense of mystical recognition."[6] During the writing of *Cane*, Toomer's affirmation of an African-American continuum shored up his complex sense of heritage. In the words of *Invisible Man*'s apparitional old slave woman, he discovered that freedom "ain't nothing but knowing how to say what [you] got up in [your] head."[7] In Georgia he saw black people who, though no longer slaves, were still in bondage. He heard them express their desire for freedom through songs sometimes veiled, sometimes open. And although a stranger, Toomer was encouraged by the people he met to participate in their life.

Inspired by folk songs and spirituals, Toomer nonetheless feared he might be witnessing their waning, and he made *Cane* a dwelling place for music. "A family of back-country Negroes," he writes, "had only recently moved into a shack not too far away. They sang. And this was the first time I'd ever heard the folk songs and spirituals. They were very rich and sad and joyous and beautiful." But he felt the noose of conformity tighten around the uninhibited performance of these songs. "I learned that the Negroes of the town objected to them. They called them 'shouting.' They had victrolas and player pianos. So, I realized with deep regret, that the spirituals, meeting ridicule, would be certain to die out." For Toomer the spirituals constituted the most authentic and moving expression of folk culture, but he saw their spirit doomed "to die on the modern desert." "That spirit" he calls "beautiful." "Its death was so tragic," he says. "And this was the feeling I put into *Cane*. *Cane was a swan song. It was a song of an end.*"[8]

Cane is a promise-song, too, for Toomer breathes the spirit of the ancestral black South into his fiction. He seeks sensuous and spiritual nourishment from an unfamiliar yet familiar landscape animate with his history and the history of the race. Responding to the powerful voices he hears, Toomer realizes the orphic potential of his artistic voice. In *Cane* Toomer bears witness to what W. B. Yeats called "heart mysteries"—experiences that illuminate one's "two eternities / That of race and that of soul."[9] *Soul* is the fusion of sensuous and spiritual energy during moments of historical transcendence in the life of an individual and a people. In *Cane* Toomer's voice becomes whole, but his characters do not overcome the division of their lives and the fragmentation of their culture. These men and women lead unrealized lives, but sometimes experience wholeness, usually in the act of song.

In the world of *Cane*, there are songs for every occasion, even "supper-getting-ready songs" (*C*, p. 2). Music informs and is informed by the daily activities of social life; its reality belongs to the community. Toomer observes a lingering African presence in black Georgia, and this is especially true of the role music plays in the culture. "In Africa," writes John Chernoff, "music helps people to work, to enjoy themselves, to control a bad person or to praise a good one, to recite history, poetry, and proverbs, to celebrate a funeral or a festival, to compete with each other, to encounter their gods, to grow up, and, fundamentally, to be sociable in everything they do." Thus, Chernoff concludes, "we may readily understand the reciprocity inherent in rhythmic call-and-response."[10] But in the black American world of *Cane* the bond of reciprocity is often broken, and the flow of call-and-response, of participation between performer and audience, interrupted. As a writer, Toomer attempts to restore that bond through symbolic, literary variations of call-and-response.

Songs are touchstones for the call-and-response pattern informing the sketches, stories, and poems of *Cane*. Throughout the opening section Toomer grounds tales of unfulfilled or tragic lives (mostly black women's) with antiphonal songs performed by solo and choral voices. In the middle section, the scene shifts to Washington and Chicago. Although Georgia folk songs stir in the soul's underground, Toomer distills the community voice into syncopated jazz songs, mocking and satiric. Lacking a consoling common voice, individuals wither and fall into silence and isolation. In "Kabnis," Toomer reinhabits his Georgia landscape. But, tragically, hearing folk songs utter the people's spirit and history, Ralph Kabnis answers with a corrosive soul and race hatred. He mocks the very reciprocity of call-and-response that might free him from his demons. His voice does not mediate between the almost dead, almost silent but still faintly oracular voice of Father John, the former slave preacher, and the lovely, nourishing but little nourished, sensuously stifled Carrie Kate. But at *Cane*'s end, Toomer, acting as a medium, proclaims that the rising sun pours a birth-song over the fallow land. Responding to the songs he has heard from both individual and communal voices, he summons those in the valley of *Cane* (and other places, too) into sensuous and spiritual, soulful wakefulness.

2

Toomer's first words in *Cane* invoke the remembered beauty of a place he is about to conjure into existence.

> *Oracular.*
> *Redolent of fermenting syrup,*
> *Purple of the dusk,*
> *Deep-rooted cane.*

In the act of writing he animates the world. He pays homage to voices he hears and imagines, and through them comes into possession of the word. The call to voice depends on silence, too, and Toomer uses blank pages to represent intervals of uninhabited verbal space. He chooses arcs as a spatial signature through which to announce each section of *Cane*. Anticipating "Karintha" and the sketches and stories of southern black women (and one white woman), the first arc curves up the page as if to trace the coming of women's voices along the path of the crescent moon.[11] In the opening section of *Cane* women's voices summon Toomer. Because they sing more readily than they speak, black women express their lives in song, and, sometimes desperately, a refrain marks the cessation of voice after a woman's dream of relationship fails.

A song, soulfully blues, opens and closes "Karintha"; along the way its verses mark Karintha's passage from girl to woman. Like Karintha, Toomer carries but does not possess the music. He calls readers to apprehend her beauty in relation to the beauty of the world.

> Her skin is like dusk on the eastern horizon,
> O cant you see it, O cant you see it,
> Her skin is like dusk on the eastern horizon,
> ... When the sun goes down. (*C*, p. 1)

We do not know who, besides Toomer, sings. Karintha's lovers, if they participate, betray the wonder of the song with their possessive appetites. But as he exposes "this interest of the male, who wishes to ripen a growing thing too soon," Toomer infuses his narrative voice with rhythms and phrases from the praise-song.

Playing off the song, Toomer's prose presents men's failure to understand that Karintha's beauty is a gift and a mystery they cannot seize. But male desire is dangerous and seductive to a young girl like Karintha because of her urge to autonomy and power. Paradoxically, Karintha's defiant, emerging individuality alienates her from the tradition of womanly expression that briefly counteracts possessive male sensibility in the story. "At dusk, during the hush just after the sawmill had closed down, and *before any of the women had started their supper-getting-ready songs*, her voice, high-pitched, shrill, would put one's ears to itching" (C, p. 2, my italics). Not yet a participant in the work or the songs of the women, Karintha disturbs the interval of silence in a voice antithetical to the beauty she carries in her person. "But no one ever thought to make her stop because of it"—not the women for unrevealed reasons, and not the men who indulge her out of sexual self-interest. Self-deceptively, men deny the bond between beauty and autonomy. Even the preacher denies Karintha's soul, acting as though "she was as innocently lovely as a November cotton flower" (C, p. 2):

> Brown eyes that loved without a trace of fear
> Beauty so sudden for that time of year. (C, p. 7)

But unlike the wild presence celebrated in "November Cotton Flower," Karintha does not love. "She played 'home' with a small boy who was not afraid to do her bidding" (C, p. 3).

Her curiosity only inflames the men, and Toomer counterpoints their delirium with an abbreviated, uptempo version of the song:

> Her skin is like dusk,
> O cant you see it,
> Her skin is like dusk,
> When the sun goes down. (C, p. 3)

The immensity of scale provided by the horizon is missing, but Karintha's essential relation to the universe is the same. "Karintha is a woman. She who carries beauty, perfect as dusk when the sun goes down." Sexually, she goes the way of many marriages, many lovers. Men take her briefly, desolately. They touch her superficially but the person and the essential woman is absent. "She has contempt for them" (*C*, p. 3), but she is a woman. She has a child, and the impression persists, thick as smoke, that she leaves her baby on an enormous smouldering "pyramidal sawdust pile" (*C*, p. 4). Coming home, Karintha now carries smoke from the baby's funeral pyre into the air of "the valley of *Cane*." In response, as a prayer for deliverance, "someone made a song":

> Smoke is on the hills. Rise up.
> Smoke is on the hills, O rise
> And take my soul to Jesus. (*C*, p. 4)

The song, spiritual as the other is blues, belongs to the community. Its voice is plural, communal, more than the apostrophic song that seems superficially the men's and profoundly Toomer's.

The song's compassionate wish for transcendence inspires Toomer to write boldly about the tragedy that has happened and is happening to Karintha and the men obsessed by her. As a woman who is a person and a sexual being, Karintha has been hurt—"ripened too soon"—but perhaps not beyond restoration. She continues to exist "carrying beauty" in the midst of the community, but her male pursuers learn nothing. They understand nothing about the freedom and mystery of beauty.

As Karintha's African name lingers in the air, Toomer sounds an ominous note with the last words of his song. He and those who sing with him pause, and after a silence close with the simple repetition

> Goes down . . .

More than the sun, Karintha descends; sexually and spiritually, she is sinking. At twenty, though carrying beauty, she is world-weary, maybe doomed. All that remains is repetition with variations of cadence but no change in the condition that divides her soul from her body and her personality from the beauty that, despite everything, continues to express her connection with the universe. Toomer responds in a voice that makes him a participant with Karintha and the community in a simultaneous act of song and story. But this moment of potential transcendence is symbolic. Aesthetically and socially, "Karintha" foreshadows the melting of speech into song in

"Blood-Burning Moon," when sexual and racial combat lead to violence so terribly final there remains little potential for relationship, only the repetition of words stripped of their former improvisatory, transformational power.

"Becky," "Carma," "Fern," and "Esther": from these stories of women flares a passion so desolate and detached that Toomer only guesses at the voices. Long suppressed, these women rarely speak, and, when they do, their words are articulate mostly as music—disembodied and indefinite but passionately, palpably real. So Toomer fills his stories with songs and the fragments of song, and joins these women in the search to elude the limits of ordinary time and space.

In "Becky" Toomer speaks in both white and black voices. "Becky had one Negro son. Who gave it to her? Damn buck nigger said the white folks' mouths . . . Who gave it to her? Low-down nigger with no self-respect, said the black folks' mouths." The white folks are more virulent, but "white folks and black folks built her cabin, fed her and her growing baby, prayed secretly to God who'd put His cross upon her and cast her out" (C, p. 8). Though white folks and black folks "joined hands to cast her out," they do not. A snatch of song intervenes: "The pines whispered to Jesus" (C, p. 9). Rich and poor, white and black, male and female seize the refrain as a prayer for Becky and themselves: "O pines, whisper to Jesus" (C, p. 11). As a participant in the story, Toomer takes personal possession of the refrain before he witnesses the crumbling of Becky's cabin. "Pines shout to Jesus!" (C, p. 12), he thinks. The variation prepares him to intensify his participation in the community, and he breaks into the first person as he tells of his new role as storyteller. "I remember nothing after that," he writes, "until I reached town and folks crowded round to get the word of it" (C, pp. 12-13). The people's belief that he carries the word confirms and quickens his reciprocal narrative voice. In "Karintha," Toomer speaks directly to readers—"you"—and leads them into the witnessing community, but in "Becky," he addresses the community directly, telling a story that, because of song and witnessing, is his as well as theirs. By ending the written text with the identical reportage with which he began,

Toomer teases his readers and challenges them to imagine him performing for those who gather around him in the streets of the town.

After pausing in "Face" and "Cotton Song," a lyric and a work song, which, like many of the poems in *Cane*, respond to the predicament of the previous story and prepare for the next, Toomer calls readers to join him.

> Wind is in the cane. Come along.
> Cane leaves swaying, rusty with talk,
> Scratching choruses above the guinea's squawk,
> Wind is in the cane. Come along. (C, p. 16).

He and the wind are the lead voices in the song that frames "Carma." His eyes "leave the men around the stove" to follow Carma. When she disappears, he gradually becomes aware of the entire transitional landscape of dusk. A girl's "sad story song" awakens him to his ancient heritage of beauty and culture. "She does not sing," Toomer tells us; "her body is a song. She is in the forest, dancing. Torches flare . . . juju men, greegree, witch-doctors . . . torches go out. . . . The Dixie Pike has grown from a goat path in Africa" (C, pp. 17-18). As Toomer listens to the woman's dance, her body transports him beyond the South to Africa. His vision and Carma's spell in the canebrake convince him that "time and space have no meaning in a canefield" (C, p. 19). And they don't unless you are open to voices and images beyond ordinary rational ideas of "time and space and cause and effect. If you are open to vision, like Toomer's of Africa, then "come along." Repeated four times, these words are a refrain that opens and closes "Carma" with Toomer in pursuit of the truth beyond his narrative. "Now he's in the gang. Who was her husband?" he writes and then overcomes sexual and storytelling conventions. "Should she not take others, this Carma, strong as a man, whose tale *as I have told it* is the crudest melodrama?" (C, p. 20, my italics). In an open voice he calls us to heed the limits of his tale and to respect the story Carma acts out in a time and space beyond his voice.

If we do "come along," we cross the threshold of *Cane* and hear Toomer's apostrophic poems, "Song of the Son" and "Georgia Dusk." "Pour O pour that parting soul in song," he calls, and that soul belongs alike to black folks and the soil. He names the people "dark purple ripened plums," and his metaphor changes plums and seed into a tree of song:

> An everlasting song, a singing tree,
> Caroling softly souls of slavery,
> What they were, and what they are to me,
> Caroling softly souls of slavery. (C, p. 21)

But in "Georgia Dusk," Toomer confronts the world of night and nightmare that casts its spell over the landscape.

> A feast of moon and men and barking hounds,
> An orgy for some genius of the South
> With blood-hot eyes and cane-lipped scented mouth,
> Surprised while making folk-songs from soul sounds. (C, p. 22)

Toomer absorbs the nightmare of violence that interrupts and joins his song of the South. He realizes that to sustain his voice, he will have to rely on the continuing songs of the people.

> O singers, resinous and soft your songs
> Above the sacred whisper of the pines,
> Give virgin lips to cornfield concubines,
> Bring dreams of Christ to dusky cane-lipped throngs. (C, p. 23)

His apostrophe calls for black voices to combine the conjuring of African juju-men with the miraculous promise of Christianity. And the dream of Christ is not simply solace but a dream of deliverance. As always, songs are the bread and wine of transformation.

"Fern" picks up the theme of "Karintha." Now Toomer is a participant—a catalyst as well as a witness to Fern's inarticulate pain. "You," he repeats, intensifying his call to readers, seeking intimacy with them partly because in the story he was not able to respond to the otherness of Fern. What is visible about her is beautiful. But her soul is mute, waiting to speak. Her beauty, like Karintha's, calls men to speak, but men, including Toomer, are slow to understand how desperately women long to use their voices reciprocally. Looking at Fern, Toomer hears the voice of a Jewish cantor. "If *you* have heard a Jewish cantor sing, if *he* has touched *you* and made *your* own sorrow seem trivial when compared with *his*, *you* will know *my* feeling when *I* follow the curves of *her* profile, like mobile rivers, to their common delta" (C, p. 24, my italics). Toomer's pronouns move in fluid mediation; like the curves of Fern's profile, they flow toward what is felt and seen but not understood. Toomer does not draw conclusions; he embodies relationship. Telling the story in the form of a half-imagined conversation, he anticipates a relationship with his audience built on his suspended contact with Fern. He implicates us in his predicament. "Your thoughts can help me, and I would like to know. Something I would do for her" (C, p. 17), he writes before he tells of their climactic encounter. His vague wish to do something is realized only in the story's ambiguous response to his and Fern's experience. He knows that the story, more his than hers as he writes it, does not reach her. For his soul's sake, he tells how Fern's presence opened him to the place so intensely that the ancestral past fuses with the present moment.

The act of writing enables Toomer's first-person voice to overlay the emotion of the present upon his memory of Fern. "I felt strange, as I always do in Georgia, particularly at dusk. I felt that things unseen to men were tangibly immediate. It would not have surprised me had I had vision. People have them in Georgia more often than you would suppose. A black woman once saw the mother of Christ and drew her in charcoal on the courthouse wall. . . . *When one is on the soil of one's ancestors, most anything can happen to one*" (C, p. 31, my italics). In danger of being overcome by his vision, Toomer shifts stiffly from *you* and *I* to a more hypothetical, impersonal *one*. As time flows forward again, he reenters the Georgia landscape where he and the countryside are held in Fern's eyes. In slow, antiphonal, bodily rhythm, he and she exist together in silent knowledge. But some reflex of possession intervenes: "I must have done something—what I don't know, in the confusion of my emotion" (C, p. 32). Does he make an abrupt move, which she associates with the empty sexual gestures of previous men? Toomer cannot remember, but he knows that his action broke the spell of companionship, and that he became a mere witness to Fern's struggle to release her long-dormant, long-denied soul. "Her body was tortured with something it would not let out. . . . Like boiling sap it flooded arms and fingers till she shook them as if they burned her." Her voice is bottled up until the volcano of her body forces up urgent orgiastic sounds more painful than pleasurable. "It found her throat, and sputtered inarticulately in plaintive, convulsive sounds, mingled with calls to Christ Jesus. And then she sang, brokenly. A Jewish cantor singing, with a broken voice" (C, p. 32). As Fern's voice becomes uncontainable and bursts into the world, Toomer returns to the safety of his metaphor. He uses the writer's artifice to become audience to the naked, quivering, frightening voice of Fern's being.

Before her eruption, Fern has gazed toward folk songs sung in the distance. Now that her voice emerges, like Celie at the beginning of Alice Walker's *The Color Purple,* she has no one to sing to except Jesus, a recurring, sympathetic masculine presence that *Cane's* women imagine listens to their stories. For his part, as the narrator, Toomer withdraws farther from Fern's actual voice. He hears not a cantor's but "a child's voice, uncertain, or an old man's." Nevertheless, her voice persists. "Dusk hid her; I could hear only her song" (C, p. 32). Toomer, who constructs the story around Fern's eyes and the power of vision, is now compelled by the presence of her song. His metaphors fall away as her voice expresses her soul's womanly condition. Fittingly, as soon as he takes her in his arms, she faints, passing back into silence. Moreover, Toomer concludes the story as if Fern has not spoken, as if he again *sees* all there is of her as he rides north on the train. "Saw her face flow into [her eyes], the countryside and something that I call God, flowing into them. . . . Nothing ever really happened. Nothing ever came to Fern, not even I" (C, p. 33). But what happened was a coming into song, a matter of voice, not sight; once again Toomer's controlling metaphor obscures Fern's act of self-expression and his ambiguous role in that act.

At the close of "Fern," Toomer retreats from his self-justifying finality as if he fears his readers may balk. He challenges us: "And, friend, you? She is still living, I have reason to know. Her name, against the chance that you might happen down that way, is Fernie May Rosen" (C, p. 33). Though mocking, his tone invites us to share his failure of intimacy with Fern. *His* song of sorrow more than hers resembles the voice of a Jewish cantor. Boiling like cane, Fern's voice burns the page. She sings "brokenly," and what eludes her is not a connection with the countryside or God, what Walker's Celie calls stars, trees, sky, peoples, everything. What shatters is her dream of a full, sensuous, spiritual relationship with a man. But in her pain she finds a fragment of her voice. Toomer, however, once again betrays Fern's trust, this time with a deeply ambivalent fictional gesture. He ends by giving readers her full name as if to mock our capacity for intimacy and to signify Fern's absence from his life by affirming her presence in a now remote world. Here, by choice, Toomer approaches the condition of many of his women characters. He divides the word from the world and exposes the hypocrisy of his (and perhaps our) sentimental wish to do something for Fern. Implicitly, it is clear that he and we must allow her her voice, and listen responsively to her song.

3

After "Fern," Toomer pauses, and in reverie dreams of a harmonious relationship with nature and women. In "Nullo" an intense sunset is not an ending but a prologue to the sexual tenderness that in "Evening Song" allows a man and his lover to mingle in harmony with the rhythms of the moon. Then Toomer resumes his prose voice, and in "Esther" the failure of a woman's voice and her subsequent renunciation of the world reach an extreme. From the first, Esther requires an infusion of energy. At nine, she is almost at the point of budding. Her "hair would be beautiful if there were more gloss to it"; "if her face were not prematurely serious, one would call it pretty." Toomer finishes the portrait provocatively: "Esther looks like a little white child" (C, p. 36). As the "near white" daughter of "the richest colored man in town," Esther appears doomed to exist apart from both black and white groups in the community. Like Toomer during his months in Sparta, Georgia, Esther is "pulled deeper and deeper into the Negro group,"[12] in her case because she witnesses an extraordinary public performance by "a clean-muscled, magnificent, black-skinned Negro, whom she had heard her father mention as King Barlo" (C, p. 36).

Nine-year-old Esther experiences Barlo's "prophet's voice," and for almost twenty years the legends woven from his blues sermon dominate her inarticulate soul. Barlo boldly reverses the pattern of call-and-response between Jesus and the individual. Unlike Cane's other characters who offer apostrophes to Jesus, Barlo claims Jesus has spoken to him in words that are simultaneously a call and a response. "Jesus has been awhisperin strange words deep down," he chants in words and cadences recalling the spirituals. "O way down deep, deep in my ears." Jesus commands Barlo to preach and become a leader of his people: "An He said, 'Tell em till you feel your throat on fire' " (C, p. 38). As they did with Fern, words become tongues of flame; unlike Fern's words, Barlo's burn and purge the ears of an audience.

With his vision of ancestral African power, Barlo turns his audience into a congregation. His sermon does not simply celebrate the African past. Addressing his racially mixed audience, Barlo relies on a subversive rhetoric of double consciousness. Offering white listeners the preacher's face, he invokes a remote, intimidating, bumbling African figure. Long ago a "big an black an powerful" African had "his head caught up in the clouds." Unvigilant, the ancestor grew oblivious to his and his people's safety. "An while he was agazin at the heavens, heart filled up with the Lord, some little white-ant biddies came an tied his feet to chains" (C, p. 38). Barlo then incorporates into his sermon the form as well as the substance of the African-American secular tradition. Specifically, as Barbara Bowen recognizes, Barlo telescopes the middle passage "into a perfect blues stanza":[13]

> They led him t the coast,
> They led him t the sea,
> They led him across the ocean,
> An they didn't set him free.
>
> The old coast didn't miss him,
> An the new coast wasn't free,
> He left the old-coast brothers,
> T give birth t you an me.
>
> O Lord, great God Almighty,
> T give birth t you an me. (C, pp. 38-39)

As Barlo pauses, "white and black preachers," now alarmed, "confer as to how best to rid themselves of the vagrant usurping fellow" (C, p. 39). They are right to worry because, carefully listened to, Barlo's sermon renounces a passive Christianity and calls black Christians to acts of radical social change.

The blues tucked away in the sermon establishes a context for Barlo's eloquence. "To the people he assumes the outlines of his visioned African," but his voice is filled with the bitter consequences of the African's fall into captivity. He summons his people to a historical and spiritual awareness of the contemporary situation in a way that deflects the suspicions of unsympathetic white (and black) listeners. "Brothers an sisters, turn your faces t the sweet face of the Lord, an fill your hearts with glory. Open your eyes and see the dawnin' of th mornin light. Open your ears—" (*C*, p. 39). If his people understand the vision in his voice, they see a future condition of freedom, equality, and love growing out of spiritual experience. In this sense Barlo supersedes the African as a presence and a performer able to overcome the disabling passivity and silence of the past through improvisational mastery of the word.

Afterward, the people prefigure in legend the transformations called for by Barlo's blues sermon. His powerful voice releases images of love and liberation sexual and racial, private and public in nature. In Esther's case what she sees and hears and is told "years afterward" of Barlo and his performance "became the starting point of *the only living patterns that her mind was to know*" (*C*, p. 40, my italics). For eighteen years Barlo's image feeds Esther's subterranean desires for sexual and racial identity. To her, he becomes "best cotten picker," "best man with his fists, . . . with dice, with a razor. . . . Lover of all the women for miles and miles around" (*C*, pp. 42-43). These centrifugal images of Barlo as hero and bad man keep her heart beating, her silent lips poised for five more years, until he swaggers back to town, now rich and changed by wartime cotton money.

Desperate to become the "black madonna" drawn "in charcoal on the court-house wall" eighteen years before by a woman inspired by Barlo's sermon, Esther pursues Barlo at midnight. Like the spiritually and sexually starved women of *Winesburg, Ohio*,[14] Esther goes, and going goes bravely against the grain of her sheltered, hothouse environment. She finds Barlo upstairs in a sporting house dive—"Blackness rushed to her eyes"—and cajoles her voice to call him. "This aint the place fer y," Barlo responds. "I know," Esther answers. "But I've come for you" (*C*, p. 47). The call-and-response form is intimately present, but the context turns it into parody. Here, as with Barlo's sermon, there is an audience present, but it is an ironic congregation that mocks Esther as a grotesque "dictie nigger." Her call is private and sexual, woman to man, but she utters it in an arena hostile to her newly emergent voice. Besides, as her veils of illusion burn off shamefully, Barlo's heroic image recedes before his actual "smile, ugly and repulsive to her" and a bodily and spiritual presence equally "hideous." Silenced, Esther metamorphoses into a "somnambulist," and the jeers of the audience banish her. Worse, she descends into an oblivion bereft of form and voice, hers and the world's. In a terrible reversal, space and place for Esther turn into a void. Without voice, something melts into nothing, and Toomer ends in minimal voice, denying even what Joyce called the "ineluctable modality of the visible."[15] "There is no air," he testifies for Esther, "no street, and the town has completely disappeared" (C, p. 48). All vanishes, particularly the younger Barlo's eloquently voiced vision fusing self and race through love. Despite the reality and legend of an enabling presence, in the present Esther loses hope of a nourishing, intimate experience. Her voice, when it flutters into speech, expresses private urgency in a public forum. She does not grasp that Barlo's former eloquence, though ahead of the crowd and short-lived, proceeded from a reciprocal relationship with his audience/congregation. Set apart from black and white experience, Esther nurtures the fantasy of Barlo as an unchanging image, and outside her mind she finds no community to nourish her too delicate voice and self.

After "Esther" Toomer enters a more dangerous and chaotic space: the ungovernable southern landscape of racial violence. He prepares for the blood and fire of "Blood-Burning Moon" with two companion poems. "Conversion" counterpoints Barlo's improvisatory, momentarily enabling blues sermon with an unflattering religious portrait. A former "African Guardian of Souls," now "Drunk with rum," yields to "new words. . . . Of a white-faced sardonic god"; bought off, he becomes an entertainer:

> Grins, cries
> Amen,
> Shouts hosanna. (C, p. 49)

Unlike Barlo, who converts Christianity to African-American ends, this anonymous *conversion* means surrender to white captivity. And if religion failed to keep blacks in subservience, there were other means. "Portrait in Georgia," the sequel to "Conversion," uses the figure-ground pattern to expose the white southern obsession behind the blood sacrifice of lynching. Through Toomer's newly made eyes, the image of a southern belle dissolves into a black man tortured and burned alive at the stake. One by one, the woman's features yield to the paraphernalia of lynching, until in a final chilling montage her white body becomes a simile for the black victim:

> And her slim body, white as the ash
> of black flesh after flame. (C, p. 50)

The poem's silent imagery summons the black folk voices of "Blood-Burning Moon" that improvise desperately against the spell of violence hovering over the land as pregnantly as the full "red nigger moon."

In "Blood-Burning Moon" Toomer's metaphor recognizes a historical pattern of violence as common to this landscape as the waxing and waning of the lunar cycle. And he achieves a *tour de force* through the speech and song of both individual and communal voices. Toomer's vision of the moon gathers shape from the articulate feelings of black folks who see it "like a fired pine knot," an "omen" indistinguishable from the landscape. Seeing is believing, but silence leads to capitulation, so from the start "Negro women improvised songs against its spell" (C, p. 51). Louisa, whose autumnal, oak-leaf color suggests the "red nigger moon" of the refrain, sings apart from the chorus of women. First, as if unaware of the evil tradition of racial violence evoked by this moon, "she sang softly at the evil face of the full moon." But soon she feels the opposing presences of her two men—Bob Stone, her white lover and "younger son of the people she worked for," and black Tom Burwell, "whom the whole town called Big Boy,"[16] a man of prowess determined to woo and marry her. Under this fearful moon, "the slow rhythm of her song grew agitant and restless" (C, p. 53). The barnyard animals "caught its tremor"; they yelp and howl so unnervingly that the songs of the other women become "cotton-wads" to stop their ears against a sudden rush of evil.

> Red nigger moon. Sinner!
> Blood-burning moon. Sinner!
> Come out that fact'ry door. (C, p. 53)

The women's song conjures the moon away from the old cotton

factory, which they know as a spot unhallowed by acts of racial violence.

Meanwhile, in the complementary space of a nearby canefield, old David Georgia's tales "about the white folks, about moonshining and cotton picking, and about sweet nigger gals" (C, p. 54) create an equilibrium until one of the black men listening breaks the spell with gossip about Louisa. Ominously, Tom Burwell's violent, verbal, and physical response calls in question the healing power of the women's song. Pumped up, Burwell heads toward Louisa's place, but hearing from a distance the animals' noises, even he, "who didn't give a godam for the fears of old women," shudders at the sight of the moon (C, p. 55). In Louisa's presence, he is inarticulate; "he wanted to say something to her, and then found that he didn't know what he had to say, or if he did, that he couldn't say it" (C, p. 56). Louisa, with the same articulate, intuitive knowledge she and the other women have about the moon, arouses Tom to an act of voice and love. "Youall want me, Tom?" she asks, and he responds suddenly able to improvise an eloquent metaphor for the risky, unpredictable, mysterious nature of the spoken word. "But words is like the spots on dice: no matter how y fumbles em, there's times when they jes wont come." He is right and his vernacular denial of his power over words is proof of his capacity for eloquence. Moved by the moment, Tom affirms Louisa's kinship with the blues grain of the countryside. He did not really see her, he confesses, until he heard her sing " 'Sometimes in a way that like t broke m heart.' " Her blues voice intensifies his will to perform the strenuous day-to-day tasks of his life. "Yassur," he brags about cotton picking: "Come near beatin Barlo yesterday" (C, p. 57). Yet Burwell does not associate the blues feeling of Louisa's voice with *her* experience. To uphold his masculine convention of female virginity, he assumes wrongly that Louisa has not known men. He does not treat her as a human sexual equal.

Perhaps fatally, they evade rumors about Louisa and Bob Stone. Burwell's threat to "cut hm jis like I cut a nigger" belongs, he thinks, to his male world; he's "been on the gang three times fo cuttin men" (C, p. 61). Tragically, Burwell separates that potential for violence from Louisa and her singing. "But that ain't th talk f now. Sing, honey, Louisa, an while I'm listening t y I'll be making love" (C, pp. 57-58) For a time, their intimacy dissolves all consciousness of conflict. Liberated from the ominous moon, Louisa and Tom are joined by an old Negress who sings as she draws water from the well. Soon black folks inside the shanties "joined the old woman in song." They all flow together in one voice: "Louisa and Tom, the whole street singing":

> Red nigger moon. Sinner!
> Blood-burning moon. Sinner!
> Come out that fact'ry door. (C, p. 58)

Individual voices become communal, singing the identical refrain sung earlier as a warning and a spell by which the women attempt to charm the loaded dice of fate and circumstances. Now for an interval, the song banishes the moon and exorcises its augury of violent evil. And something else happens as these many voices gather in a single act of song. The song no longer belongs exclusively to the women. Men and women sing together and create a space for love. The collective voice is so strong that no one thinks its power may be overthrown by the racially charged passion of Louisa's white lover—Bob Stone.

Nevertheless, Toomer adapts his voice to include Sempter's white folks—first Bob Stone and then the mob that Toomer, recalling King Barlo's vision of African captivity, imagines as so many ants. Until his climactic, deadly encounter with Tom Burwell, Bob Stone's voice remains an interior monologue—the arrogant, half-cracker idiom of a northern-educated southerner who longs for slavery's apparently uncomplicated days of *droit de seigneur*. Contemptuous of black men, Stone recognizes paradoxically that "it was because Louisa was nigger that he went to her. Sweet . . . the scent of boiling cane came to him" (C, p. 61). Moving through space, he comes face to face with the landscape's sweet yield—black men grinding and boiling the freshly cut cane. As he overhears talk of him and Tom Burwell, his ears and blood figuratively burn and boil as Burwell's literally do before the night is over. Thrashing around in a canebrake on the way to his rendezvous with Louisa, he cuts his lips. When he finds her absent, he tastes blood, his blood, but in his inflamed mind, it becomes Tom Burwell's blood. Meanwhile, Toomer registers changes in mood and action through arresting, alternating images of sound and silence. As they have earlier this night, before the Negro women fought off the moon's spell, barnyard animals raise insensate cries "heralding," in the tale's prophetic words, "the bloodshot eyes of southern awakening." In a single, brilliant, succinct stroke reminiscent of Chesnutt's conjurations, Toomer calculates the limits of Negro voices, songs, and charms against Bob Stone and the collective presence and power of white folks. Even before Stone enters the Negro street of factory town, his presence, signaled by the animals, breaks the spell cast by Tom and Louisa and all the men and women of shantytown when they exorcised the evil possibilities of the night with one voice, one jagged blues incantation.

Suddenly, all changes fatally. The "singers in the town were silenced," and "palpitant between the rooster crows, a chill hush settled upon the huddled forms of Tom and Louisa" (*C*, p. 63). The consequent bitter dialogue between Burwell and Stone displaces the life-giving, community-building call-and-response pattern into a dead-end ritual. Although Stone and Burwell ostensibly fight over Louisa, her presence recedes utterly while they contend. Though physically present, she is silent. Moreover, the absence of her voice and energy recalls that women's songs have mediated between the community and the violent possibilities of the night. Left out and ignored as a person, Louisa fails to try to bring her female improvising power to bear on this male battleground.

> "Whats y want?"
> "I'm Bob Stone."
> "Yassur—an I'm Tom Burwell. Whats y want?"
> Bob lunged at him. Tom side-stepped, caught him by the shoulder, and flung him to the ground. Straddled him. (*C*, p. 63)

In both verbal and physical, individual combat, Tom Burwell bests Bob Stone at every turn. Burwell, having found a metaphor for voice with Louisa, rolls the verbal dice like a gambling man. He counters Stone's announcement of his identity with an obligatory "Yassur" but undercuts the formula with the assertion of his own name and the repetition of his terse question: "Whats y want?" Unable to take even this challenge from a black man, Stone escalates the conflict. Burwell responds easily, almost playfully to Stone's lunges until the white man ups the ante with a racial insult. "Get off me, you godam

81

nigger you," he calls in a last retort, and in response Burwell "began hammering at him" (C, p. 64).

The denouement occurs on a more dangerous male ritual ground. Again, Stone raises the stakes, arbitrarily, unilaterally. He draws his knife and is amazed when Burwell responds by flashing the black ace of death from his own hand. Words, fists, knives, the outcome is the same. Man to man, Burwell proves Stone's better. But the sequel overrides Burwell's individual voice and prowess:

> They don't come by ones,
> they don't come by twos,
> But they come by tens.[17]

Tragically, the contest extends to an arena of power beyond two individuals. Stone speaks the last word to a group of white men who accost his staggering body on Broad Street. "Tom Burwell . . . ," he tells them, falls, and dies. No further word passes among them as, antlike, they swarm into a lynch mob. Against the grain of African-American oral culture, "the moving body of their silence . . . flattened the Negroes beneath it" (C, p. 65). While they drag Burwell to the factory, sink a stake, pour kerosene, they utter "no words." Whereas voice enables black Americans in Cane, the calculated absence of human speech propels the white mob as if a single spoken word might unnumb it and blunt its murderous purpose, as if the spoken word might recall some of these people to human individuality and morality.

Only when "Tom's eyes popped," only then "the mob yelled." Like the moon's enlarged visual presence over this landscape, the yell magnifies into the sound of "a hundred mobs yelling." The mob empties the countryside of logic, symmetry, and proportion. There is no living voice. Only the "ghost of a yell . . . fluttered like a dying thing down the single street of factory town." The only Negro about, the stunned and devastated, moonstruck Louisa on "the step before her home, did not hear it, but her eyes opened slowly." She sees but cannot hear because there is no voice, speaking or singing. No one is present. Worse, "the full moon, an evil thing, an omen," now propitiated by human sacrifice, becomes a thing "soft showering the homes of folks she knew" (C, p. 67).

Dazed out of her mind by the lynching and the silence, by the

absence of human voice and presence that follows, Louisa seeks
somehow to restore the condition of love and song that she remembers
from before Stone's intrusion:

> Where were they, these people? She'd sing, and perhaps they'd come
> out and join her. Perhaps Tom Burwell would come. At any rate, the
> full moon in the great door was an omen she must sing to:
>
> > Red nigger moon. Sinner!
> > Blood-burning moon. Sinner!
> > Come out that fact'ry door. (*C*, p. 67)

For the third and last time the words of the song float toward the
moon. But the song sounds solitary and desolate, Louisa's voice more
formulaic than improvisational. Now its repetition merely reinforces
the dissolution of the spell conjured briefly when she and Tom sang
in unison with all the other black folks in shanty town. That moment
of voice harks back to *The Conjure Woman*. The power of African-
American speech and song, like Aunt Peggy's (and Uncle Julius's)
conjuring, sustains the community's culture but stands only briefly
against the sudden storm of racial violence. For Louisa, the worst
has happened. Necessarily aware that in this racial context, she bears
an indelible responsibility, she sings a solace song to keep her devastated life in touch with human feeling and expression. To her call,
however, there is not yet a response. But unlike the *privately* devastated Esther, she persists in singing, now with inflections of grief.
Her only chance to overcome her pariah's role and compel an answer
from "folks she knew" is to repeat the self-same words and acknowledge a reality neither she nor the community can control. In
this way Louisa tries to exorcise some of the night's terror and sing
a healing song for her and the still silent, appalled black citizens of
Sempter. Voice and song return on a reduced scale in this tragic
landscape as the only comfort once the mob's fury of racial hate and
violence runs wild, wrecks havoc and murder on both individual
lives and the black community, and subsides. Her refrain seeks to
disengage the moon's cosmic force from the irrational tidal pull of
white folks toward the orgy of lynching. But Louisa cannot have
Tom back, and she cannot bring back the choice between her two
lovers, one white and transitory, the other black and willing to affirm
her in a commitment to lifelong, strong-voiced love. So Toomer leaves

this song and story of passion and racial madness to reverberate testamentally through the air breathed by Louisa and everyone else on this blood-red soil of Georgia, where the stench of burning flesh sometimes overpowers the sweet smell of boiling cane.

4

Toomer wrote the northern section of *Cane* last. Then he placed it in the middle between the stories of southern women and "Kabnis," his tale of a northern Negro's encounter with his bitter, static self in the beautiful and terrifying, richly fluid ancestral landscape of Georgia. This section links black experience in Washington, D.C., and Chicago with the rural exodus and the sexual and artistic awakening taking place all over America in the 1920s. Yet everywhere in these stories strong southern roots, images of cane and cotton, push up their stalks through cracks in the street or the floorboards of northern cabarets.[18] In the first two pieces, call-and-response serves as a figure for sensuous energy. But soon a shadow falls over *Cane* because of the loss of communal voice and, worse, the absence of any response to the urgent calls by Dorris in "Theater" and by the men in "Box Seat" and "Bona and Paul" as they awaken to the sexual, spiritual, and aesthetic potential of African-American identity.

Toomer prepares for these stories by calling Washington's Seventh Street to awaken. In response, this bastard street of Prohibition and World War I bawls an irreverent, syncopated, fast jazz refrain. Toomer's defiant metaphor of "black reddish blood . . . flowing down the smooth asphalt of Seventh Street" emancipates "a crude-boned, soft-skinned wedge of nigger life" and celebrates the improvisational energy of jazz. The metaphor recalls Tom Burwell's blood boiling and flowing over southern ground, and also the Great Migration to the North undertaken to escape southern poverty and violence and seize the prosperity offered by the postwar boom. In "Seventh Street," Toomer observes the transition to a more skeptical and secular, less spiritual experience. "A Nigger God!" he exclaims in response to doubts about the conventional white God's presence on this turf. But a "Nigger God," too, "would duck his head in shame and call for the Judgment Day," so, in a sassy jazz voice Toomer frees Seventh

Street from even that image of authority and restraint. "Who set you flowing?" he asks again and answers with a brash refrain.

> Money burns the pocket, pocket hurts,
> Bootleggers in silken shirts
> Ballooned, zooming Cadillacs,
> Whizzing, whizzing down the streetcar tracks. (*C*, p. 73)

On this illegitimate urban street money excites the blood toward clothes and Cadillacs and other possessions of the fast life. Fluid and unstoppable, this intense energy writes a jazz signature appropriate to the newly evolving landscape.

In counterpoint to Karintha, Toomer first portrays Rhobert, a man who forces his soul to tote a "dead thing, stuffed." Possessed by the stolid, dead-weight of his bourgeois house, Rhobert's soul is deaf and dumb, like a diver sinking into mud. "Brother, life is water that is being drawn off," rescuing voices call, but Rhobert does not respond. Toomer addresses his fellow singers, and together they mock Rhobert's passing with a playful version of "Deep River."

> Brother, Rhobert is sinking.
> Lets open our throats, brother,
> Lets sing Deep River when he goes down. (*C*, p. 75)

Instead of the great spiritual's celebration of crossing over to Camp Ground, Toomer and his chorus sign off on a deadened man of property.[19] So far Toomer follows the pattern of the southern stories; his images supply leading choral lines but the community's rescuing voice fades out, and even individual voices become more and more interior. The words actually spoken by Toomer's northern characters often sound like counterfeit imitations of the impressions and thoughts seething in underground deep rivers of self.

Toomer follows the withering of voice to its root in "Avey," a transitional piece, and perhaps the most personal tale in *Cane*. In "Fern" voice follows vision; and though it strikes the narrator's ears as inarticulate and inaccessible, Fern's voice is powerfully present. Avey, though, falls silent when the aspiring young artist walks with her to a hill in Soldier's Home and lectures her on the future. "One evening," the narrator says of his recent encounter, "in early June, just at the time *when dusk is most lovely on the eastern horizon,* I saw Avey, indolent as ever, leaning on the arm of a man; strolling under the recently lit arclights of U. Street" (*C*, p. 84, my italics). Toomer's quest remains the pursuit of passion and tenderness. The evocation of dusk recalls the song in "Karintha" and perhaps recapitulates what might have become of Karintha or Fern if either had migrated to northern streets and cabarets. Like Fern's eyes, Avey's testify to an ebbing soulful beauty within. When the narrator hums a folk tune to drown out some harsh band music, she slips her hand in his. But in response, he tells her his story or, rather, in Toomer's deliberately stuffy words, "traced my development from the early days up to the present time, the phase in which I could understand her" (*C*, p. 86). Encouraged by Avey's polite silence, he discusses her need to develop "an inner life against the coming of that day" when there would "be born, an art that would open the way for women the likes of her" (*C*, p. 87). Though he comes to know it, if he does, only as he writes the story, the narrator is in love with his artistic vision, not Avey's elusive, stubbornly particular, womanly reality.

"I recited some of my own things to her," he recalls, and strangely, speaking written words quickens his voice into song. "I sang," he continues, "with a strange quiver in my voice, a promise-song." Oblivious to Avey, he "begins to wonder why her hand had not once returned a single pressure." His words lull her to sleep, and perhaps like some of the black men Toomer has written of fleetingly in the southern stories, his anger and hurt yield to a lonely, desolate desire. But when he looks at Avey, her face—now she reminds him of a child—drives away his hostile passion. But it does not seem to occur to him that his speeches may have reminded her of how interminably she listens to men during her daily assignations. Sadly, his last words estrange her. "Orphan woman . . . ," he writes and pauses, short of an ending. In that he is right, but Avey's response to him when he hummed the folk song should have told him that she is open to the beauty of African-American culture but deaf to his obscure, self-centered, self-serving imaginings of some vague, disembodied art.

In "Avey" Toomer depicts the marginal relationship between men and women in his northern landscape. Without speech or song, at the end both Avey and the narrator are orphans lacking the nourishment of love and culture. Between "Avey" and "Theater," in the poems, "Beehive" and "Storm Ending," Toomer pauses, and wishes for a quiet corner of nature sheltered from the urgency of work and love. "Theater" follows, and there Toomer's jazz syncopations build on southern folk songs. His voice turns the black walls of the Howard Theater into "throbbing jazz songs." Breathed from street life and performed by road shows, at night these songs penetrate "the mass heart of black people" and "seep out to the nigger life of alleys and near-beer saloons, of the Poodle Dog and Black Bear cabarets" (C, p. 91). You'd think such a wild landscape would wake the characters' walled-in souls. This is true for Dorris but not for John, the manager's "dictie" brother whom she tries to love, and sees, deep down, desires to love her. She dances a love song for him, for her, for the two of them. In a creative moment of improvisation, "she forgets her tricks." Suddenly free, she sings, too, and "her singing is of canebrake loves and mangrove feastings"—of the earthy, passionate South. Joining her, "the walls press in, singing," and compel John to dream of her and feel transported to a "southern canefield." Called by these fragments, John's eyes do duty for his voice. "'Glorious Dorris.' So his eyes speak." But like the narrator of "Fern," at the climactic moment John swerves away from Dorris in favor of making her image a living presence in his writing. He cannot fuse the dancer with the dance, while Dorris, her intimate public performance over, quivers, vulnerably alive to the risk of the moment. "His whole face is in shadow. She seeks for her dance in it. She finds it a dead thing in the shadow which is his dream" (C, p. 99). Inhibited by her passionate aesthetic enactment of love and desire, he crawls back into the silent space of overinsulated private walls. The dangerous "center of physical ecstasy" (C, p. 93), embodied by Dorris in her dance, scares John off. He retreats into an abstract dream, which denies Dorris and seems fated to shrivel his body as well as his mind.

Toomer follows Dorris's unanswered call to sexual love with a poem equal to her dance in sexual intensity. In "Her Lips Are Copper Wire" he asks a lover to touch him with words and breath, and completes his electric metaphor by calling on her to strip the insulation from her white-hot lips:

> then with your tongue remove the tape
> and press your lips to mine
> till they are incandescent. (C, p. 101)

"Her Lips Are Copper Wire" reinstates the experience of reciprocal passion, and answers the will to property and abstract passion of "Rhobert" and "Theater" before, in "Calling Jesus," Toomer imagines a woman's soul reduced to "a little thrust-tailed dog that follows her, whimpering." She leaves the dog her soul in the vestibule of her large house till morning, and in the daytime when the woman is oblivious to her surroundings, "you hear a low scared voice, lonely, calling, and you know that a cool something nozzles moisture in your palms." In these moments Toomer feels her breath as "sweet as honeysuckle whose pistils bear the *life of coming song*" (C, p. 102, my italics). But in this landscape, divided apparently between vitality and respectability, you hear songs only "up alleys where niggers sat on low door-steps before tumbled shanties and sang and loved." Looking to close the fissure between Negro and nigger Washington, Toomer ends with a lullaby that carries the woman South for the interval of her dreams. "Someone . . . eoho Jesus . . . soft as the bare feet of Christ moving across bales of southern cotton, will steal in and cover it that it need not shiver, and carry it to her where she sleeps: cradled in dream-fluted cane" (C, p. 103). Unlike "Rhobert," where a male chorus sings in mockery, Toomer turns a potentially insulting, derisive fable into a song affirming some small remaining possibility of wholeness. Unlike the first version of the song where the woman slept upon "clean hay cut in her dreams," she rests now "cradled in dream-fluted cane"—a song realized in her dreams and also in the shanties by recent migrants from the South.

"Calling Jesus" anticipates Toomer's quest for sexual love through acts of song and speech in "Box Seat" and "Bona and Paul." In "Box Seat" the estrangement of public from private voice and speech from thought signifies the estrangement of man from woman. The landscape, too, is partitioned, for Toomer locates "Box Seat" in a lace-curtain Negro neighborhood deaf to and distant from Seventh Street's earthy jazz songs. On these affluent streets, "houses are shy girls whose eyes shine reticently upon the dusk body of the street. Upon the gleaming limbs and asphalt torso of a dreaming nigger." And Toomer calls on the male street to "stir the life-root of a withered people" (C, p. 104). He calls Dan Moore—born in a canefield—to become one of those "street songs that woo virginal houses." But

Dan Moore feels like a displaced person on this neat, locked-in Negro residential street.

"Come on, Dan Moore, come on," Toomer calls. But Dan's "voice is a little hoarse. It cracks. He strains to produce tones in keeping with the houses' loveliness. Can't be done. He whistles. His notes are shrill. They hurt him" (C, pp. 104-5). Intimidated, inhibited, Dan Moore fumbles silently at the iron gate. His fantasies fluctuate between paranoia—"baboon from the zoo"—and messianic self-confidence—"come to a sick world to heal it" (C, pp. 105-6). He knocks so hard on the door of the respectable boardinghouse that the owner, Mrs. Pribby, his girl Muriel's benefactor and keeper, thinks the thick glass may break. To Dan, Mrs. Pribby is the spirit of this "sharp-edged, massed, metallic house." She is both jailed and jailer. More than a woman or a person, Mrs. Pribby is a repressive condition. "Bolted. About Mrs. Pribby. Bolted to the endless rows of metal houses. No wonder he couldn't sing to them" (C, p. 107). Although mute, Dan intensifies his resolve to rescue Muriel from her environment. Waiting for her, he chooses hearing over the prying and prurience he associates with seeing. Suddenly, shuddering under the vibrations of a passing streetcar, he hears "the mutter of powerful underground races," and imagines "all the people rushing" to hear the word of "the next world savior" (C, p. 108).

Once Muriel comes downstairs, she keeps their talk superficial, their voices safely proper and public. "Let's talk about something else," she interrupts when Dan speaks about their volatile, painfully unresolved relationship. She keeps hidden the intimate thoughts that boil away in her silent, subterranean self. "Dan, I could love you if I tried. I don't have to try. I do. O Dan, don't you know I do? Timid lover, brave talker that you are. . . . She [Mrs. Pribby] is me, somehow. No, she's not. Yes she is. She is the town, and the town won't let me love you, Dan. Don't you know? You could make it let me if you would" (C, p. 110). Sensing Muriel's underground deep river of vitality, Dan sees her lips as "flesh notes" and his thoughts become spoken challenges to the platitudes uttered by her genteel voice. For a minute they speak honestly and touch. But the voice of the community speaks repressively through Mrs. Pribby's rustling newspaper in the next room. Muriel withdraws toward conformity, but Dan declares his love in defiant anger: "Muriel, I love you, whatever the world of Pribby says. Damn you, Pribby" (C, p. 114). Meanwhile the newspaper answers with loud rapping sounds and sends into hiding the passionate words Dan has dared to speak. They "gaze fearfully at one another," and when the clock strikes eight, "Muriel fastens on her image" (C, p. 115); as planned, she leaves for the Lincoln Theater with her friend, Bernice.

Like Mrs. Pribby's confined and confining house, the interior of the Lincoln intensifies the theme of captivity. In sight of each other, Dan and Muriel sink into separate, subterranean selves. "Prop me in your brass seat," Dan thinks as he sees Muriel. "He-slave. Slave of a woman who is a slave. I'm a damned sight worse than you are. . . . A slave, thou art greater than all Freedom because I love thee" (C, p. 121). Dan's archaic, apostrophic diction belongs to the dramatic tradition of soliloquy, but, unspoken, his words command no audience. Still, his passionate energy disturbs those who want to surrender their minds to the vaudeville entertainment. In this context the reciprocity of performance is missing; locked into identical box seats the members of the audience seem surreal fragments of the disjointed theatrical action. A "portly Negress," whose "strong roots" Dan imagines "sink down and spread under the river and disappear in blood-lines that waver south," has eyes that "don't belong to her" (C, p. 119). The world and Dan's metaphors distort each other. Hurt still and distracted by the dwarfs on stage, Dan wishes he had responded to "those silly women arguing feminism" (C, p. 123) with wild prophecies of a bloodless sexuality driven by technology and ideology. At last, when he yields to the balm of inner silence, the image of a former slave he has seen and spoken to on the streets of Washington struggles into his reverie. Snatches from spirituals flow through Dan's mind and enable him to reexperience his encounter with the old man and seek ancestral wisdom against the desolation of the present.

Hearing applause, Dan turns to the stage where the dwarf, who outlasts the others in a mock heavyweight prizefight, returns to sing a sentimental love song. With an effort Dan stifles fantasies of destroying the theater and rising with two signs of triumph—a dynamo in his right hand and an ebony god's face in his left. Drifting from his psychological mooring, he focuses on the dwarf's attempt to present a white rose to a woman in the audience. In characteristic revulsion from the unsightly, the unseemly, the grotesque, Muriel flinches at the dwarf's approach. She sees only ugliness, but Dan, illuminated by his memory of the slave, sees the dwarf's enormous brow undergo transformation. "It grows profound. It is a thing of wisdom and tenderness: of suffering and beauty. Dan looks down. The eyes are calm and luminous. Words come from them" (C, p. 128). Like other Toomer characters who struggle to discover a voice, Dan has a vision first. He sees words form in the dwarf's eyes, hears sounds and an accent. In Toomer's South the women see visions, sing, and sometimes speak in tongues; but here Muriel bolts her heart against the images and words of the dwarf's oracular figure. But Dan hears a call issue from the man's eloquent eyes and reciprocates with silent words of response:

> Do not shrink. Do not be afraid of me.
> *Jesus*
> See how my eyes look at you.
> *the son of God*
> I too was made in His image
> *was once*
> I give you the rose. (C, p. 128)

Though attenuated, call-and-response survives in this mute dialogue between two outsiders. Now, watching Muriel deny all connection to the dwarf as she "daintily reaches for the offering," Dan uncorks his bottled up words. "JESUS WAS ONCE A LEPER," he shouts. His line explodes, and Dan does not amplify or explain. He strides outside, a free man.

Dan's solitary illumination and utterance testify to the desolation of this landscape. His words defy but do not call because these people have shut their ears against the voices of challengers or pariahs, whether Dan, the dwarf, or Jesus the leper. Dan's isolation recalls and rivals "Fern"; though he utters a brief forceful public expression, he changes nothing, reaches no accommodation with this slavishly overrefined environment.[20] In his mind, he nurtures a connection between the dwarf and the old ex-slave who saw Grant and Lincoln and heard Walt Whitman's lonely nineteenth-century American voice call for individuality and community, and for sexual liberation. What he sees in the dwarf's eyes he hears, too, and he forms words of spiritual connection in response to the dwarf's call. In "Box Seat" there is communing but no community, only the huddling together of the puny, whimpering tag-along souls Toomer pities and shelters in "Calling Jesus." Dan keeps going at the end — no more but no less. No one — not Muriel, not Toomer, not the reader — follows because no one, not even Dan, knows where he is going. Unlike Toomer's women who, receiving no response, stay put, condemned to be oracular presences in the same static place, Dan Moore takes off, lights out toward some unknown territory. Even in silence, rejected by respectable society, he keeps a measure of freedom and mobility. And from his box seat he spoke sufficiently to break out of captivity, whereas Muriel remains behind in her genteel, gilded bourgeois cage.

Between "Box Seat" and "Bona and Paul" Toomer places two poems about the need for intimacy and the danger of isolation for the person and the writer. "Prayer" celebrates the presence of spirit in earthly spaces. Here, too, the primary act of relation is speech and song grounded in bodily reality:

> My voice could not carry to you did you dwell in stars,
> O spirits of whom my soul is but a little finger... (C, p. 131)

In "Harvest Song" Toomer is a reaper whose harvest of oats corresponds to his writing. After doing his work, he seeks fraternity with "other harvesters but fear[s] to call." He fears he would not be a responsive listener yet "strains to hear the calls of other harvesters." Toomer calls for a community, of writers, yes, and also a society in which we are brothers ("O my brothers") and citizens and, on that basis, audience to each other's work and lives. Toomer cautions against the artist's tendency to self-indulgence or self-pity. "My pain is sweet," he confesses but closes by writing that "it will not bring me knowledge of my hunger" (C, p. 133). "Harvest Song" is a pause in the unfolding of *Cane*. From it, Toomer confronts the continuing conflict between intimacy and the assertion of African-American male identity in "Bona and Paul."

Like differences in social status in "Box Seat," racial differences lead Bona and Paul to express their passion in unspoken, interior voices. Bona, a young southern white woman, senses that Paul, a mystery man, has African blood. "He is a harvest moon. He is an autumn leaf," she thinks, recalling Toomer's description of Louisa in "Blood-Burning Moon." And she goes on, as Bob Stone did, to add elements of hostility and the forbidden to her fantasy. "He is a nigger" (C, p. 136). Though he passes for white in Chicago, Paul's secret images bear him south. In the midst of thoughts of Bona, he imagines a scene in rural Georgia where "a Negress chants a lullaby beneath the mate-eyes of a southern planter. Her breasts are ample for the suckling of a song. She weans it, and sends it, curiously weaving, among lush melodies of cane and corn" (C, pp. 137-38). Taken sexually but not possessed by the southern planter, the black woman sings and sends her story beyond his "mate-eyes" into the valley of Cane. Her song distances Paul from a stereotypical context in which his white acquaintances, male and female, look to his African-American blood for confirmation of their own sexual identity.

On his way to the Crimson Gardens with Bona, Paul feels the presence of black people in "clapboard homes which now resemble Negro shanties in some southern alley." In this scene Bona and Paul speak intimately to each other. "Paul, I love you" (C, p. 143), she suddenly declares. In response, he tells her, "I cannot *talk* love. Love is a dry grain in my mouth unless it is wet with kisses" (C, p. 144, my italics). Bona starts to respond, remembers they are in the street, asks for reassurance in the form of a declaration of love, and when Paul cannot give it "yet," she catches up with the other couple. Their private drama becomes public as soon as they enter Crimson Gardens and feel the stares and whispered questions. Paul realizes that friends and strangers alike "saw not attractiveness in his dark skin, but difference" (C, p. 145). When an entertainer, "a girl dressed like a bare-back rider in flaming pink" (C, p. 147), sings "Liza, Little Liza Jane," Paul's interior voice probes Bona's southern ambivalence. For the sentimental, unnourishing commercial song, his inner ear substitutes the healing song of the Negro woman in Georgia. "O song!" he thinks, and then, imagining that Bona hears the same song on her earthy, southern lower frequencies, he names her as a participant in the dialogue of his thought.

> "And you know it too, don't you Bona?
> "What, Paul?"
> "The truth of what I was thinking." (C, p. 148)

Without hesitation, she answers that she'd "like to know I know —
something of you." Her response answers his earlier sexual challenge
with a call of her own focused on his personality, not merely his
body or his racial identity.

The frantic gaiety of the Crimson Gardens interrupts the flow of
intimacy between Bona and Paul. Out of rhythm they dance, and
their attraction dissipates into the bickering, contentious words of
shallow conversation. But the act of dancing rescues their desire.
Suddenly, words yield to spontaneous movement, and "they are a
dizzy blood clot on a gyrating floor" (C, p. 151). When it appears
that they will leave Crimson Gardens and go off to make love, the
need to articulate the vision behind his desire comes over Paul. For
him, the "knowing eyes" of the huge Negro doorman are a sudden
catalyst. "Too many couples have passed out, flushed and fidgety,"
Paul realizes, "for [the doorman] not to know." He cannot bear for
another black man to imagine his and Bona's sexual encounter as
anything other than an act of beauty and vision. Earlier, Paul sensed
the doorman's likely awareness of his African-American blood. For
this reason, too, he now drops his disguise, and, with a word of
salutation, expresses racial kinship with the man:

> "Youre wrong."
> "Yassur."
> "Brother, youre wrong." (C, p. 152)

For sir, Paul returns brother — an assertion of fraternity that opens
the way for his intimate revelation.

Painfully for Paul, the doorman's leer responds accurately to what
is happening. On one level he is using the complexity of race to
hustle a white girl to bed. With Bona, he has been strategically cagey,
implying that he will reveal his racial identity as a complement to
their love-making. But now, at the risk of forfeiting his night with
Bona, Paul bursts into a lyrical speech intended to transform the
black doorman's impression. "I came back to tell you, to shake your
hand, and tell you that you are wrong. That something beautiful is
going to happen" (C, p. 152). Apparently, Paul needs to declare his
racial identity and sexual integrity to another black man before
consummating his passion for Bona. His rhetoric, in part a response

to the prurience of onlookers, points to his confusion of motives. His sudden euphoria seems too self-conscious, his language too contrived to engender a spontaneous dialogue with the doorman. That man, accustomed to the nightly, urgent comings and goings of many couples, listens silently to Paul's bizarre, literary speech.[21] As a Negro who is no longer passing, Paul pursues metamorphosis into a lover and an artist. The "petals of roses" (white faces) and "petals of dusk" (dark faces) he would gather are metaphors for the sexual, racial, aesthetic wholeness he seeks to experience. But, like other Toomer men, he seems more in love with words and images than with an actual woman.[22]

Perhaps Paul tests Bona when he leaves her outside, beyond the reach of his voice. Perhaps he knows she may disappear. Surely he is aware that her ambivalence raises the possibility that she requires the fantasy of his blackness to arouse her and the reassurance that it is only an illusion to consummate their passion. Nevertheless, leaving her behind, Paul jeopardizes the fragile beginnings of their intimacy. Moreover, without Bona and the possibility of their sexual love, he would not have a story to tell the doorman. Paradoxically, he ends the story before it has a chance to unfold. Bona sees but cannot hear, and who knows but that she imagines Paul bragging about his approaching conquest?

> Sex and race
> are private dominions,
> memories and modal
> songs, a tenor blossoming.[23]

Bona gone, Paul's sexual condition contradicts the lavish, lyrical possibilities he has expressed to the doorman. Racially, too, for the moment, he resides in an isolated, painfully private space. Because sexuality and race remain an unfulfilled polarity, Paul's words are hypothetical. They do not yet blossom in a consummate healing version of the folk song his inner ear heard a black woman sing in Georgia. For that, he will have to go South more nakedly and profoundly, as Toomer does in "Kabnis," the last and most ambitious tale in *Cane*.

5

"Kabnis" doubles as a swan-song and a birth-song. "Begun shortly after Toomer's return from Sparta in November 1921, 'Kabnis,' the synoptic piece of *Cane*," as Onida Estes-Hicks observes, "was the most difficult for Toomer and the last to be revised for publication."[24] By chronicling the folk past, Toomer anticipates a new awakening for the black South. His oracular voice mediates among several individual voices and an occasional community voice. His collaborative impulse bears witness to the unfolding of African-American oral forms in everyday experience. But when his characters respond with cynicism, madness, flight, or, worse, betray his vision through an alien silence, Toomer as the returning (and departing) son of the soil, sings a birth-song. Acknowledging the intimate creative power of silence, he calls us to listen for other voices as they awaken to life, song, and story in the future.

In a storytelling voice of call-and-response intimate with and detached from Ralph Kabnis, Toomer turns the elemental energy of the countryside into song. Alone in his cabin, unable to sleep, Kabnis reads. But the winds call him away from the mute words of his book toward the personal and artistic awakening he seeks in the South. "Night winds in Georgia," Toomer writes, conjuring breath into the written word, "are vagrant poets, whispering." Against his will, Kabnis lets his book fall and listens to "the weird chill of their song":

> White-man's land.
> Niggers, sing.
> Burn, bear black children
> Till poor rivers bring
> Rest, and sweet glory
> In Camp Ground. (*C*, p. 157)

The song moves Kabnis to a vivid response. To an imaginary sweetheart he muses that to be an articulate presence in this land requires a "bull-neck and a heaving body." He dreams of eloquence as "a soft face that fits uncertainly upon" the "body of the world." Buoyed by the promise of language, he finds words to express passionately his emerging mission. "God, if I could develop that in words," he thinks. "If I, the dream (not what is weak and afraid in me) could become the face of the South. How my lips would sing for it, my songs being the lips of its soul" (*C*, p. 158). Kabnis longs to sing, and knows that his song depends on the character of his participation in the community whose life he would express. He dreams of voice as a collaborative, enabling force. Issuing from such a voice he imagines a new body and soul strong enough to transcend and maybe transform the historical condition alluded to in the song he has absorbed from the southern night winds. But Kabnis is divided, and his other unbelieving voice denies the potentiality of self. "Soul. Soul hell. There ain't no such thing" (*C*, p. 158).

Toomer mediates between Kabnis and the South. He challenges Kabnis to conjure the swan-song he hears into a birth-song announcing a human presence far more powerful and loving than anything in his experience. Toomer's call is disturbingly intimate as well. He asks Kabnis to respond to the southern countryside, its voices and conditions, in a voice simultaneously private and public, individual and collaborative. He urges Kabnis to forget his psychological self-preoccupation long enough to absorb his and the region's terrors into a beauty both painful and uplifting. As Kabnis steps outside, clutching an intruding chicken by the neck, Toomer reenters and again collaborates with the voices in the landscape. He utters the spirit of place in a medley. "The half-moon is a white child that sleeps upon the tree-tops of the forest. White winds croon its sleep-song":

> rock a-by baby . . .
> Black mother sways, holding a white child in her bosom.
> when the bough bends . . .
> Her breath hums through pine-cones.
> cradle will fall . . .
> Teat moon-children at your breasts,
> down will come baby . . .
> Black mother." (*C*, p. 160)

Between the lines of the traditional lullaby, Toomer's antiphonal form identifies the contending forces and feelings in the South. He hints at stories waiting to be told if Kabnis would listen and shape his formless feelings. And because Kabnis is in but not of the place, Toomer challenges him to discover and love his own soul sufficiently to join the South and the people he finds there. With *croon* Toomer identifies the danger tucked away in the lullaby. If the wind blows hard, down will come baby, cradle and all. The original lyric expresses every woman's ambivalence toward caring for her babies; Toomer's new lines observe a black mother as she sings to a white baby instead of her own. His improvisation acknowledges the subversive power of black women even in roles considered safely subservient by whites.

In the meantime, Kabnis yanks the head off the squawking chicken. He calls himself a "bastard son" and implicitly joins his fate to the black mother in the song. Suddenly, moved by the night, he prays for "an ugly world." His bitter prayer testifies to his inability to respond openly, resiliently, to the beauty and misery around him, the love and hate within him. Spontaneously, he calls: "Dear Jesus, do not chain me to myself and set these hills and valleys, heaving with folk songs, so close to me that I cannot reach them. There is a radiant beauty in the night that touches . . . and tortures me" (*C*, pp. 161-62). His prayer for deliverance from the pain and beauty of black song ironically confirms his capacity for burning, purging eloquence. Speech liberates him briefly from the frozen time and space of his worst self and allows him to absorb the fluidity of the countryside, its presences and voices. Nevertheless, fearful of a lynch mob of white minds, he travels north in reverie until "impotent nostalgia grips him" and "becomes intolerable." In an act of will he strains to imagine the Negroes in "a cabin silhouetted on a knoll about a mile away. . . . They sing. They love. They sleep. Kabnis wonders if perhaps they can feel him. *If perhaps he gives them bad dreams*. Things are so immediate in Georgia" (*C*, p. 164, my italics). But this inner reciprocity with the people does not banish the ghosts of racial violence. After another interval of anxious sleeplessness for Kabnis, Toomer repeats the song and reinforces the continuing presence of black folk voices and hovering spirits of place. Perhaps now the song will strengthen Kabnis's desire to encounter the palpable, painfully beautiful environment of Negro Georgia. Comparing the night winds to "soft-voiced vagrant poets," Toomer implies that, sleeping, Kabnis prepares to participate in the singing of the song.

Toomer elaborates the song's perspective on the South with stories told by Layman, "by turns teacher and preacher, who has traveled in almost every nook and corner of the state and hence knows more than would be good for anyone other than a silent man" (*C*, p. 169). Unsure of himself with Layman, Kabnis flatters what he thinks are the other man's expectations. "Things are not half bad," he tells him and Layman responds by dropping his mask and telling him the truth. To Kabnis's pathetic fantasy that whites "wouldn't touch a gentleman—fellows, men like us three here—" Layman responds laconically, "Nigger's a nigger down this away, Professor. And only two dividins: good an bad. An even they aint permanent categories. They sometimes mixes um up when it comes t lynchin. I've seen um do it" (*C*, pp. 171-72). Kabnis's response to Layman's first account of sadistic racial violence is categorical and hostile. Negroes are a "preacher-ridden race," he says, echoing James Joyce's view of the Irish as a "priest-ridden race."[25] But Kabnis misunderstands the complex role of the black church and makes matters worse by excepting Layman from his denunciation. "Preacher's a preacher anywheres you turn" (*C*, p. 174), Layman answers, and his stress on the shared consequences of African-American identity exposes Kabnis's tendency to follow nullifying, dead-end generalizations with convenient, superficial distinctions. As a storyteller rooted in lore and experience, Layman offers Kabnis rescue from his shallow, abstract preconceptions.

The stories Layman tells show black people falling back on the wit of the animal tales as a recourse against mob violence. On one occasion Layman drawls, the white folks "had jis knocked two others like you kill a cow—brained um with an ax, when they caught Sam Raymon by a stream." But Sam recalls Br'er Rabbit's trick in "Tar Baby." "They was about t do fer him when he up and says, 'White folks, I gotter die, I knows that. But wont y let me die in my own way?'" Grudgingly, they agree, and as if to fulfill the night winds' refrain about crossing over into Camp Ground, Sam Raymon "fell down ont his knees and prayed, 'O Lord, Ise comin t y,' and he up and jumps int the stream" (*C*, pp. 174-75). Sam's prayer enables him to survive, and Layman's tale reinforces the worldly uses of black Christian tradition in the South. As Layman finishes the story, his listeners hear the swelling moans of a shout from the black church next door. In a sudden reflex Kabnis's "face gives way to an expression of mingled fear, contempt, and pity" (*C*, p. 175). Like a man ignorant of the participatory nature of black oral culture, Kabnis scorns the call-and-response of the spirituals. He would prefer to abstract the songs' beauty from the cares, feelings, and problems of everyday lives. Likewise, Kabnis resists Layman's storyteller's office, rejects the possibility that Layman's tales might have meaning for his life.

Kabnis keeps his distance from the passionate witness of African-American culture even as he pesters Layman to break his disciplined silence and tell the story of a particularly hideous lynching. Meanwhile, in church the preacher's sermon yields to an old spiritual that, because it is sung by the choir and the entire congregation, gives rest to a distraught, shouting sister. But Layman agitates Kabnis, because he counterpoints his tale of Sam Raymon's trickster's escape with the story of Mame Lamkins in which even her unborn child falls victim to the murderous wrath of a lynch mob. When Kabnis asks what Mame Lamkins had done, Layman replies with calculated understatement. "Tried to hide her husband when they was after him" (C, p. 179). Like Chesnutt's Uncle Julius, Layman does not cheat; he testifies to annihilation and escape as conditions of African-American experience. Along with Layman's tale, the continuing, complex flow of experience feeds Kabnis's apprehension of the existing world. As the men in Halsey's parlor hear the sister's individual voice interrupt the congregation to tell that she has found Jesus, a stone with a message wrapped around it crashes through the window. Kabnis, startled, then terrified when the words are read out loud — "You northern nigger, its time fer y t leave" (C, p. 174) — runs away without a word. He does not sort out his feelings of fear and complicity. Inside and out, he believes he is about to be annihilated.

The other men follow him knowing that down here whites would not bother with such a warning. While they move silently through space, Toomer fills the air with a song now sung by the church choir

> My Lord, what a mourning
> When the stars begin to fall. (C, p. 91)[26]

At that moment dusk is falling and stars are beginning to appear, but inside the black church, a choir sings of the end of the world. The song faces the terror Kabnis flees — and worse, for this is a community randomly and savagely marauded when white folks have the urge. Some of their stars — their heroic rebel angels — have already fallen; doubtless more will in coming struggles. Toomer thus frames Kabnis's purely individual response to this landscape's dangers with the continuing, solacing call of spirituals that people sing with one and many voices to sustain their souls and history. The variations sung in response to the spiritual's refrain testify to the black community's will to overcome the conditions of its existence. "You'll hear de trumpet sound," and "you'll hear de sinner moan," and "you'll hear de Christians shout." All the verses have the same refrain, one reminiscent of Dan Moore's mission in "Box Seat": "To wake de nations under ground." Like many spirituals, this one fuses spiritual and historical reality and in the meantime holds the people together through the participatory form of call-and-response.

After they track Kabnis back to his cabin, Halsey and Layman educate him explicitly about contemporary southern violence. "These aint th days of hounds an Uncle Tom's Cabin, feller. White folks aint in fer all them theatrics these days" (*C*, p. 183), Halsey tells him, and then uses moonshine as a metaphor for the discipline required in any craft. "Th boys what made this stuff—are y listenin t me, Kabnis? Th boys what made this stuff have *got th art down like I heard you say youd like t be with* words" (*C*, p. 184, my italics). He challenges Kabnis to distill his words into a substance at once textured and quickening. Later in a fierce manly voice Halsey holds at bay the pompous black headmaster, Hanby, who comes to fire and evict Kabnis. As another example to Kabnis of the power of the spoken word, Halsey, who has had literary interests of his own, bests Hanby by mimicking and manipulating his bullying, impotent voice and empty, oratorical style.

Kabnis understands that no one can confer or nullify manhood. He, therefore, "wants to rise and put both Halsey and Hanby in their places. He vaguely knows that he must do this, else the power of direction will completely slip from him to those outside" (*C*, pp. 188-89). But his gestures are inarticulate and misunderstood until Lewis, a more open and courageous northern Negro, enters. Lewis embodies the possibilities of manhood; "he is what a stronger Kabnis might have been, and in an odd faint way resembles him" (*C*, p. 189). Although there on his own business, Lewis is not too preoccupied to see the complexity of Kabnis's unrealized voice and soul. "Kabnis," Lewis thinks, possesses "a promise of soul-soaked beauty; uprooted, thinning out. Suspended a few feet above the soil whose touch would resurrect him." Silently, Kabnis and Lewis recognize each other in "a swift intuitive interchange of consciousness" (C, p. 191). Perhaps aware of similar divisions in his own being, Toomer mediates the silent communication between these two strangers who seem the nearest of kin. For his part, "Kabnis has a sudden need to rush into the arms of this man. His eyes call, 'Brother' " but his voice is mute as if to allow his fear of intimacy to recover its strength. "And then a savage, cynical twist-about within him mocks his impulse and strengthens him to repulse Lewis" (C, pp. 191-92). But as Lewis leaves, Toomer breaks the silence with the testimony of a woman who, "miles down the valley, begins to sing." Oblivious to the drama of opposing male wills inside the cabin, the woman's voice affirms and extends the human bond. "Her song is a spark that travels swiftly to the near-by cabins. Like purple tallow flames, songs jet up" and ride the air until other voices join her song. Toomer's words recall "Blood-Burning Moon" and herald a soulful transformation: "Now the whole countryside is a soft chorus. Lord. O Lord" (C, p. 192).

Moved, Kabnis participates by trying twice to draw Halsey into the song's community of feeling. "Do you hear it?" he asks, "Jesus, do you hear it" (C, p. 193), and his question recalls "Karintha's" refrain: "O cant you see it?" But Halsey keeps on talking about mobs and danger and Lewis as a manly man; in effect, he belittles Kabnis's wonder at the song and stirs his fears of lynching. Treated like a child, "Kabnis submits, wearily. *He has no will to resist him*" (C, p. 194, my italics). As they did briefly to Lewis, Kabnis's instincts respond to the song's evocation of the sensuous beckoning landscape; he wants to collaborate with the people in the making and the singing of the song. But Halsey's harsh-toned world of male combat intervenes. Instead of remaining an active witness, willing to testify to his half-articulate voice and its aspiring craft, Kabnis caves in. He yields to Halsey, who in his impatient, too simple, stultifying protection forgets his admonition that Kabnis distill his words from the soil in a voice of his own making. So far, then, the black songs of Georgia touch Kabnis, but his eloquence remains a potentiality seeking a responsive audience and a true occasion.

A month later, the scene is Halsey's wagon shop, which serves as a gathering place for the black men of the town. Here, too, Kabnis is stifled. A white man's pun about Kabnis getting "the hang of it" burns his neck and weighs him down with "the whole white South" (*C*, p. 201). No songs penetrate this place, but Halsey's sister, Carrie Kate, appears, and like some of the women in earlier stories, "her body is a song" (*C*, p. 17). Though mostly a silent presence, she is kin to those black women whose songs stir the community into a chorus momentarily at one with the place. As he did with Kabnis, Lewis is the only man to see her in the round, complexly. Outwardly stunted, Carrie Kate carries a light as she performs her chores and serves Father John, an old former slave preacher. She and Lewis call to each other in a "swift sunburst," and Lewis sees into the interior of life. "His mind flashes images of her life in the southern town. He sees the nascent woman, her flesh already stiffening to cartilage, drying to bone. Her spirit bloom, even now touched sullen, bitter. Her rich beauty fading." But the future recedes when he takes her hands, and she responds wholly. "The sun-burst from her eyes floods up and haloes him. Christ-eyes, his eyes look to her. *Fearlessly she loves into them*" (*C*, p. 205, my italics). All of "Kabnis," all of *Cane*, informs this moment. In her awakening, Carrie Kate recalls other women who yearn for sensuous and spiritual love in the same act of experience, while Lewis revives the image of Christ summoned previously in *Cane*—an unmartyred messiah who lives in the world as a man—and evoked by later novels like *The Autobiography of Miss Jane Pittman* and *Meridian*.

No song comes to bless the unsought, intense union. Instead, ominous voices enter stealthily. Like other black women in *Cane*, Carrie Kate hears reproving voices warn her of bodily desire. They dissipate her vision and with it the passionate actuality of the moment. "The sin-bogies of respectable southern colored folks clamor at her: 'Look out! Be a *good* girl. A *good* girl. Look out!'" (*C*, p. 205). Living in her brother's world, Carrie Kate is remote from the womanly voices that fuse human passion with a consciousness of earth and sun and sky. She internalizes the voices of convention and stultification and retreats from a chance to move beyond her life of generous, decent service toward a passion and experience of her own.

Soon Toomer, not any of his characters, especially not Kabnis, moves beyond the voices of denial and revoices the elemental song of place heard earlier in the night winds' song:

Night, soft belly of a pregnant Negress, throbs evenly against the torso of the South. Night throbs a womb-song to the South. Cane-and cotton-fields, pine forests, cypress swamps, sawmills, and factories are fecund at her touch. Night's womb-song sets them singing. Night winds are the breathing of the unborn child whose calm throbbing in the belly of a Negress sets them somnolently singing. Hear their song.

> White-man's land.
> Niggers, sing.
> Burn, bear black children
> Till poor rivers bring
> Rest, and sweet glory
> In Camp Ground. (C, pp. 208-9)

The song's words are identical to what the night winds sang to Kabnis in Part 1. But now Toomer calls his readers to become witnessing listeners, hear what they have read earlier, and vary the inflection and rhythm according to their developing interpretation of his tale. The "night winds," formerly "vagrant poets," metamorphose into the breathing of an "unborn child." Again, the song testifies to black folks singing, bearing children, being burned alive in a white man's country, and aspiring to "rest" after toil and to "sweet glory" after a life of pain, humiliation, and often violent death. Again the words acknowledge a continuing unresolved conflict between murder and creation, brutality and tenderness, silence and song. But Toomer's revised metaphor joins the fertility of black women to the life and soul of the South in all of its manifestations. Specifically, the figure breathes life into Mame Lamkins, the murdered Negress whose unborn child was ripped alive from her belly and knifed to a tree. Furthermore, the shift from "vagrant poets" to "unborn child" signifies Toomer's awareness that African-American song and story reside essentially in the people and can never be put in the keeping of a few "vagrant poets." Presently, the outside night world participates vitally in the cycle of life, whereas the human characters within descend to the underground depths of "the Hole" below Halsey's workshop. There, in homage to past defeats, their aimless party stays remote from the passion heard in the framing voices of a black woman and her unborn child—voices meant to signify Mame Lamkins and her child haunting the land, and the possibility that they will be avenged and the South redeemed by future acts of creation.

Meanwhile underground, Lewis and Kabnis contend. As often happens in *Cane*, voice is the correlative of personality. Lewis seeks to rekindle the spirit of the word, while Kabnis seeks oblivion or at least forgetfulness; and, if he cannot have either, then annihilation of his own soul. Alert to the presence of a former slave called Father, Lewis prepares responsively but silently to receive the word. He wonders if the old man is merely "a tongue-tied shadow of an old" faith or "a mute John the Baptist of a new religion" (*C*, p. 211). The old man's silence calls Lewis to speak but speak cryptically. By naming the old man Father John, Lewis answers Kabnis's bitter designation, "Father of hell," and testifies to the ancestral gift of tradition available to those who would carry on black culture.

Lewis follows this naming with a call to Father John. Like earlier calls to Kabnis and Carrie Kate, this one is interior, as if Lewis requires a private vision to speak to the assembled individuals. As yet there is no community, no congregation, though, if spoken, his thoughts might move the others to participate in the essential continuum of African-American experience:

> Slave boy whom some Christian mistress taught to read the Bible. Black man who saw Jesus in the ricefields, and began preaching to his people. Moses- and Christ-words used for songs. Dead blind father of muted folk who feel their way upward to a life that crushes or absorbs them. (*Speak*, Father!) Suppose your eyes could see, old man.
>
> (The years hold hands, *O Sing!*) Suppose your *lips* . . .
>
> Halsey, does he never *talk?* (*C*, p. 212, my italics).

The others hear Lewis's few spoken words but not his thoughts, though shortly Kabnis, sensing something is up, calls them back to the party. "Drink corn licker, love the girls, and listen t th old man mumblin sin," he urges as if the old man is part of the entertainment. But his call is flat and false. His pathetic voice restores "no good-time spirit to the party." "Lewis, seated now so that his eyes rest upon the old man, *merges with his source and lets the pain and beauty of the South meet him there*" (*C*, p. 214, my italics). The landscape lives in his bodily imagination as, so far, it does not for any of the others.

Lewis bides his time. After a while, he answers Kabnis's continuing ridicule of Father John with a variation of his previous interior monologue. "The old man as symbol, flesh, and spirit of the past," he preaches, "what do [you] think he would say if he could see you? You look at him, Kabnis" (*C*, p. 217). But Kabnis scorns the old man as another preacher whose words, like Layman's, return him to a past he wishes were dead and forgotten. In the exchange that follows, Lewis smokes out Kabnis's fantasy of an aristocratic past and testifies eloquently, out loud this time, to the actual forces pressing in on Kabnis and others who struggle against the South and its legacy of slavery. "My ancestors were Southern blue-bloods," Kabnis crows:

> Lewis: And black.
> Kabnis: Aint much difference between blue and black.
> Lewis: Enough to draw a denial from you. Cant hold them, can you? Master; slave. Soil; and the overarching heavens. Dusk: dawn. They fight and bastardize you. (*C*, p. 218)

Kabnis chooses silence, but the others begin to tell stories that connect their experience to the painful history of the race. Stella, one of the women enlisted for the night, looks at Father John and hears her father's voice singing and "when he could sing no mo, . . . aswayin an aleadin every song. A white man, took m mother an it broke th old man's heart" (*C*, pp. 218-19), she says and testifies about the shallow, bitter nature of her relations with men. In turn, Halsey responds with the story of his failure to pursue truly complex intimate relationships. "Common wench—na she aint, Lewis," he says of Stella. "I used t love that girl. Yassur. An sometimes when th moon is thick an I hear dogs up th valley barkin *an some old woman fetches out her song*," he confesses, "I sometimes get t thinkin that I still do" (*C*, pp. 220-21, my italics). Again, song communicates the spirit of place, and Lewis's speech turns these stunted individuals into a congregation and Halsey's basement into a queer Amen corner. Listening but not hearing the others' words, Kabnis reenters in the same bragging voice as before. "I was born and bred in a family of orators, that's what I was," he begins, and denounces preachers, this time denying any connection between sermons and oratory. Drunk, he is more determined than ever to isolate his life from those around him. But suddenly, honest words burn through his pose, and he joins the witnessing.

Kabnis feels his quest for "beautiful an golden" words contradicted by his experience of the world and his self-knowledge. He opens the cage of his soul and sees "some twisted awful thing" branded there that "wont stay still unless I feed it. An it lives on words," he declares, and not the "beautiful words" he seeks to shape lyrically. To keep the demon quiet, Kabnis paradoxically delivers a heavy load of "misshapen, split-gut, tortured twisted words." Moreover, in another abdication of responsibility, Kabnis accuses everyone else in Georgia of shoring up his inner monster. "Layman was feedin it back there," he accuses. "White folks feed it cause their looks are words. Niggers, black niggers feed it cause theyre evil an their looks are words. Yallar niggers feed it. This whole damn bloated purple country feeds it cause its goin down t hell in a holy avalanche of words" (C, p. 224). Looks are words, they nourish Kabnis's malignant spirit and so, he thinks, do the sermons preached in black churches. Kabnis's peroration takes no heed of the songs that suffuse the landscape and express the beauty and pain of the people's soul.

In truth, Kabnis is the keeper of his soul. But he does not feed the nightmare thing terrorizing him the many-voiced songs of *Cane*. Instead, he feeds his soul a stream of abusive words and abdicates his mission to shape the life around him into a complex, inclusive vision of the South. He refuses to acknowledge the relationship between pain and beauty; foolishly, he believes he can separate the hideous "thing" from his soul. In surrender to terror, he composes a coda to Layman's tale of Mame Lamkins and her murdered unborn child that makes the "twisted awful thing" coextensive with his soul. "I wish to God some lynchin white man ud stick his knife through it [his soul] an pin it to a tree. An pin it to a tree. You hear me?" (C, pp. 224-25). His approach to voice mirrors his approach to personality. He misuses call-and-response so profoundly that he aborts its living, improvisatory soul. His words demand that those who hear him do so in a final, absolute way and make no response lest they contradict him. Here Kabnis acts out the distinction between a closed version of oratory and the open participatory sermons of the black church. For in an uncreative, dead-end way he is an orator. Perhaps most terrible of all, he calls a "lynchin white man" to murder the soul he cannot face and, as he utters this wish, deadens his being. *His words,* not the looks or words or acts of anyone else, white or black, paralyze him and reduce his voice to a stuttering agent of disintegration.

Kabnis's soul-denying, soul-destroying testimony silences the Amen corner. Because his catalytic voice and presence are now "completely cut out" (*C,* p. 226), and because he feels so intensely the failing promise of those he meets, Lewis leaves, abruptly and silently—for good. Though he departs without speech, his plunge into the night is not a negative act, not simply an escape. For his soul's sake Lewis ascends and reenters the elemental, passionate reality of a landscape resonant with the soul of the people, the earth, and the universe. The song heard above in the night releases Lewis from the limited, shrinking voices in the hell-hole within. But Toomer does not accompany Lewis. Lewis goes into the night alone to discover its song. As if partly under the influence of Kabnis's nullifying words, Toomer grants Lewis only a symbolic acknowledgment of the desire to seek the people's song and soul in the open.

Lewis's going signifies Kabnis's failure to use call-and-response truly. No more words are spoken in the reader's presence until morning when Halsey tells the women to leave and Kabnis to get to work. Alone with Father John, Kabnis parodies the reciprocal call-and-response pattern. As if feeding his malignant, hungry soul, "words gush from Kabnis" at Father John. He pretends to ask questions, but his monologue offers the old man no chance to respond. Moreover, his words attack Father John. He would "burn an rip your soul," like the whites did to Mame Lamkins' baby. "Your soul. Ha. Nigger soul. A gin soul that gets drunk on preachers' words. An screams. An shouts. *God Almighty, how I hate that shoutin"* (*C,* p. 232, my italics). Rejecting the old former slave and scorning the shouts, the original spirituals of slavery time, Kabnis turns away from the mission of voice—"Caroling softly souls of slavery"—that Toomer embraced in "Song of the Son." Meanwhile, Carrie Kate appears, and when the old man's lips begin to move and he responds to Kabnis with the single word, "sin," Kabnis tries to shut him up. Even in front of Carrie Kate, he abuses Father John. Then, in an apparent attempt to recover her respect, he tells her, ironically in the voice of a preacher, that "th only sin is whats done against th soul." Forgetting his offenses against his and others' souls, he adds absurdly, self-absolvingly, "Th whole world is a conspiracy t sin, especially in America, an against me. I'm the victim of their sin. I'm what sin is" (C, p. 236). Again, Kabnis trivializes the idea, the word, and the act of oppression by reducing it to the scale of his existence. "Sin," repeats Father John and responds to Kabnis's repeated calls to "shut up" by slowly speaking his brief text in answer to Carrie Kate. Despite Kabnis, she and Father John create a genuine call-and-reponse, whose intimacy is a long-shared regard and silent communication across a gulf of unspoken words, thoughts, and feelings.

Implicitly, Toomer testifies to the residual power of call-and-response. Slowly, in fragments encouraged patiently and lovingly by Carrie Kate, who also foils Kabnis's attempts to silence the old man, Father John answers: "The sin whats fixed . . . upon the white folks— . . . f telling Jesus—lies. O th sin th white folks 'mitted when they made the Bible lie" (C, p. 237). But his words evoke a dual response from his audience. "Carrie Kate is wet-eyed. Kabnis, contemptuous" (C, p. 238). What Carrie Kate calls sarcastically Kabnis's "best Amen" is another insult. Father John's cryptic revelation might become a healing-song if Kabnis absorbed the old man's historical and spiritual experience and understood that the old man's words vindicate his conviction that the only sin is what is done against the soul. Father John experienced sin as a curse upon the sacred words first spoken by the prophets and then written down in the Bible. To justify slavery's terrible injustice, white folks distorted the Bible into a profound spiritual lie. Against the odds, African-Americans held together as a people, partly through their interpretation and revision of the Bible in the oral tradition of their songs and sermons. With his failing strength Father John subtly calls Kabnis to reconsider his categorical distinctions between preaching and oratory. He knows that sermons and speeches are complementary forms of African-American culture. To become a black American artist able to express the people's experience, Ralph Kabnis needs to embrace both secular and spiritual oral traditions, and maybe fuse them in a new voice—as Ralph Ellison was to do a generation or two later.

Father John's text identifies the continuing historical and spiritual significance of the crime of slavery. Because of his ancestral voice and experience, Father John becomes an oracular presence whose words anticipate the fusion of new and old meanings. But who will carry on his oracular role? Lewis is gone; and after Carrie Kate draws "the fever out" of Kabnis's "hot cheeks," he trudges upstairs in silence. Tragically, Kabnis succumbs to a false myth of deliverance. Neither he nor any single individual can rescue the black South. His work is the artistic work of finding a suitable voice and form through which to express and imagine the world. But he reacts guiltily to the wish of others that they be delivered from evil; mired in ambiguities and ambivalence, he despairs and perversely makes his home in a labyrinth of belittling words. Still, Kabnis's silent pasage upstairs may signify a desire to purge his voice of its egotism.

Now only Carrie Kate remains with Father John, and on her knees she murmurs the last words spoken in *Cane*: "Jesus, come" (*C*, p. 239). But there is no one to fulfill the old man's mission and build a new testament on traditions nourished during slavery. Throughout "Kabnis," and for that matter *Cane*, Jesus is invoked as an actual historical figure and a potential force for change. Carrie Kate's call quietly, patiently, intimately testifies to her faith in such a person as a force of life and love. Her call is an imperative, too; perhaps one or two or many will come to lead, if not in her time, then after, and perhaps the word will become flesh in acts performed by the people, as prophesied both by the scriptures and the African-American oral tradition. Her prayer is the prayer of Toomer's black madonna, the prayer of his black South, the prayer, too, of his book of the people.

After a silence Toomer responds to Carrie Kate's call; and his "song of an end" carries the rhythm of beginning as well. The human figures left on stage are Father John and Carrie Kate—an old man and a young woman whose vitality wanes with his approaching death. In answer to her call to Jesus, Toomer looks to the world and finds what Gerard Manley Hopkins called the "dearest freshness deep down things."[27] "Outside," Toomer writes, "the sun arises from its cradle in the tree-tops of the forest. Shadows of pines are dreams the sun shakes from its eyes. The sun arises. Gold-glowing child, it steps into the sky and sends a birth-song slanting down gray dust streets and sleepy windows of the southern town" (*C*, p. 239). Through an enabling metaphor Toomer keeps faith with Carrie Kate's call. His response hints at miraculous possibilities: perhaps the unborn child throbbing in the Negress's womb will awaken the black South to the promise of a new day. Meanwhile, as an artist Toomer pours out his song. His voice becomes a nesting place for Kabnis and other missing voices until they are ready to take up the story. As a tale "Kabnis" heightens the intensity of Toomer's quest for vocation in *Cane*—all the more so because he allows Ralph Kabnis the freedom to pause in the pursuit of his form and voice. Absorbing Kabnis's pain, Toomer discovers a healing personal voice possessed of but not beholden to the voices of the past.

6

Like Lewis in "Kabnis," briefly and movingly Jean Toomer touches the soul, "merges with his source and lets the pain and beauty of the South meet him there" (*C*, p. 214). Perhaps this is why *Cane* is so central and why black writers who follow speak of it as a promise-song they answer in their work.[28] In a transitional time of artistic experiment and black awakening, Toomer absorbed nuances of call-and-response, especially the inspiration of breath and spirit between speech and silence. Hearing the people's song, he experienced the intimate intervals before interior individual voices dare to join in and improvise variations on the song. In *Cane* Toomer listened to and collaborated with voices of the dead, the living, and the unborn; in *Cane* Jean Toomer discovered the possibilities and, for him, the limits of reciprocal voice.

NOTES

1. Jean Toomer to Waldo Frank, quoted by Brian Benson and Mabel Dillard in *Jean Toomer* (Boston: Twayne Publishers, 1980), p. 29, and by Nellie Y. McKay in *Jean Toomer, Artist* (Chapel Hill: University of North Carolina Press, 1984), pp. 46-47. McKay's book, which I read after writing this chapter, is an important study of both Toomer's work and life.

2. Frederick Douglass, *My Bondage and My Freedom* (1855; rpt., New York: Dover, 1969), p. 98, my italics.

3. Jean Toomer to Claude Barnett, quoted in Benson and Dillard, *Jean Toomer*, p. 33, and in McKay, *Jean Toomer, Artist*, p. 180.

4. Barbara Bowen, "Untroubled Voice: Call-and-Response in *Cane,*" *Black American Literature Forum* 16, no. 1 (Spring 1982), 15. I have one difference with Bowen's indispensable, groundbreaking essay. Call-and-response is a pattern and technique central to the forms of Afro-American oral culture, i.e., the spirituals, the work songs, and often in their testamental quality, the sermons, the blues, sometimes the tales. Certainly, African-American writers use symbolic variations of the call-and-response pattern within literary forms and genres, but I think Bowen overstates the case when she names call-and-response "a distinctively Afro-American literary form." Call-and-response accounts for the brilliant design of *Cane,* and this is not exclusively an African-American or an American vernacular quality, though Toomer's particular use of call-and-response is "distinctly Afro-American."

5. Jean Toomer, *Cane* (1923; rpt., New York: Harper and Row, 1969), p. 21. All references to *Cane* are to this edition; the volume will be cited hereafter as *C.*

6. Quoted by McKay in *Jean Toomer, Artist,* p. 47.

7. Ralph Ellison, *Invisible Man* (1952; rpt., with author's introduction, New York: Random House, 1982), p. 9.

8. Jean Toomer, *The Wayward and the Seeking,* ed. Darwin T. Turner (Washington, D.C.: Howard University Press, 1980), p. 123, my italics.

9. W. B. Yeats, *The Collected Poems of W. B. Yeats* (New York: Macmillan, 1956), pp. 336, 341.

10. John Miller Chernoff, *African Rhythm and African Sensibility* (Chicago: University of Chicago Press, 1979), p. 167.

11. For some reason this arc, which appears on the second of two otherwise blank pages preceeding "Karintha" in the first edition, is missing from the 1969 reprint issued by Harper and Row as a Perennial Classic. This is perplexing because this reissue includes Toomer's arcs on the otherwise similarly blank pages that divide the southern from the northern stories and the northern stories from "Kabnis." The only other difference between the 1923 first edition and the 1969 reissue is that the latter substitutes an introduction by Arna Bontemps for Waldo Frank's original foreword. Incidentally, on the configuration of form, region, and race in *Cane* there is no better study than Charles T. Davis's "Jean Toomer and the South: Region and Race as Elements within a Literary Imagination," *Studies in the Literary Imagination* 7, no. 2 (Fall 1974), 23-37.

12. Toomer to Frank, quoted in Benson and Dillard, *Jean Toomer,* p. 29.

13. Bowen, "Untroubled Voice," p. 12; this blues arrangement of Barlo's words is Bowen's.

14. For Toomer's account of the impact of *Winesburg, Ohio* on his work see *The Wayward and the Seeking*, p. 120, and a letter to Anderson quoted in Benson and Dillard, *Jean Toomer*, pp. 23-24.

15. James Joyce, *Ulysses* (rpt., New York: Random House, 1961), p. 37.

16. Whether eight or eighty years of age, black men have had to contend with the epithet of boy; African-Americans and their writers have responded to this humiliation with the counter epithet, "Big Boy." In the poetry of Sterling Brown and the fiction of Toomer and Richard Wright, for example, "Big Boy" connotes sometimes craft and confidence and always power and defiance of white rules and conventions, often to the death. Zora Neale Hurston, however, cites a quite different meaning for "Big Boy" in her "Glossary of Harlem Slang." "But in the South," she writes, "it means fool and is a prime insult." See her *Spunk: The Selected Stories of Zora Neale Hurston* (Berkeley: Turtle Island, 1985), p. 91.

17. Sterling A. Brown, "Old Lem," *The Collected Poems of Sterling A. Brown* (New York: Harper and Row, 1980), p. 180.

18. See Sterling Brown's brilliantly voiced counterpoint between southern and northern racial landscapes in "Cabaret," a complex poem that in its fragmentation and dislocation of past and present idiom and history recalls and responds to T. S. Eliot's *The Waste Land*. Brown, *Collected Poems*, pp. 101-3.

19. In "Kabnis" Toomer makes the passage to Camp Ground a folk song at once religious, secular, and ironic, as if to remind us of the urgent, historical roots driving many expressions of black Christianity.

20. See Michael S. Harper's recontextualization of this predicament in "Christian's Box Seat: So What," in *Images of Kin: New and Selected Poems* (Urbana: University of Illinois Press, 1977), pp. 175-76.

21. At times in *Cane*, Toomer's determination to sing in prose may lead to a strained and overwrought lyricism, a needlessly artificial language.

22. See Michael G. Cooke's discussion of intimacy in *Cane* in *Afro-American Literature in the Twentieth Century: The Achievement of Intimacy* (New Haven: Yale University Press, 1984), pp. 177-99, and specifically in "Bona and Paul," pp. 177-86.

23. Michael S. Harper, "Here Where Coltrane Is," *Images of Kin*, p.160.

24. Onida Estes-Hicks, "Jean Toomer and the Aesthetic Adventure," manuscript, p. 172. For a suggestive discussion of "Kabnis," see Maria Isabel Caldeira's "Jean Toomer's Cane: The Anxiety of the Modern Artist," *Callaloo*, 8, no. 3 (Fall 1985), 546-50.

25. James Joyce, *A Portrait of the Artist as a Young Man* (rpt., New York: Viking, 1964), p. 37.

26. Toomer uses "mourning" for "morning," although "morning," as

James Weldon and J. Rosamond Johnson point out, is the correct word in the song. For the complete text of the song see *The Books of American Negro Spirituals* (1925-26; rpt., New York: Viking Press, 1969), 1: 162-63. Nevertheless, Toomer heard the song sung "mourning," and the pun serves his purposes in "Kabnis."

27. Gerard Manley Hopkins, *Poems and Prose,* ed. W. H. Gardner (London: Penguin Books, 1953), p. 27.

28. Alice Walker views Toomer as a person with a "soul surprised by nothing." "I did not read *Cane* until 1967, but it has been reverberating in me to an astonishing degree," she writes. "I love it *passionately;* could not possibly exist without it." *Interviews with Black Writers,* ed. John T. O'Brien (New York: Liveright, 1973), p. 200. Also see Walker's comments on Toomer and *Cane* in *In Search of Our Mothers' Gardens* (San Diego: Harcourt Brace Jovanovich, 1983), pp. 60-65, 231-35, 258-59.

Ernest J. Gaines, too, came to Toomer late—the mid-1960s—after he'd set his course as a writer. Still, he has said that "if I had read Jean Toomer earlier, he would have been the greatest influence on me as a writer. His *Cane* would have influenced me." Asked why, Gaines answered: "Because of its short chapters, the songs between the stories, the roads, the South" (Ernest Gaines to the author in Baton Rouge, La., May 17, 1985).

CHAPTER 4

"Mah Tongue Is in Mah Friend's Mouf": The Rhetoric of Intimacy and Immensity in *Their Eyes Were Watching God*

1

The act of storytelling is as important in Zora Neale Hurston's *Their Eyes Were Watching God* as antiphonal songs are in Jean Toomer's *Cane*. Like Toomer, Hurston adapts call-and-response to fiction, but in her case oral storytelling is the inspirational, instrumental form. Unlike Toomer, she grew up inside the oral tradition of the South. As a girl in the all-black town of Eatonville, Florida, she relished the repartee between the men gathered on the porch of Joe Clarke's store and the women passing in and out. What she "really loved to hear was the menfolks holding a lying session." From them she heard tales of the Creation and the animal stories of Br'er Rabbit and Br'er Fox, Sis Cat and Sis Goose. And sometimes black women told folktales. Hurston first heard the story of color—God's "Git back!" misunderstood as "Git black!"—wonderfully embellished by Gold, a new woman in town and a bold enough performer to come forward in public as a storyteller.[1]

At a young age Hurston had visions and began to make up "little stories." She told stories to her mother, and, though her interfering grandmother urged that she be whipped for her "lying tongue," her mother "never tried to break" her spirit. Her mother was an open but unindulgent audience. "She'd listen sometimes, and sometimes she wouldn't. But she never seemed displeased."[2] As her daughter's primary early audience, Lucy Hurston sensed the girl's extraordinary power of voice. On her deathbed she gave Zora "solemn instructions that no one was to take a pillow from under her head as she was dying, and neither the clock nor the looking glass in the room was to be covered with cloth."[3] "She depended on me for voice,"[4] Hurston wrote later of her mother's reliance on her as the only one willing to defy the townspeople's folk customs and honor her wish to die like an individual. At the time no one listened. Her father forcibly restrained her, and Hurston grew up feeling the double burden of her mother's trust and reproach because she had failed to make her voice an instrument of action and change in the local world of Eatonville.

In her autobiography Hurston also acknowledges her later struggle for voice as a writer. *Their Eyes Were Watching God* "was dammed up in me, and I wrote it under internal pressure in seven weeks. I wish that I could write it again," she confesses, implying that, like spoken tales, stories told on paper are not necessarily final. Those who hear or read a story, including sometimes its author, complete and also continue it by virtue of their response. Intriguingly, in view of the collaborative artifice at work in *Their Eyes Were Watching God*, Hurston testifies to the presence of a call from outside as well as from within. "Anyway," she declares, "the force from somewhere in Space which commands you to write in the first place, gives you no choice. You take up the pen when you are told, and write what is commanded."[5] Hurston's observations reinforce *Their Eyes Were Watching God*'s thematic fusion of intimacy and immensity, personal and impersonal reality; her words also direct attention to the novel's fusion of individual and collaborative narrative authority as adapted from the call-and-response of oral storytelling. In *Their Eyes Were Watching God* Hurston's voice is the lead voice. She performs with her characters, autonomously and separately yet collaboratively, in an asymmetrical relation reminiscent of the polyrhythms of African music and early African-American antiphonal songs. Hurston imbues her voice with the narrative identity and personality associated with oral storytellers who performed and embellished the stories they told. Through a double act of storytelling and narrative, Hurston calls readers to respond to Janie Crawford's story and her novel with "new thoughts" and "new words."[6]

In the immediate act of reading I was a friend to the novel. I flowed with its story, lived in its world, listened to its voices. I was audience to Hurston and Janie simultaneously. And I felt like a participant about to break into my own voice and continue the story. But afterward, like Janie, I had to overcome other voices, in my case voices of scholarly authority, before I could listen to my own. For a while, influenced by Robert Stepto, a critic vitally concerned with "authorial control" as an agent in the African-American "quest for freedom and literacy," I questioned my response. For Stepto, "the one great flaw" in *Their Eyes* is the use of third-person point of view. He argues that Hurston's "curious insistence on having Janie's tale—her personal history in and as a literary form—told by an omniscient third-person, rather than by a first-person narrator, implies that Janie has not really won her voice and self after all— that her author (who is quite likely the omniscient narrating voice) cannot see her way clear to giving Janie her voice outright."[7] But eventually I realized that Hurston, always eclectic, original, idiosyncratic, individual, experimental, had decided to challenge the once innovative and generative but by the mid-1930s increasingly pat and closed modernist position against fraternization between novelist and character. I realized that in a personal way Hurston's form asks readers to trust their voices, and that to trust her voice I had to trust my own.[8]

Their Eyes Were Watching God is Hurston's novelistic Emancipation Proclamation as, earlier, *Mules and Men* had been her Declaration of Independence from the conventions of anthropology. In *Mules and Men* Hurston applied to anthropology an insight about perception and perspective going back at least to Henry James. She realized, in ways her precursors and many successors have not, that her method of observation and manner of self-presentation influenced the people's (or subjects') expression and revelation of their culture. So she abandoned the premise of impersonal, third-person scholarly objectivity and made *Mules and Men* into a first-person story about her initiation into the practice of fieldwork as well as a collection of the tales she gathered. She became a character in *Mules and Men* as she had been a participant in the black communities of Eatonville and Polk County. Her experience of Negro folklore as "not a thing of the past" but part of a culture "still in the making"[9] mediates between her story and the tales told by her "subjects." Her slowly developing relationships with the people under study and theirs with her authenticate *Mules and Men* both as anthropology and as an autobiographical tale.

Mules and Men establishes Hurston's familiarity with the possibilities of first-person narration as well as with the ambiguous implications of the so-called third-person omniscient voice, i.e., what voice, however impersonal in tone or objective in method, can be all-knowing in the face of reality's chaos and contingency? In *Their Eyes Were Watching God* Hurston breathes into her third-person narration the living voice of a storyteller. Implicitly, she puts her personality on the line. For the fashionable value of authorial control she substitutes a rhetoric of intimacy developed from the collaborative habit of call-and-response. Moreover, her performance gives the impression that she is embellishing a story she has heard before, if not from Janie, perhaps from Pheoby, Janie's immediate, responsive audience. Because of her intimate yet impersonal form, Hurston invites her readers to respond as listeners and participants in the work of storytelling.

2

Like Janie Crawford's self-presentation as an autonomous black woman simultaneously in and against the Eatonville grain, Hurston's narrative is deliberately anomalous. Authorial control implies a struggle for the story among two or more different voices, analogous to the spirit of competition that sometimes animates oral storytelling. But the two major voices in *Their Eyes Were Watching God* do not contend; rather, they cooperate and collaborate. Hurston's novel tells the story of a black woman's struggle to chart her life and choose the tones of her voice—a quest familiar to Hurston.[10] And Janie first masters, then seeks to transcend the tradition of verbal combat. For her and for Hurston, storytelling and narrative lead to an intimate mutual response. Each seeks to overcome the jarring distraction of narrow competitive voices with a lyrical serenity subtly keyed to liberation, autonomy, and, finally, honest reciprocal contact. The shared rhetorical space of *Their Eyes Were Watching God* leads to the fusing of Janie's silent interior consciousness with Hurston's outspoken, respectful, lyrical voice when, at the end, Janie is alone in her bedroom and her "thought pictures" become present in Hurston's written words.

By beginning with the utterly impersonal designation "the woman" for Janie and then moving into an intimate narrative collaboration with her storyteller, Hurston takes on the highly individual, personal characteristics of many oral storytellers. Soon Janie wrests "from menfolk some control of the tribal posture of the storyteller,"[11] but her tale does not project the values of Eatonville. Rather, in collaboration with Hurston, she projects a new and different community, first for black women, second for women, and, finally, for both women and men. In so doing Janie and Hurston challenge the conventional premises of storytelling as well as the rules governing relationships between women and men. Appropriately, Janie's act of storytelling begins as a private autobiographical act true to her position as an outcast from both the women and the men of Eatonville. Her audience consists only of Pheoby, who acts as a friend to Janie and, after the tale and her transformation, becomes a bridge between Janie and the estranged community. Janie's voice articulates her unfolding self; her grandmother, Nanny, and her first two husbands, Logan Killicks and Joe Starks, suppress her personality by stifling her right to speak. On occasion, she insists on using her voice, but only when she meets Tea Cake Woods do voice and self burst openly and strongly into eloquence, and after his death and her return to Eatonville Janie maintains it by virtue of the creative act of storytelling.

Throughout *Their Eyes Were Watching God* Hurston works out the relationship between her voice and Janie's on grounds of cooperation and support—that condition of intimacy sought by women. Hurston frames Janie's storytelling as a necessary action in the struggle for freedom—in this case a struggle for verbal as well as social equality. To succeed, women must change values, not places, and so authorial control is a false premise, a dead letter in the radical context Hurston and Janie build for the word in the world. Instead of having Janie seize authorial control (a sometimes too simple and arbitrary act in fiction and in life), Hurston improvises an intimate rhetoric of call-and-response. Author and character work together; each shares authorship and authority—collaboratively. Hurston wants to show

119

Janie openly and continuously in the round, both as she sees herself and as others see her. So she calls for Janie's story; Janie responds, and the two women, narrator and storyteller, share voices and perspectives throughout the novel.

As the novel flows along, it becomes "more like a conversation than a platform performance,"[12] but Hurston opens with a parable uttered in an improvisatory public voice.

> Ships at a distance have every man's wish on board. For some they come in with the tide. For others they sail forever on the horizon, never out of sight, never landing until the Watcher turns his eyes away in resignation, his dreams mocked to death by Time. That is the life of men.
>
> Now, women forget all these things they don't want to remember, and remember everything they don't want to forget. The dream is the truth. Then they act and do things accordingly. (*TE*, p. 9)

Audibly, Hurston declares that the story about to unfold follows from her reconsideration of the old ways of seeing, living, and telling. About men's dreams she is metaphorical in a public, oratorical style. About women she is conversational as if to insinuate her intention to abandon authorial control in favor of a more fluid and intimate style of storytelling. Her voice becomes partisan to women's experience as if foretelling that moment in the novel when Janie realizes that her image of her husband Joe Starks "never was the flesh and blood figure of her dreams," and she begins "saving up feelings for some man she had never seen." Like Janie, the woman, Hurston, the storyteller, has "an inside and an outside now"; like Janie, "she knew how not to mix them" (*TE*, pp. 112-13) and when to mix them. Like Janie, she is committed to keep the dream alive in imaginative experience. Hurston seeks immensity and intimacy, and from the start, her third-person voice is speculative as well as descriptive, personal as well as impersonal.

Peopled by abstract presences, at first the novel's world seems almost mythical, its space cloudy and inchoate. Although Hurston transforms the void into a particular place, before Janie's entrance, Eatonville is without intimacy or immensity.[13] The traditional call-and-response form between individual and community cannot work yet because the men and women of Eatonville are unable to listen or respond openly to Janie's story. They do not share her experience or her values. So, as her first task, Hurston shapes a narrative form responsive to folk and literary traditions, and fluid and improvisational enough to tell Janie's story and inspire a new tradition. By making storytelling and the narrative act collaborative and continuing, she simultaneously launches a new community of values and performs a revolutionary literary act.

Hurston's action words people the landscape and evoke the social and moral life of Eatonville. But her rich, lyrical imagery is not pastoral or uncritical; she marks the limitations of the community in ways that explain but do not justify its petty response to Janie. The time is sundown, reminiscent of dusk in Toomer's *Cane*, a transitional time for people and nature. Space, too, is transitional, ambiguous, and evasive — half-cosmic, half-historical. "Tongueless, earless, eyeless conveniences all day long," these black folks now "felt powerful and human." Nevertheless, they tell stories and pass judgment, jaundiced by the subservience of their days. As a black town, Eatonville is an island surrounded on all sides by tides of racism as treacherous and violent when Janie returns in the 1920s as when Hurston grew up there around the turn of the century. The people respond to Janie's self-assertive presence with the bitterness of the oppressed. They make "killing tools out of laughs. It was mass cruelty" (*TE*, p. 10). There is violence in the people's talk. They prefer an adversarial stance to the intimate responsiveness required to imagine or hear Janie's story, but their cowardly voices assault her pathetically and vicariously after she passes through their gauntlet of silence.

The revelation of how men and women see Janie relocates Hurston's opening presentation of male and female dreams and prepares for Janie's tale of her struggle for love and autonomy. Still "the woman," Janie may be unidentified but her identity is well known to all who watch her.

> The men noticed her firm buttocks like she had grape fruits in her hip pockets; the great rope of black hair swinging to her waist and unraveling in the wind like a plume; then her pugnacious breasts trying to bore holes in her shirt. They, the men, were saving with the mind what they lost with the eye. The women took the faded shirt and muddy overalls and laid them away for remembrance. It was a

121

weapon against her strength and if it turned out of no significance, still it was a hope that she might fall to their level some day. (*TE*, p. 11)

The men figuratively undress Janie and parse her body according to a lustful male syntax, whereas the women, desperate to deny her sexuality, make her fieldworker's clothes a reductive metonymy for her person. "But nobody moved, nobody spoke, nobody even thought to swallow spit until after her gate slammed shut" (*TE*, p. 11). Perhaps because they use words falsely and meanly, without spirit, the onlookers are compelled into lifeless silence by Janie's presence. Not only are these people afraid of the "bossman" by day; at dusk they fear the vital, realized self of one of their own who has broken their rules and survived to tell the story.

The women of the community recede before Janie's actual presence, yet, when she is absent, name her an "ole woman" and demand to know her story. Theirs is a false call. They would have but not hear her story, because in the closed space of their envy they think they know it already. Only Pheoby remains open, both as Janie's friend and as a friend to her story, whatever its gist and whether it confirms or denies her expectations and values. "Well, nobody don't know if it's anything to tell or not," she tells the townspeople. "Me, Ah'm her best friend, and Ah don't know" (*TE*, p. 12). Pheoby is a sympathetic, rigorous audience. Even though she is Janie's "best friend," she will not vouch for her story until she has heard it. Were she to do so before Janie's performance, she would abdicate her right to a full, free response. For her, hearing is believing. Nevertheless, as a friend to Janie and her act of storytelling, Pheoby creates a nest for the story. When Mrs. Sumpkins volunteers to accompany her to Janie's, Pheoby refuses and asserts Janie's right to choose her space and her audience. "If she got anything to tell yuh, you'll hear it" (*TE*, p. 13). She then leaves the crowd and goes to Janie. But not at the formal entrance—the front gate. Instead, she "went in at the intimate gate with her heaping plate of mulatto rice" (*TE*, p. 14). Pheoby makes this entrance deliberately. "Janie must be round the side" (*TE*, p. 14), she figures, for during Janie's absence Pheoby remains a friend. Though she does not know the particulars of Janie's story, she stays in touch imaginatively, just as Hurston the writer

keeps in touch with the thoughts in Pheoby's mind. "Intimate gate,"
"mulatto rice": these words reify the friendship flowing again between the two women and between them and Hurston, for Hurston's
rhetorically intimate voice reveals her as a friend to the story. Her
narrative *donnée* and Pheoby's personal *donnée* strive for friendship.
Hurston knows and does not know her characters, but intimacy
requires that she be responsive to their revelations. In this way all
have freedom to come and go. Her characters' minds become part
of the narrative space, and Hurston's voice moves easily toward and
between the voices of Janie and Pheoby. Theirs is a collaborative
eloquence.

Against the grain of Eatonville, Hurston, Janie, and Pheoby evolve
a potential community committed to freedom of voice and experience. Janie and Pheoby talk first of small things, each comfortable
enough with the other to let the big thing on their minds go for a
while. When they do speak of it, they focus on how and whether
Janie should tell her story, the framing of the tale rather than the
tale. As a friend to Janie and, potentially though not yet actually,
to her story, Pheoby advises her to "make haste and tell 'em 'bout
you and Tea Cake" (*TE*, p. 17). Pheoby wants to comb the people's
curiosity out of her hair; as one of them in her conventional self,
she feels accountable. But Janie, who is sufficiently a friend to her
own story and its telling to resist the prurient interest of Eatonville,
understands and accepts Pheoby's position. She is unthreatened by
Pheoby's double identity as a friend to her and a fully accepted member of the community. True to intimacy, Janie does not ask for total
allegiance from Pheoby; in her proud, confident autonomy, she seeks
only that fair, open, honest hearing appropriate to friendship and
storytelling. Rather than set ground rules, Janie allows Pheoby the
freedom to retell what she will hear.

Go ahead, "You can tell 'em what Ah say if you wants to," Janie
tells Pheoby. "Dat's just de same as me *cause mah tongue is in mah
friend's mouf*" (*TE*, p. 17, my italics). Janie's extravagant figure for
call-and-response affirms the intimate sympathetic imagination as an
essential faculty for telling someone else's story truly. Because she
and Pheoby are friends, Janie trusts Pheoby to be a friend to her
story. Janie goes on to tell Pheoby she will not volunteer her story
to the people of Eatonville because they have violated the spirit of

intimacy. "If they wants to see and know, why they don't come kiss and be kissed? Ah could then sit down and tell 'em things" (*TE*, p. 18). Janie proposes civility, courtesy, and hospitality as preconditions for intimacy and the minimum standard for a listener's contribution to storytelling. An audience earns the right to hear a story, as Pheoby has done with her acts and words of hospitality and friendship. No one should take for granted the right to hear someone else's story simply because they live in the same place, or share the same race, gender, or class. Hurston embodies these values for the hearing and telling of stories in the experiential frame she builds for Janie's tale. The common values she and Janie discover as women, as African-Americans, and as storytellers inspire genuine call-and-response.

As Janie's audience, Pheoby departs from convention in another way. As a friend who has heard Janie tell stories before, though not her story, Pheoby asks for help *before* Janie begins her tale:

> "It's hard for me to understand what you mean, de way you tell it. And then again Ah'm hard of understandin' at times."
>
> "Naw, 'tain't nothin' lak you might think. So 'tain't no use in me telling you somethin' unless Ah give you de understandin' to go 'long wid it. Unless you see de fur, a mink skin ain't no different from a coon hide." (*TE*, p. 19)

The two women explore the relation between language and experience, storyteller and audience. As language, particularly metaphor, expresses the shimmer and radiance of reality, so the dialogue of call-and-response embodies the flux of human personality. Each individual has responsibilities, and before Janie begins, she tells Pheoby that she depends on her, too. She expects her to listen intimately while she tells her story. "Pheoby, we been kissin-friends for twenty years, so Ah depend on you for a good thought. And Ah'm talking to you from that standpoint" (*TE*, p. 19). Janie's perspective challenges the impersonality sometimes mistakenly associated with oral storytelling and the authorial control identified with the practice of narrative craft. Janie in her storyteller's dialect and Hurston in her lyrical vernacular look after each other's needs. Because of their mutual, radical transformation of values, Janie and Hurston together reconstruct the theory and practice of storytelling and narrative; in imaginative, narrative space, Hurston exists with Janie, alongside her, not in front of her or behind her.

To underscore the intimate mix of separate and kindred voices as a positive narrative value, Hurston ends the first chapter with a response to Janie's kissing metaphor. "Time makes everything old so the kissing, young darkness became a monstropolous old thing while Janie talked" (*TE*, p. 19). Hurston animates the cycles of day and night, of individual lives, and of storytelling into concentric circles of meaning and experience. Each moves continuously, palpably, openly, according to its own rhythm and Hurston's polyrhythmic artifice of call-and-response.

After bearing witness to the conjunction of Janie's storytelling with time's immensity, Hurston invents a companion figure for the spatial scale of Janie's life.

> Janie saw her life like a great tree in leaf with the things suffered, things enjoyed, things done and undone. Dawn and doom was in the branches.
> "Ah know exactly what Ah got to tell yuh, but it's hard to know where to start at." (*TE*, p. 20)

Like Pheoby, Hurston enters as a friend to Janie before Janie struggles to utter the first words of her story. But the relation between their two voices depends on "abrupt and unexpected changes." In her remarks on the asymmetry of Negro art, Hurston provides a suggestive description applicable to the polyrhythmic quality present in *Their Eyes Were Watching God*. "There is always rhythm," she observes of African-American music and dancing, "but it is the rhythm of segments. Each unit has a rhythm of its own, but when the whole is assembled it is lacking in symmetry." Likewise, Hurston's juxtaposition of voices highlights what she calls angularity: the African-American determination "to avoid the simple straight line."[14] Sometimes, like the polyrhythms of African and African-American music, the separate voices in *Their Eyes Were Watching God* fuse with one another, but each quickly breaks free and pursues its different individual beat, its own voice line and lifeline.[15]

Although separate, Hurston's and Janie's voices sometimes meet in the space beyond the lines of the text. From images in her character's mind, Hurston composes an extended simile linking Janie's struggle with her story with the tree of life. For Janie's beginning rambles, perhaps because of a sudden fear that, despite Pheoby, she is on her own in storytelling as she was in childhood without the presence of her mother and father. She tells a few anecdotes of girlhood: her unawareness of race ("Ah couldn't recognize dat dark chile as me"); her nickname Alphabet, signifying many nullifying names; black children's ridicule of her "'bout livin' in de white folks backyard"; her shame at her fugitive father and her puzzled resentment at what is left out in accounts of him ("Dey didn't tell about how he wuz seen tryin' tuh git in touch wid mah mama later on so he could marry her"); and, finally, her memory of her grandmother's decision to buy land and a house because she "didn't love tuh see me wid mah head hung down" (*TE*, pp. 21, 22). At this point Hurston's voice reenters and testifies to the sympathetic effect produced by Pheoby, Janie's immediate audience. "Pheoby's hungry listening helped Janie to tell her story. So she went on thinking back to her young years and explaining them to her friend in soft, easy phrases while all around the house, the night time put on flesh and blackness" (*TE*, p. 23). Though silent, Pheoby's response to the call of the scarcely begun tale challenges Janie. The intimacy between them nurtures Janie's conversational style ("soft, easy phrases") and offers Hurston the freedom and narrative space to reconstruct, imagine, and revoice what Janie thinks and feels between the words of the story she tells Pheoby. And in confirmation of the transforming power of their collaboration, the night, too, becomes a sympathetic black presence.

From now on, Hurston and Janie function respectively (and respectfully) as composer and performer of the story. Hurston speaks for Janie because Janie speaks for Hurston, too. And Hurston also participates in the intimacy between Janie and Pheoby. Because she writes in a shared, complementary narrative space, Hurston conveys the impression that her embellishments are inspired and sustained by Janie and her spontaneous oral storytelling. Hurston's form also depends on an improvisatory, creative tension, a becoming; her third-person voice is personal but not proprietary. In form and theme, *Their Eyes Were Watching God* pursues the evolving possibilities of intimacy and autonomy. The novel presents Janie's experience and perspective as realities perhaps not yet realized but aspired to on some submerged level of feeling, thought, and speech by black women, women generally, and — such is Hurston's imaginative power — by men as well. For these reasons it is crucial that Hurston's collaborative voice be free to explore not only what Janie said, but things she might have thought but not said, and, not least, that "gulf of formless feelings untouched by thought" (*TE*, p. 43).

There is another reason for Hurston to break in on Janie's voice and story at this early point. So far, her entrances have framed Janie's tale. To that extent the narrative relationship seems conventional enough. But now Hurston's lyrical tone signals an intimate conversation between her voice and Janie's *in the telling* of Janie's story. That is, when Hurston's voice emerges from Janie's chamber of thought and memory, her words testify to a common experience, sometimes lived, sometimes imagined, an experience both women need to articulate. They share what Hurston, describing Janie, calls "that oldest human longing — self-revelation" (*TE*, p. 19), and referring to her condition before writing *Their Eyes Were Watching God*, describes as the "agony" of "bearing an untold story inside you."[16] Hurston realizes that Janie knows her comments to Pheoby about her childhood are essential prologue to her experience and her tale. "She thought awhile and decided that her conscious life had commenced at Nanny's gate" (*TE*, p. 23). Reexperienced, those details lead to reconsideration of Janie's "conscious life," and collaboration becomes possible without fear of condescension or control by the author's third-person voice. The form works because Janie stands between Pheoby's immediate responsive silence and Hurston's distanced but intense personal imagination. Finally, Hurston's acknowledgment of "Pheoby's hungry listening" raises the possibility of similar but different responses by a more removed but unremote, potential audience of readers.

3

In *Their Eyes Were Watching God* Hurston and Janie revoice the continuing American/African-American theme of identity. Who am I and how shall I live? And how should a black woman live? To whom does she dare tell her story? These questions pose an old riddle: how does an individual make her voice count in the world, and the world newly present in her words, especially when other voices work to sustain the status quo of speech and experience, the old patriarchal values? Only with a struggle and, Hurston's form argues, through collaboration, can Janie resist others' efforts to control her life and, therefore, her story. In the novel human beings inevitably live out one or another version of the word. Janie discovers early and repeatedly that others expect her life and her voice to conform to their text, however contrary it is to her experience and desires. To be free she must formulate her own scripture and learn to be articulate about it in a voice of her own.

And Janie does imagine a text that then becomes accessible and eloquent through collaboration between her voice and Hurston's. At sixteen, her orgiastic experience of spring inspires an original metaphor, expressed first in Hurston's voice and then, directly by Janie when, desperate to make Nanny feel her loathsome nights and days as Logan Killicks's wife, she bursts into verbal bloom: "Ah wants things sweet wid mah marriage lak when you sit under a pear tree and think" (TE, p. 43). As a young and then an older woman, Janie counters the false calls of Nanny, Logan Killicks, and Joe Starks with a visionary burgeoning text of her own. Throughout the story her responses to the narrow, belittling, condescending texts of others become a call to her sensuous imagination, a call answered and amplified in the equality of voice and experience she shares with Tea Cake Woods, her third husband. And after his death, her voice, in the act of storytelling, evolves into an instrument able to reach the world and her soul.

Few voices are more important than Nanny's in *Their Eyes Were Watching God*. Hers is a black female ancestral text and tale to be absorbed and overcome. Her call begins as a response to Janie's emerging, expectant womanhood and the consequences of her sudden, sensuous, orgiastic communion with the living world. Tragically, Nanny sees only a "breath-and-britches," "trashy nigger" neighborhood boy "lacerating her Janie with a kiss." Her call is really a command that Janie marry old Logan Killicks. When Janie protests that "he look like some ole skull-head in de grave yard," Nanny assaults her verbally, and in response to Janie's pouting, defensive silence, "she slapped the girl violently, and forced her head back so that their eyes met in struggle." In place of intimacy, Nanny resorts to confrontation, in place of call-and-response, a stringent authorial control. Nonetheless, Nanny's soul presently melts before Janie's "terrible agony," and she stands there "suffering and loving and weeping *internally,* for both of them" (*TE,* pp. 27, 26, 28, 29, my italics).

Nanny's sudden rush of sympathy leads her to tell Janie her version of the scheme of things behind the black woman's place in the world. "Honey," she says, "man is de ruler of everything as fur as Ah been able tuh find out. Maybe it's some place way off in de ocean where de black man is in power, but *we don't know nothin' but what we see.* So de white man throw down de load and tell de nigger man tuh pick it up. He pick it up because he have to, but he don't tote it. He hand it to his womenfolks. De nigger woman is de mule uh de world so fur as Ah can see." Nanny ends by testifying in a way deceptively like the call-and-response common to the black church. "Ah been prayin' fuh it tuh be different wid you. Lawd, Lawd, Lawd!" She seems deaf to the fact that for Janie marriage to Killicks is surrender to the very fate Nanny would protect her from—namely, transformation into "de mule uh de world." Moreover, Nanny fights Janie's aspirations with a metaphor whose meaning is contradicted by the young woman's sensuous intuitive experience, if not by her lineage. "You know, honey, us colored folks is branches without roots," Nanny declares, and, lest her words belittle her own strong, stubborn existence, she confides to Janie her dream of "whut a woman oughta be and to do." Like many slaves, Nanny saw Emancipation as a beginning: "Ah wanted to preach a great sermon about colored women sittin' on high but they wasn't no pulpit for me." She hopes her daughter "would expound what Ah felt," and when she loses the way, Nanny transfers her ambition to Janie, the newest bastard child in her lineage. "'So whilst Ah was tendin' you of nights Ah said Ah'd save de text for you'' (*TE,* pp. 29, 31, 32, my italics).

Contrary to the view that *Their Eyes Were Watching God* "takes place in a seemingly ahistorical world,"[17] Nanny's parable of race follows from the historical context of her experience. As a slave, she was forced into concubinage by her master and bore him a daughter. In his absence his wife threatens to whip Nanny to death and sell the child. Nanny runs away to the swamp and with help from "uh friend or two" hides out until Sherman's army liberates the black folks of Savannah. After the war she refuses offers of marriage and moves to West Florida, but there her daughter's rape by a black schoolteacher destroys her dream of uplift. But not entirely, for Nanny names Janie the successor to her dream. Nanny's capacity for eloquence is clear, but her way of knowing and seeing is narrow and limited. Although she lives somewhat independently and autonomously, perhaps with fatal help from "some good white people" (*TE*, p. 36), her life has beaten her down into one of the dimmest flickering sparks later invoked in Janie's folk version of the Creation and Fall.

In the end Nanny's eloquence is false and static. Despite all that has happened to her and her daughter, and what she imagines may happen to Janie, her text remains the same. She is content to hand it down to the descendents she assumes will come from Janie and Logan Killicks. She grieves that preaching the "great sermon about colored women sittin' on high" (*TE*, p. 32) will have to wait, but she sees her time and Janie's governed by unchanging social and historical circumstances. And there is another thing: her text, if experienced, would revise the past and present inequality between women and men, black women and white women within a hierarchical context. For Janie, a rich view of life's possibilities begins with rejection of Nanny's epistemology. As she retells Nanny's tale, she, along with Hurston, preaches a "great sermon" to Pheoby in which she overcomes the burden of her grandmother's expectations. And her text is her own, not her grandmother's. Before she learns to speak with conviction and eloquence, she begins to compose her own text, her call to the world. It becomes imperative for her to embody love and autonomy, intimacy and immensity in both her story and her experience. Once her soul reemerges after her marriages to Logan Killicks and Joe Starks, she rejects completely Nanny's text in favor of her desire "to be a pear tree — any tree in bloom" reaching for the "far horizon" (*TE*, pp. 25, 50).

Meanwhile, in the aftermath of her tale, Nanny makes a request calculated to discourage Janie from responding according to her emerging perspective and experience. "Have some sympathy fuh me," she pleads. "Put me down easy, Janie, Ah'm a cracked plate" (*TE*, p. 37). Her sentimental metaphor reinforces Janie's silence. In the days before her marriage to Killicks, Janie keeps unspoken her metaphor about marriage, self, and the pear tree. Instead, she hopes Nanny and the other old folks are right when they tell her that "Yes, she would love Logan after they were married" (*TE*, p. 38). But they are wrong, and when Janie comes to tell Nanny, the old woman at first improvises variations on her polar texts: the one of nightmare ("nigger woman de mule uh de world"); the other her dream of "colored women sittin' on high." On the one hand, "everybody got tuh tip dey hat tuh you and call you Mis' Killicks," she tells Janie; and on the other she characterizes the male body as a weapon on which women are often impaled: "Dat's de very prong all us black women gits hung on. Dis love!" (*TE*, p. 41). Nanny, though, has escaped this fate, and perhaps that is one reason she softens under the poetry of Janie's newly uttered, womanly text: "Ah wants things sweet wid mah marriage lak when you sit under a pear tree and think. Ah" (*TE*, p. 43).

Janie's eloquence and her moving pause compel Nanny to respond with an ambiguous acknowledgment of the possibility of change. "Better leave things de way dey is," she tells Janie. "Youse young yet. *No tellin' what mout happen befo' you die.* Wait awhile, baby. Yo' mind will change." Although Nanny's last words half-heartedly invoke the old certainties, they do not take away the hope she gives Janie. After Nanny dies, largely from her "infinity of conscious pain," Janie waits. She hears "the words of the trees and the wind," and speaks to "falling seeds" as she has heard them speak to each other. The articulate vitality of the living world mocks her static life with Killicks. "She knew now that marriage did not make love. Janie's first dream was dead, so she became a woman" (*TE*, pp. 43, 44, my italics).

Through Hurston's voice Janie's unheard words articulate her discovery that for Killicks and, later, Joe Starks, Nanny's text is a code word for women's subservience. Killicks, for instance, eventually gives his young reluctant wife the choice of satisfying his illusions and desires convincingly if not happily, or chopping wood, plowing, and helping him move manure piles. In the midst of this struggle, Joe Starks comes down the road. To Janie, "he acted like Mr. Washburn or somebody like that," i.e., well-to-do white folks, but it is his voice that calls boldly and distinctively—so much so that Hurston, in her continuing collaboration with Janie, makes his voice briefly hers. "Joe Starks was the name, yeah Joe Starks from in and through Georgy. Been workin' for white folks all his life. . . . *He had always wanted to be a big voice,* but de white folks had all de sayso where he come from and everywhere else, exceptin' dis place dat colored folks was buildin' theirselves" (*TE*, pp. 47, 48, my italics). Now Hurston picks up Janie's mimicry of Joe; without Janie's tale, Hurston could not do Joe, but because of their collaboration Hurston fuses these voices in her narration before resuming the past dramatic moment of Janie's encounter with Joe and her recreation of that experience as she tells her tale to Pheoby.

Janie runs off with Starks to escape from the puny, straitened space she occupies with Killicks and because Joe "spoke for far horizon." But she is also aware of the things she does not hear in his voice. She "pulled back a long time because he did not represent sun-up and pollen and blooming trees"; in the end she goes because at least "he spoke for change and chance." "With him on it," the seat in the hired rig he takes her away in "sat like some high, ruling chair," but Janie does not notice the echo of Nanny's sermon. Instead, she covers Joe and herself with the sweet pollen of her vision. "From now on until death she was going to have flower dust and springtime sprinkled over everything. A bee for her bloom." Fortunately, Janie keeps in mind the need to adapt her voice to changes in experience. "Her old thoughts were going to come in handy now," Hurston imagines her musing, "but new words would have to be made and said to fit them" (*TE*, pp. 50, 54). The call-and-response going on so fluidly and implicitly between Hurston and Janie parallels Janie's former readiness to create an original discourse in her marriage to Joe Starks, beginning with her invention of the more intimate name, Jody.

In her life with Starks in the new black town of Eatonville Janie discovers that Jody views her as an appendage. "Ah told you in de very first beginning dat Ah aimed tuh be a big voice," he reminds her, and follows with a logic antithetical to her vision of reciprocal experience. "You oughta be glad, 'cause dat makes uh big women outa you" (*TE*, p. 74). Because Joe loves being Mr. Mayor, Janie should gratefully accept the name and identity of Mrs. Mayor. She should live in his space within the sound of his voice. In this context Janie becomes a listener and absorbs the voices and stories of Eatonville's oral culture, so that later on she and Hurston bring the flowing talk to life in her story. Biding her time, Janie looks for an opening to speak in a circumstance not in the least threatening or competitive to Joe. She finds such an occasion when Joe, overhearing her disgust at the mule-baiting by the men on the front porch, buys Lum's mule for more than it is worth. "Freein' dat mule makes uh mighty big man outa you. Something like George Washington and Lincoln. Abraham Lincoln, he had de whole United States tuh rule so he freed de Negroes. You got uh town so you freed uh mule. You have tuh have power tuh free things and dat makes you lak uh king uh something" (*TE*, pp. 91-92). On the male ritual ground of the *front* porch, Janie's irony is ungrasped by her audience. Only when she tells her tale to Pheoby from the female space of the *back* porch is her audience aware that Janie is calling attention to the unfree condition of women.

Freedom is Janie's text, and her speech of praise enlists Joe in the cause. Her audience of male townspeople salutes her for putting "jus de right words tuh our thoughts," and Starks "beamed all around," but he "never said a word" (*TE*, p. 92). His silence is significant. It suggests his lack of verbal reciprocity or genuine call-and-response with Janie or anyone else. It also implies embarrassment at Janie's words, for Starks, as he makes clear, expects Janie to sit on high as his possession. Sometimes functional, sometimes ornamental, she is supposed to act and speak at his command; even her psychological inner space should be peopled with his thoughts. A public exchange between him and Janie reveals Starks's perverse reversal of Nanny's text "about colored women sittin' on high":

> "Somebody got to think for women and chillun and chickens and cows. I god, they sho don't think none theirselves.
> "Ah knows uh few things, and womenfolks thinks sometimes too."
> "Aw now they don't. They just think they's thinkin'. When Ah see one thing Ah understands ten. You see ten things and don't understand one." (*TE*, pp. 110-11)

Such is Joe Starks's absolute rejection and denunciation of Janie's courageous but almost pathetically modest variation on her theme of freedom and reciprocity.

Henceforth, Janie hushes her soul and sustains her womanhood by ceasing to act fully as a woman toward Joe. "The bed was no longer a daisy-field for her and Joe to play in." When a meal of Janie's turns out soggy and tasteless, Joe slaps her hard and humiliatingly across the face, and from that moment she abandons all traces of her quest for intimacy with Joe Starks, instead "saving up feelings for some man she had never seen." In her role as Mrs. Mayor, Janie mostly holds her tongue on the front porch, but when provoked, she proves Joe's and the other men's better at verbal combat. On one occasion, tired of hearing variations on Joe's theme of women and chickens, Janie challenges the male voices. "Sometimes," she says, "God gits familiar wid us womenfolks too and talks His inside business." And she testifies to an intimate conversation with God. "He told me how surprised He was 'bout y'all turning out so smart after Him makin' yuh different; and how surprised y'all is goin' tuh be if you ever find out you don't know half as much 'bout us as you think you do" (*TE*, p. 117). Her text warns against male hubris and foreshadows the volcanic potential of women's voices.

Fittingly, given Joe's identity as a public man, the climax of the contention between him and Janie occurs in front of a large audience of mostly male townspeople. Once again, their conflict is expressed on the essential level of maleness and femaleness, but this time Janie plays the dozens in place of her previous attempts to nudge Joe toward reciprocity through an intimate, tentative, conversational response. Now, their words are weapons of war.

> "Tain't no use in gettin' all mad, Janie, 'cause Ah mention you ain't no young gal no mo'. Nobody in heah ain't lookin' for no wife outa yuh. Old as you is."
>
> "Naw, Ah ain't no young gal no mo' but den Ah ain't no old woman neither. Ah reckon Ah looks mah age too. But Ah'm uh woman every inch of me, and Ah know it. Dat's uh whole lot more 'n you kin say. You big-bellies round here and put out a lot of brag, but tain't nothin' to it but yo' big voice. Humph! Talkin' 'bout *me* lookin' old. When you pull down yo' britches, you look lak de change uh life." (*TE*, pp. 122-23)

Janie does not simply reveal Joe's impotence. Her words proceed from her earlier witty claim that God has told her that women, not men, were the norm at creation. She calls Joe a woman and not a woman like she is, still in the prime of womanhood, but a woman no longer fully a woman because of the change of life. Addressed to a man, her allusion to "de change uh life" has a devastating sexual force it lacks for a woman. In response Joe can only strike her; henceforth he keeps his distance and relies on other women for comfort in his sickness. When he is near death, Janie breaks the silence between them with tough words that express bluntly the mind that "had tuh be squeezed and crowded out tuh make room for yours in me." ' Joe responds with a pathetic command for silence and the wish that lightning strike Janie dead. But she keeps on talking and *her voice* hastens his death.

Starks dies by the text he spoke and lived by, and Janie proclaims it as his epitaph. " 'Dis sittin in de rulin' chair is been hard on Jody,' she muttered out loud" to no audience but herself; though, in her act of storytelling, Pheoby, and in Hurston's act of narrative, a succession of readers hear her. "She was full of pity for the first time in years," Hurston says. From this moment Janie opposes Nanny's female dream of "colored women sittin' on high" and Jody's male dream of "sittin' in de rulin' chair." Instead, she proposes an experience able to mingle the sensuously intimate "pear tree" with the immensity of "far horizon." For the first time in years Janie looks at herself. Seeing and admiring the "handsome woman" who takes the place of the "young girl" who had arrived in Eatonville some twenty-five years before, Janie frees her hair from the kerchief required of her by her late husband. But Janie has learned a thing or two about performance in her role as Mrs. Mayor. So "she starched and ironed her face, forming it into just what people wanted to see"; then, her hair tied back for effect, she issues a public call. "Come heah! Jody is dead. Mah husband is gone from me" (*TE*, pp. 134, 135). Her words are true in different ways for her private and public selves, her past and forthcoming experience, her former and current audiences. Her factual but ambiguous language encourages self-revealing responses from the townspeople, Pheoby, and the rest of us who hear her.

4

With his "big voice" Joe Starks, in effect, became Nanny's successor, and so it is appropriate that after his death and burial

Janie discovers her true feelings about Nanny. Here, as a witness, Hurston tells of Janie's unceasing anger; as a participant in the story, she distills a portion of compassion for Nanny, an act impossible for Janie. But only after Hurston helps Janie remove the "cloak of pity" from her feelings is her long-disguised emotion revealed as an abiding hatred. Janie's reasons, spelled out by Hurston, center on her grandmother's transgression of space. "Here Nanny had taken the biggest thing God ever made, the horizon—for no matter how far a person can go the horizon is still way beyond you—and pinched it in to such a little bit of a thing that she could tie it about her granddaughter's neck tight enough to choke her. She hated the old woman who had twisted her so in the name of love" (*TE*, p. 138). Janie expected intimate allegiance from Nanny. Consequently, Nanny's womanly complicity with the patriarchal scheme of things took special advantage of Janie's girlhood vulnerablility. Janie realizes that in her determination to prevent "de menfolks white or black" from "makin' a spit cup outa [her]," Nanny had set her "in the market place to sell," had set her "for still bait" before the repulsive Logan Killicks.

Now, inspired by her experience of Janie's passionate feelings of betrayal, Hurston, without transition, collaborates with Janie on a folk myth of Creation and the Fall:

> When God had made The Man, he made him out of stuff that sung all the time and glittered all over. Then after that some angels got jealous and chopped him into millions of pieces, but still he glittered and hummed. So they beat him down to nothing but sparks but each little spark had a shine and a song. So they covered each one over with mud. And the lonesomeness in the sparks make them hunt for one another, but the mud is deaf and dumb. Like all the other tumbling mud-balls, Janie had tried to show her shine. (*TE*, pp. 138-39)

This myth recapitulates the theme of the confining power of those who deny individuals their free human expression. Against the fall, the original damage done, a person has to struggle to keep alive "a shine and a song"—an independent articulate existence. In fact, Janie's experience calls for revision of this tale as it has the previous texts of Nanny and Joe Starks. Because "the mud is deaf and dumb," the human sparks within need both strong voices and the alert ears of good listeners. To survive and thrive in the world as an articulate presence and personality, Janie (and everyone else) needs to restore and recreate a reciprocal tradition of call-and-response. To call others and generate a response, an individual has to overcome the deaf-and-dumb proclivity of mud-balls—a figure for the unawakened, unresponsive prosaic conventions human beings fall into so easily. So the old tale is a commencement, its possibilities acted out and extended by the collaboration between Hurston and Janie, and per-haps by readers who also seek to show both "a shine and a song."

Meanwhile, a new text of male authorial control is spoken to Janie. " 'Uh woman by herself is uh pitiful thing,' she was told over and again," and such talk is bound up with the townspeople's corollary point that Janie owes her well-being to Joe Starks's money and worldly success. "Throwin' away what Joe Starks worked hard tuh git tuhgether" (*TE*, p. 61), Sam Watson tells Pheoby. But Janie has every right to Joe's store and his other worldly possessions; her labor and brains as well as his brought them to fruition. Shrewdly, Janie avoids confrontations and commitments in her responses to numerous male suitors. When Pheoby, her new fishing friend, tries to persuade her to marry an undertaker, Janie responds by turning an honest negative into an eloquent positive, "Ah jus' loves dis freedom" (*TE*, pp. 139, 143). Increasingly, Janie's identity comes not in rebellion against someone else's text but from the pleasure she takes in her reencounter with the world. Left to herself, she will not sit anywhere; hers is to explore, to move out from the sanctum of the pear tree. Alone, at forty, she dreams of integrating the im-mensity and intimacy of experience in the unfolding story of her life.

When Tea Cake arrives, Janie and her soul are ready; though, with his dark skin, empty pockets, and traveling-man ways, he seems an unlikely candidate for a husband. Easy conversation is the first thing between them. Tea Cake does not ask Janie for a match. Instead, he revivifies the thing named: "You got a lil piece uh fire over dere, lady." He teaches her to play checkers, a game Eatonville convention reserves largely for men, and while they kid around, he performs gently and humorously for her. When he leaves, Janie remembers their intimacy of speech: "Look how she had been able to talk with him right off!" (*TE*, pp. 145, 151). And in her third-person way,

Hurston changes once more from a witness to a participant in Janie's inner life. For his part, Tea Cake is a man like Janie is a woman: on the terms of his essential existence and experience. "You needs tellin' and showin', and dat's what Ah'm doing" (*TE*, p. 162), he says to Janie after turning up at daybreak to tell her the story of his love. Voice and experience are one for him, and when he definitely, fulsomely declares his love, he makes his words a text of praise. "You got de keys to de kingdom" (*TE*, pp. 165, 181), he tells her and repeats the refrain after their marriage. For the first time, Janie hears a voice and text celebrate her in her own right, because of who she is. Like her text of the pear tree and far horizon, his embodies autonomy and equality, intimacy and immensity.

When Janie runs off with Joe Starks, she tells herself that "new words would have to be made and said to fit" her "old thoughts" (*TE*, p. 55). But now telling Pheoby the story of her life with Tea Cake, she says that "in the beginnin' new thoughts had tuh be thought and new words said" (*TE*, p. 173). She is right. She calls Tea Cake to think and speak "new words" appropriate to their relationship:

> "So you aims tuh partake wid everything, hunh?"
> "Yeah, Tea Cake, don't keer what it is."
> "Dat's all Ah wants to know. From now on you'se mah wife and mah woman and everything else in de world Ah needs." (*TE*, pp. 186-87)

For her part, Janie accepts Tea Cake's gambling; violence and all, "it was part of him, so it was all right" (*TE*, p. 188). In marriage, they talk and work things out mutually and compatibly.[18] They change each other, and, as their love dissolves jealousy and possessive authority, each becomes a freer individual by virtue of their life together.

On the Muck picking beans with Tea Cake in "her blue denim overalls and heavy shoes," Janie "got so she could tell big stories herself from listening to the rest" (*TE*, p. 200). Moreover, as Janie comes to the Tea Cake section of her story, Hurston's third-person narrative grows increasingly able to mesh with the voices of Janie and the people around her. Again, as if she is more a participant than a witness, Hurston does the townspeople of Eatonville in her vernacular. "Poor Joe Starks. Bet he turns over in his grave every day. Tea Cake and Janie gone hunting. Tea Cake and Janie gone fishing" (*TE*, p. 166). Equally, Hurston becomes a presence on the Muck with Janie and Tea Cake: "Wild cane on either side of the road hiding the rest of the world. *People wild too* (*TE*, p. 193, my italics). The inversion suggests that in the act of writing Hurston moves from seeing *what* Janie sees to seeing (and writing) as Janie sees (and speaks). Likewise, Hurston modulates without warning into the dialect of the "great flame throwers" on the Muck, "handling Big John de Conquer and his works. How he had done everything big on earth, then went up tuh heben without dying atall" (*TE*, p. 232). Here and elsewhere,[19] Hurston's diction and rhythm are one with her characters' voices, and then each goes its separate way. The point is that, as in *Mules and Men*, Hurston has been influenced by her characters, so that their oral performances are interwoven with her continuous novelistic act of composition.

Just as Hurston dissolves arbitrary lines of idiom and voice, so Janie crosses lines of class and color in her marriage to the black workingman, Tea Cake. "You always did class off," Pheoby tells Janie to support her argument against her friend's involvement with Tea Cake. "Jody classed me off. Ah didn't," Janie responds and in the same conversation argues vehemently against hierarchical demarcations. "Dis is uh love game," Janie declares and, having earlier faced her feelings about her grandmother, connects the old woman's perspective with the institution of slavery. But she rejects her grandmother's "sittin' on porches" because of her experience. "Ah got up on de high stool lak she told me, but Pheoby, Ah done nearly languished tuh death up dere" (*TE*, pp. 169, 171, 172). And later on, Janie answers Mrs. Turner's denunciation of Tea Cake and dark Negroes generally. "We'se uh mingled people and all of us got black kinfolks as well as yaller kinfolks" (*TE*, p. 210). The spirit of mingling imbues Janie's personality and her voice. On all levels of her relationship with Tea Cake, Janie rejects classification for points of being that are fluid. She prefers a contingent over a categorical response to people and the world.

Their Eyes Were Watching God dissolves the hard lines of voice and idiom, gender, class, and color into a vernacular mosaic of language and experience. But it is not always easy or even possible for Janie to integrate the essential, contradictory bits and pieces of assertion and action strewn in her path. Sometimes, the space of the world contains unfamiliar, hostile way stations; at times self is the only home and its only form a chaotic polyrhythmic version of collage. Janie's trial, after she shoots the tragically rabid, suddenly murderous Tea Cake in self-defense, is such an occasion, and in Hurston's and Janie's hands, a complementary, asymmetrical performance. In the courtroom Janie's intimate experience clashes with the consequences of Jim Crow legal and social space. Reminiscent of the folk tale of "Old Sis Goose," judge, jury, and attorneys are all white men. As Janie notices the "eight or ten white women," "nobody's poor white folks" who "had come to look at her," she wishes "she could make them know how it was instead of those menfolks." Like the well-to-do white women sitting in front, "all of the colored people standing up in the back of the courtroom" are excluded from participation; they are tolerated only if they remain silent. That's the institutional context behind Janie's personal hurt when she sees that the black folks, people she and Tea Cake lived among, "were all against her" (*TE*, pp. 274-275). Without power, they seek refuge in false categories. In life they loved Tea Cake; now in death he seems a hero destroyed by his love for a light-skinned, wealthy woman from a strange place.

To make matters worse and better, the black spectators begin to talk among themselves. They mutter a jaundiced version of the story and insist that justice cannot be done without their participation. "They talked all of a sudden and all together like a choir," in a desperate parody of the black church, "and the top parts of their bodies moved on the rhythm of it" (*TE*, p. 276). In sympathy with their right to testify, though not with their false story, Hurston's voice briefly flows into their folk speech. But just as quickly, her voice shifts back to a dramatic enactment of the exchange between the prosecutor and Sop-de-Bottom, the spokesman for Tea Cake's friends. Sop-de-Bottom's emergence is both predictable and appropriate. Back when Tea Cake gives Janie a mostly symbolic beating because he fears losing her and his standing in the community, Sop exclaims: "Wouldn't Ah love tuh whip uh tender woman lak Janie!" (*TE*, p. 219). A vengeful powerlessness now displaces Sop-de-Bottom's prurient sexual fantasies into a political stance. When he speaks out, "anonymously from the anonymous herd," the state's attorney silences him with a generalized racist threat: "Another word out of *you*, out of any of you niggers back there, and I'll bind you over to the big court" (*TE*, p. 277). In ironic confirmation of Hurston's metaphor of "tongues cocked and loaded" as "the only real weapon left to weak folks" (*TE*, p. 275), "Yassuh," crawls out as a one-word response to Mr. Prescott.

In this Jim Crow context the bond of community is broken, the participation interrupted between Janie and the other blacks. To Janie, her spirit's survival depends on her ability to make people hear her story. "She was in the courthouse fighting something and it wasn't death. *It was worse than that.* It was lying thoughts." She is encouraged to tell her story, rather than simply answer questions put to her. But the actual words are neither spoken nor written by Janie or Hurston in their subsequent acts of storytelling and narrative. Pheoby and, later, Hurston's readers are meant to feel the spell cast on the court by Janie's tale. "She had been through for some time before the judge and the lawyer and the rest seemed to know it" (*TE*, p. 278, my italics). When the spell wears off, those who have listened to Janie fail to see her on her own individual terms, except perhaps for the white women. For if the black folks do not believe what they hear, the white male authorities believe her but do not understand her words. The judge instructs the jury to choose whether Janie is a "wanton killer" or "a poor broken creature" (*TE*, p. 279). The fact that she is neither further alienates the blacks. If forced to choose between the two stereotypes, they are willing to regard her as a "wanton killer," but they have participated too much in her life and heard too much of her story to believe that any circumstances, however devastating, would turn her into "a poor broken creature." Janie remains a free woman, even in this Jim Crow space, by virtue of her voice.

The court's innocent verdict reinforces an opposition between the two groups excluded from the official judicial process. "And the white women cried and stood around her like a protecting wall and the Negroes, with heads hung down, shuffled out and away" (*TE*, pp. 279-80). Because they "had realized her feelings," Janie visits the white women "to thank them"; she bears witness to their effort to participate imaginatively in her womanly experience. Later, at the boardinghouse, Janie overhears the dogmatic, false text preached

141

in a bitter call-and-response by some black men. "Well, long as she don't shoot no white man she kin kill jus' as many niggers as she please," one begins. In response, another adds an aphorism that recalls and contradicts Nanny's long ago declaration that "de nigger woman is de mule uh de world." "Well, you know what dey say 'uh white man and uh nigger woman is de freest thing on earth' " (*TE*, p. 280). This declaration has nothing to do with Janie or her experience. It falsifies historical reality and denies the oppression of black women by white men not only during slavery but also at the very moment this man speaks. It is poison distilled from the bitter spirits of powerlessness—the word unrelated to any space outside the abyss in the speaker's mind.

True to her polyrhythmic form, Hurston lets these asymmetrically voiced opinions stand. The very disjointedness testifies to the strength and coherence of Janie's voice. She hears false and bitter accusations yet is undeflected from her grieving, rejuvenating memory of Tea Cake. All else is trivial. Afterward, she invites Tea Cake's friends to the funeral. They come, shamed and apologetic, and Janie quietly makes them welcome. "Sop and his friends had tried to hurt her but she knew it was because they loved Tea Cake and didn't understand" (*TE*, p. 281). All this is unspoken. Janie does not embellish her story with accounts of reconciliation. Neither does Hurston, and neither does Pheoby intrude on Janie's most vulnerable, intimate thoughts. For Janie, space is peopled now by thoughts more than people. Though Tea Cake's friends beg her to stay on the Muck, she cannot because, with him gone, "it was just a great expanse of black mud" (*TE*, p. 283)—an ooze of silence. She leaves with Tea Cake's package of garden seed in her breast pocket and returns to the place that is closer to home than anywhere else—the space where she unveiled her wings before her flight with him from the branches and blossoms of the pear tree toward sun-up and far horizon.

5

The story told but not over, Janie and Pheoby engage in an epilogue of call-and-response so inviting that when Pheoby leaves, Hurston remains imaginatively in her place. "Ah done been tuh de horizon and back," Janie tells Pheoby, and her voice testifies to her ability to recover and repeople her former space in Eatonville. Her house, often desolate before when inhabited, is now "full uh thoughts, 'specially dat bedroom," and those thoughts follow from her experience and her imaginative act of storytelling. Returning to the question of audience with which she began the prologue to her tale, she tells Pheoby to tell the others her story and offers her a little more "understandin' to go 'long wid it." Preaching a short sermon on love, she begins by renouncing a false, static simile reminiscent of Nanny, Killicks, and Starks: "love ain't somethin' lak uh grindstone dat's de same thing everywhere and do de same thing tuh everything it touch." Though a rhetorical straw man, Janie's figure recalls the vision of love and marriage imposed on her experience. But she improvises a new figure: "Love is lak de sea. It's uh movin' thing, but still and all, it takes its shape from de shore it meets, and it's different with every shore" (*TE*, p. 284). Janie's words are horizons away from Nanny's text about "sittin' on high"; hers is a sermon of praise for the ebb and flow of love according to the passionate, reciprocal discovery of another, *different* personality.

In response, Pheoby announces her transformation of values and self. "Ah ain't satisfied wid mahself no mo'. Ah means tuh make Sam take me fishin' wid him after this," she declares, referring to an action whose small, personal quality signifies genuine, lasting change. She ends on a combative note, affirming her intimate, collaborative relationship with Janie: "Nobody better not criticize yuh in mah hearing." Janie, sensing how fired up Pheoby is, softens her attitude toward the community, Pheoby's prospective audience. "Don't feel too mean wid de rest of em," Janie advises Pheoby as she hands her "de keys to de kingdom" of storytelling. She does not excuse others in the community for their lack of experience and imagination, but she does remind Pheoby of the limits and possibilities of storytelling. "They got tuh find out about livin' fuh theyselves" (*TE*, p. 284, 285) are her words, and, as the last words spoken in the novel, they remind Pheoby to try to be a friend to her audience as their lives evolve in response to the story she will tell. A storyteller may launch an audience, but everyone listening journeys to experience on their own.

At this fluid, transitional point, Hurston's voice returns and holds in suspension the serenity of space and time shared by Janie and

Pheoby. In their "finished silence" they hear nature's song and story told by "the wind picking at the pine trees" like a blues player— Tea Cake, too, played blues guitar. This is a moment responsive to what Hurston earlier called that "gulf of formless feelings untouched by thought" (*TE*, p. 43). Janie and Pheoby share an intense intimacy because they have experienced as well as heard the story. Each has been alternately witness and participant in a call-and-response deepened by Janie's story. But the sea of consciousness is never still. Separate thoughts flow strongly again, and Pheoby goes home to her man and the rhythm of her life, her collaboration with Janie consummated but not ended.[20]

In the "finished silence" of Janie's bedroom, collaboration between her interior voice and Hurston's lyrical voice comes to another, still more intense climax. Hurston's words come and go in harmony with the rhythms of Janie's most intimate images. Suddenly, everything swings in perfect motion as Tea Cake enters the room from Janie's imagination in Hurston's voice. "Every corner of the room," "each and every chair and thing" vibrates "a sobbing sigh." Then "Tea Cake came prancing around her where she was and the song of the sigh flew out of the window and lit in the top of the pine trees" (*TE*, p. 286). Here and now grief becomes a praise-song. ("Doncha know de road by de singin' uh de song?")[21] The song puts all hurts, including Tea Cake's lapse into beating Janie and her act of self-defense, into the cosmic flux of love and life. In the midst of these inarticulate/articulate sounds, Janie realizes that Tea Cake "could never be dead until she herself had finished feeling and thinking" (*TE*, p. 286).

Janie's presence is Tea Cake's presence, Hurston's presence our presence, and from a most intimate inner voice the last words of *Their Eyes Were Watching God* come to consciousness. "Here was peace. She pulled in her horizon like a great fish-net. Pulled it from around the waist of the world and draped it over her shoulder. So much of life in its meshes! She called in her soul to come and see" (*TE*, p. 286). Together Hurston and Janie reimagine the horizon in a metaphor woven from the threads of Janie's experience. "The net is not the world," Robert Duncan has written; "it is the imagination of the world."[22] Earlier Hurston imagines Janie "getting ready for her great journey to the horizon in search of people" (*TE*, p. 138);

now, that image of immensity becomes animate and intimate. The world has a waist, a body, and Janie is a fisherwoman. In memory she catches her life and sees the forms of the world still becoming, still unfolding in response to her imagination. Janie calls her soul, and in the ending of *Their Eyes Were Watching God*, Hurston calls readers from the written word to the call-and-response pattern on which her text is built.

As a novel, *Their Eyes Were Watching God* is a "great fish-net" whose meshes are woven into a skein of voices. True to a net and a text, there is plenty of open space between the lines. Moreover, Hurston does not intend her voice or her novel to be Janie's voice or Janie's story. Rather, the novel is an "imagination of [Janie's] world" — a net that holds much but not all of "life in its meshes" and then releases its catch back into the sea of consciousness. Equally, the novel is the imagination and experience of voice. In the beginning, Hurston's voice and parable stand alone. But through Janie's act of storytelling and in the act of earned, easeful collaboration between her and Pheoby, her and the other characters, her and Hurston, the novel weaves Hurston's voice into the woof of Janie's speakerly dialect, Janie's voice into the warp of Hurston's writerly vernacular. Neither voice needs or wants to be dominant, and so authorial control is overthrown in favor of a more equal, democratic *womanist*[23] idea of voice and form. On that basis, on the merits, a new story joins the canon. As a black woman and a novelist, Zora Neale Hurston dreams of love and personality fused in a landscape at once intimate and immense. She dreams also of fiction as a quilt of possibility for both individual and community, fiction able to inspire a tradition of intimate collaboration in literature and experience. In her closing vision of Janie's call to her soul, which not even Pheoby hears but also must imagine, Hurston calls readers and writers. She calls us, especially the black women in the audience, to imagine and create a place suitable for our voices, our stories, our lives.

NOTES

1. Zora Neale Hurston, *Dust Tracks on a Road* (1942; ed. and with an introduction by Robert E. Hemenway, Urbana: University of Illinois Press,

1984), pp. 62, 66-69; for Hurston's comments on her reading as a child, see pp. 53-56.

2. Ibid., pp. 52-55, 70-72.

3. Robert Hemenway, *Zora Neale Hurston* (Urbana: University of Illinois Press, 1977), p. 16.

4. Hurston, *Dust Tracks on a Road*, p. 87.

5. Ibid., pp. 212-13.

6. Zora Neale Hurston, *Their Eyes Were Watching God* (1937; rpt., Urbana: University of Illinois Press, 1978), p. 173. This volume will be cited hereafter as *TE*.

7. Robert B. Stepto, *From Behind the Veil: A Study of Afro-American Narrative* (Urbana: University of Illinois Press, 1979), pp. ix, 166.

8. Anyone writing on Hurston benefits from the revival set in motion by Alice Walker's essay, "Looking for Zora" (1975; rpt., in *In Search of Our Mothers' Gardens* [San Diego: Harcourt Brace Jovanovich, 1983], followed by Hemenway's biography, *Zora Neale Hurston*, with a foreword by Walker. This work led to the paperback reissue of *Their Eyes Were Watching God*, with a foreword by Sherley Anne Williams, and to *I Love Myself When I Am Laughing: A Zora Neale Hurston Reader* (Old Westbury: Feminist Press, 1979), edited by Alice Walker with an introduction by Mary Helen Washington. Other works of Hurston's to appear or reappear include *The Sanctified Church* (Berkeley: Turtle Island, 1983); *Dust Tracks on a Road; Moses, Man of the Mountain* (Urbana: University of Illinois Press, 1984); *Spunk: The Selected Stories of Zora Neale Hurston* (Berkeley: Turtle Island, 1985). In addition, there are a number of useful recent thematic studies of *Their Eyes Were Watching God*: Barbara Christian's *Black Women Novelists* (Westport: Greenwood Press, 1980), pp. 57-60; Cheryl Wall's "Zora Neale Hurston: Changing Her Own Words," in *American Novelists Revisited*, ed. Fritz Fleischman (Boston: G. K. Hall, 1982), pp. 371-93; Lorraine Bethel's " 'This Infinity of Conscious Pain': Zora Neale Hurston and the Black Female Literary Tradition," in *But Some of Us Are Brave*, ed. Gloria T. Hull, Patricia Bell Scott, and Barbara Smith (Old Westbury: Feminist Press, 1982), pp. 176-88; Wendy J. McCredie's "Authority and Authorization in *Their Eyes Were Watching God*," and Maria Tai Wolff's "Listening and Living: Reading and Experience in *Their Eyes Were Watching God*," both in *Black American Literature Forum* 16, no. 1 (Spring 1982), pp. 25-33; Missy Dehn Kubitschek's " 'Tuh de Horizon and Back': The Female Quest in *Their Eyes Were Watching God*," *Black American Literature Forum* 17, no. 3 (Fall 1983), pp. 109-15; Michael G. Cooke's *Afro-American Literature in the Twentieth Century: The Achievement of Intimacy* (New Haven: Yale University Press, 1984), pp. 71-88; and Houston

A. Baker's *Blues, Ideology, and Afro-American Literature* (Chicago: University of Chicago Press, 1984), pp. 56-60. See also *Modern Critical Interpretations: Their Eyes Were Watching God*, ed. and with an introduction by Harold Bloom (New York: Chelsea House, 1987), a volume that includes many of the articles cited above as well as Barbara Johnson's "Metaphor, Metonymy, and Voice," Barbara Johnson and Henry Lewis Gates, Jr.'s "A Black and Idiomatic Free Indirect Discourse," and Elizabeth Meese, "Orality and Textuality in *Their Eyes Were Watching God.*"

9. Hurston, *The Sanctified Church*, p. 56.

10. See Hemenway, *Zora Neale Hurston*, particularly chap. 5, "Godmother and Big Sweet: 1927-31," pp. 104-35, for Hemenway's discussion of Hurston's difficulties with her patron, Mrs. Rufus Osgood Mason.

11. Stepto, *From Behind the Veil*, p. 166.

12. Walter J. Ong, *Orality and Literacy: The Technology of the Word* (New York: Methuen, 1983), p. 160. Ong argues that "early women novelists and other women writers generally worked from outside the oral tradition because of the simple fact that girls were not commonly subjected to the orally based rhetorical training that boys got in school." But in the United States there is evidence suggesting that nineteenth-century women writers like Harriet Beecher Stowe were exposed to and skilled at the rhetoric of "platform performance" because of their work in the evangelical movement and also the abolitionist and women's rights movements (see the *rhetorical* similarity between the Declaration of Sentiments adopted by the Seneca Falls Convention in 1848 and the Declaration of Independence). Furthermore, Hurston was influenced by the public rhetoric of the African-American oral tradition. Women testified in the black church and were also storytellers in their communities, at least among the women. Hurston modulates her oratorical gifts to a rhetoric of conversation and intimacy in *Their Eyes Were Watching God.*

13. Gaston Bachelard's *The Poetics of Space* (Boston: Beacon Press, 1969) is highly suggestive, especially chaps. 2 and 8.

14. Hurston, *The Sanctified Church*, pp. 55, 54.

15. This connection occurred to me as I recently watched and listened to a demonstration of African drumming by the Ghanaian, now African-American musician, Obo Addy.

16. Hurston, *Dust Tracks on a Road*, p. 213. In *Their Eyes Were Watching God* and elsewhere in her work, Hurston connects the gestation period often involved in storytelling with the cycle of pregnancy.

17. Stepto, *From Behind the Veil*, p. 165.

18. Inevitably, conflicts arise: in particular, Janie and Tea Cake deal with jealousy in different ways. Angry at Tea Cake's apparent response to Nun-

kie's flirting, Janie fights with him, and they end up making love. Later, Tea Cake, insecure and jealous of Mrs. Turner's lighter-skinned brother, slaps Janie around in a ritual assertion of possession intended for the black men and women on the Muck. (See Walker's provocative interpretation of the possible imaginative relationship between Tea Cake's beating of Janie and Janie's killing of Tea Cake, *In Search of Our Mothers' Gardens*, pp. 305-7.) These episodes suggest some of the threats posed to women and men in love as well as their qualitatively different responses.

19. Hurston also shows the extent to which the speech of white people is influenced by their contact with African-Americans. Dr. Simmons, whom Janie summons to cure Tea Cake, converses in a speech as resonant with black dialect as it is with standard English or white southern patois. His language, like that of the black characters, suggests the unfolding richness and complexity of American vernacular speech.

20. A word is in order about the relationship between the manuscript of *Their Eyes Were Watching God*, written in pencil on thin, inexpensive white typing paper and signed by Hurston on the day she finished, December 19, 1936, and the published version of the novel. In the handwritten draft the ending is as follows:

> Janie thrust her feet into a pair of old slides and Phoeby rose to go. Sam would be worried about her.
>
> This is the end of what was said on the back porch.
>
> (Ms. of *Their Eyes Were Watching God*, Box 1, Folder 3, Hurston special collection, James Weldon Johnson Collection, Beineke Library, Yale University, New Haven, Conn.)

In the published version Hurston expands the parting scene between Janie and Pheoby to include Pheoby's resolve to make Sam take her fishing. She also mutes Sam's worrying as a motive for Pheoby leaving. Finally, Hurston omits her original closing sentence about "the *end* of what was said" (my italics) in favor of a continuing collaboration with Janie's inner voice. She enacts call-and-response as an imaginative pattern rather than letting Janie's dialogue with Pheoby signify the end of the story or the novel.

21. Here and in the scene under the pear tree, the song and the act of singing signify the presence of vitality and a consequent sensuous, imaginative awakening for Janie and, Hurston hopes, the reader. In this context I am reminded of the spiritual, "De Ol' Sheep Done Know de Road," found in *The Books of American Negro Spirituals*, ed. James Weldon Johnson and J. Rosamund Johnson (1925-26; rpt., New York: Viking, 1969),

2: 160-61. But I quote the variation improvised by Bessie Jones for the album, Georiga Sea Island Songs, collected by Alan Lomax.

22. Robert Duncan as quoted in Sherman Paul's *The Lost America of Love* (Baton Rouge: Louisiana State University Press, 1981), p. 175.

23. Alice Walker, *In Search of Our Mothers' Gardens* (San Diego: Harcourt Brace Jovanovich, 1983), pp. xi-xii. Here I wish to express my gratitude to Rudolph Byrd and Elizabeth Frank for their helpful comments on an early draft of this chapter, and to Deborah E. McDowell for reading successive drafts. McDowell made several particularly helpful suggestions about Hurston's and Janie's use of voice in relation to their female identity.

CHAPTER 5

Frequencies of Eloquence: The Performance and Composition of *Invisible Man*

1

In *Their Eyes Were Watching God* Zora Neale Hurston is her own narrator in collaboration with Janie Crawford. But Janie remains a storyteller and a participant solely in the oral tradition; it is Hurston who brings that tradition to bear on the written word and the literary form of the novel. For the sake of rhetorical intimacy, Hurston adapts the call-and-response between Janie and Pheoby (and potentially the community) to her relationship with the individual reader and perhaps a constituency of readers. But in Ralph Ellison's *Invisible Man*, the narrator is a failed orator. Because he is unable to communicate directly with those he meets in American society, Invisible Man abandons the oral tradition in favor of a "compulsion to put invisibility down in black and white."[1] Yet Invisible Man moves back and forth over frequencies of both the spoken and the written word. After giving up as a speechmaker, he writes an improvisatory, vernacular narrative of utterance. Both the prologue and epilogue with which he frames his tale reveal a continuing, obsessive pursuit of an audience. In the prologue he is too hurt and vulnerable to risk intimate address even with readers he cannot see. So he puts on a defiant, sometimes hostile mask of invisibility impenetrable to readers except on his terms. Then, as he writes down his story, he does the tough psychological rhetorical work of creating a resilient, genuine voice. After he has told his story, he feels liberated enough to write an epilogue. There he converses with readers in an intimate, ironic voice whose democratic eloquence calls us to respond with our own dangerous, courageous, socially responsible verbal acts.

Three decades after the 1952 publication of *Invisible Man*, Ellison explores the fluctuating, often ambiguous, sometimes contentious relation between his novel and the oral tradition in an introduction that is both a meditation and a tall tale about the birth of *Invisible Man*. In the beginning, there were only Ellison and his protean character's voice. And they faced each other not in friendship but opposition, not in intimacy but confrontation. Ellison reveals that *Invisible Man*'s passage from the spoken to the written word involved an initial struggle between his voice and Invisible Man's until, in a sustained act of "antagonistic co-operation,"[2] Invisible Man performed and he composed the novel. Earlier, Ellison observed that "although *Invisible Man* is *my* novel, it is really *his* memoir."[3] Now, still the trickster, he writes his introduction as a factual and fictional interpretive response to Invisible Man's last call: "Who knows but that, on the lower frequencies, *I* speak for *you?*" (*IM*, p. 439, my italics).

Thirty-seven years after Invisible Man announced his presence, Ellison identifies the improvisational beginnings of his form. As he tells it, Invisible Man intruded on him in a barn in Vermont during the summer of 1945 while he was "on sick leave from service in the merchant marine" (*IM*, p. ix). Looking to identify the interloper, Ellison found "nothing more substantial than a taunting disembodied voice" (*IM*, p. xiv) who cried out without preliminaries: "I am an invisible man." The upstart voice compelled Ellison to stop writing and listen. "Therefore," he recalls, "I was most annoyed to have my efforts interrupted by an ironic, down-home voice that struck me as being as irreverent as a honky-tonk trumpet blasting through a performance, say, of Britten's *War Requiem*" (*IM*, p. xv). Ellison, who came to New York in 1936 as an aspiring symphonic composer, knows what he is talking about. Nevertheless, as riffs from the honky-tonk trumpet invaded his imagination, they challenged him to seize the fire and energy of Invisible Man's jazz voice.

Like Dostoevski's narrator in *Notes from the Underground*,[4] Invisible Man spoke up, uninvited and unannounced. His was the last voice Ellison wanted to hear. So he jammed Ellison's frequency because it was the only way he could be heard. For although Ellison

151

quickly sensed "that the voice of invisibility issued from deep within our complex American underground," he held back, "still inclined to close my ears and get on with my interrupted novel" (*IM*, p. xvii). Ellison tried not to hear because, in his tradition, hearing carries with it a responsibility to respond to what has been said, however marginal the speaker, however discordant and threatening his voice and message. But the jazz voice spoke in an insistent, syncopated rhythm that lured Ellison to imagine "what kind of individual would speak in such accents" (*IM*, p. xvii). Consequently, for Ellison as a "fledgling novelist," the problem of voice became the problem of character and form. To *write* a novel, he needed to *hear* this disturbingly familiar voice. And for Invisible Man to exhibit his skill in performance, Ellison needed to create an identity for the "taunting, disembodied voice." "I decided," he writes, "that it would be one who had been forged in the underground of American experience and yet managed to emerge less angry than ironic" (*IM*, p. xvii).

Ellison is no longer a resisting or reluctant listener. He becomes a responsive audience and a potentially collaborative author. He openly coaxes Invisible Man to tell the story behind his riff. Soon Ellison sees as well as hears the spokesman for invisibility. He imagines him as "young, powerless (reflecting the difficulties of Negro leaders of the period) and ambitious for a role of leadership; a role at which he was doomed to fail" (*IM*, p. xviii) because, among other reasons, he is so slow to grasp what Ellison elsewhere calls "the ambiguity of Negro leadership in the United States" (*SA*, p. 18).[5] Retrospectively, even as he performs, Ellison distinguishes the task of composition from performance. He tells of his effort to tease out the character and story behind the solo voice: "*I* began to structure the movement of my plot while *he* began to merge with my more specialized concerns with fictional form and with certain problems arising out of the pluralistic literary tradition from which I spring" (*IM*, p. xviii). Slowly, Ellison arrives at a form resilient enough to advance both Invisible Man's distinct, uncategorical voice and identity and the novel's craft.

Ellison is explicit about the new ground he wanted to break with the unsought, unexpected, unwanted, unexpurgated voice of Invisible Man. Meditating on the state of the novel in the 1940s, he wondered "why most protagonists of Afro-American fiction (not to mention

the black characters in fiction written by whites) were without intellectual depth" (*IM*, p. xviii), which for him was bound up with
a democratic idea of eloquence. "One of the ever present challenges
facing the American novelist," he writes, "was that of endowing his
inarticulate characters, scenes and social processes with eloquence.
For it is by such attempts that he fulfills his social responsibility as
an American artist" (*IM*, p. xviii). From his first "taunting, disembodied" utterance, Invisible Man challenges Ellison to write in an
urgent vernacular voice and in a form simultaneously novelistic and
autobiographical.

Ellison's quest is for eloquence. So is Invisible Man's. Because of
the unfinished business of self and American democracy, the act of
eloquence is not simple; at times the pursuit of eloquence calls
Invisible Man to think while he is acting and, at others, to act while
he is thinking. Eloquence is bound up with persuasion, and therefore,
Invisible Man's eloquence turns on his ability to improvise in genuine
response to a situation and an actual audience. In a *tour de force*
near the end of his introduction, Ellison identifies the improvisatory
forms and forces urging him to experiment with the novel: "Having
worked in barbershops where that form of oral art flourished, I knew
that I could draw upon the rich culture of the folk tale as well as
that of the novel, and that being uncertain of my skill I would have
to improvise upon my materials in the manner of a jazz musician
putting a musical theme through a wild starburst of metamorphosis"
(*IM*, p. xxi). Who in America is not "uncertain of his skill"? And
as a test of creative poise and energy, is not improvisation a potential
act of eloquence? Ellison's reliance on improvisation reinforces his
(and Invisible Man's) theme of identity, and the urgent appearance
of an invisible voice in protean form calls for techniques of performance. Furthermore, as a novelist whose sense of improvisatory
eloquence is informed by jazz as well as speech, Ellison looks to the
jam session for confirmation of his collaboration with Invisible Man.[6]

Ellison's writing on jazz provides a provocative clue to his intentions and highlights the significance of performance in his novel.
"In improvised jazz," he said a few years ago, as if to describe
Invisible Man, "performance and creation can consist of a single
complex act."[7] And in a piece on Charlie Christian, Ellison calls jazz
a form of combat: "true jazz is an art of individual assertion *within*

153

and against the group" (*SA*, p. 234, my italics). A jazz group achieves its full effect only if the musicians test each other's skills and, through improvisation explore the full range of each member's untapped potentialities. "Each true jazz moment (as distinct from the uninspired commercial performance) springs 'from a contest in which each artist challenges all the rest; each solo flight, or improvisation, represents (like the successive canvasses of a painter) a definition of his identity: as individual, as member of the collectivity and as a link in the chain of tradition" (*SA*, p. 234). Likewise, in the context of the novel, Invisible Man's "taunting, disembodied voice" challenges Ellison to try his skill to the utmost. So, too, Ellison prods Invisible Man to tell of his efforts to be eloquent simultaneously within and against the grain of his different audiences: black and white, southern and northern, Americans all, optimistic and often confused about the workings of individual and institutional power.

Through his experience as orator and rabble-rouser, Invisible Man discovers the combination of luck, will, and skill ("shit, grit, and mother wit") and the coincidence of self and other required in order for "performance and creation" to merge in a "single, complex act." He is so thoroughly a performer that he defines and tests his identity on those occasions when he becomes a public voice. In his speeches, Invisible Man's voice evolves into an instrument more and more keyed to the necessities, limits, and possibilities of call-and-response. To persuade others and move them to action, he relies mostly on techniques of improvisation. Sometimes after the jolt of reversal he learns that his words have consequences dramatically and drastically opposed to his intentions. Several times his speeches lead to unintended actions. For a long time he underestimates the dynamic mutual awareness required between performer and audience for an improvisation to become eloquent. But gradually—too late for a career as an orator, in time for his vocation as a writer—he learns to challenge his audience's skills as well as his own.

Despite his failure to be eloquent with the spoken word, Invisible Man ends up committed to self-reliance as an optimist as well as an ironist. In the novel's paradox, he learns how and why the power of speech can be the power of action only when his potential eloquence falls on closed ears during the chaos of a race riot. In time he comes to see eloquence in much the same way as Ellison's literary ancestor and namesake, Ralph Waldo Emerson, understood it. "There is no orator who is not a hero," Emerson declared. "He is challenged and must answer all comers," and his words evoke Invisible Man's struggle for identity through improvisatory oratory. But the comparison also breaks down because Invisible Man has been too obsessed with advancing "to the top" to embody Emerson's heroic conception of eloquence. "The orator's speech," wrote Emerson in the 1840s when he and others believed in the power of the word to persuade Americans to live out their democratic ideals and free the slaves, "is not to be distinguished from action. *It is the electricity of action.*"[8] Nonetheless, Invisible Man attempts to make Emerson's metaphor work for him. He sends out words like so many charges intended to flow through his audience in a current of action. He misjudges the explosiveness of language and fails as an orator. But later, underground, solitary and silent, he taps into a literal power line and drains off enough electricity from Monopolated Light and Power to provide light and heat while he generates the energy and symbolic action of his autobiography. He tells us this in a voice at once brooding and insulting, peremptory and inquiring, in a prologue that is the self-conscious "portrait of the artist as rabble-rouser" (SA, p. 179). In his prologue, Invisible Man does not seek conversation; responsive voices might talk back to him, disagree with him, belittle his point of view, question his motives, undermine his vulnerable, evolving self. Only in the epilogue, having made ironic peace with his identity and his voice, is he ready for response, for conversation, ready to risk verbal acts of intimacy, ready, in short, for eloquence.

In between, eloquence has a range of Emersonian meanings for Invisible Man. He sets out to be a leader whose speech is action, and not just symbolic action. Later, when he discovers the tricks of false eloquence and the conditions of genuine eloquence, he descends, and aspires, during the interim it takes to write his memoirs, to the symbolic action possible through literary form.[9] His transformation from "an orator, a rabble-rouser," who succeeds or fails, lives or dies through eloquence, to a writer learning his craft in underground hibernation involves a reversal of form and identity. As an orator, first free-lance and later an employee of the Brotherhood committee, Invisible Man misses the subtle connections between speech and action, performer and audience. In the world, he fails

at eloquence and political leadership because he is out of touch, too
much an isolated, solitary traveler, too much in the grip of illusion
(his own and that of others), and because he does not yet understand
that he and his words are variables in the American equation of
power. Afterward, in the epilogue, he approaches the question of
language and action as a writer able to affirm the very contradictions
he resists during his quest for heroic political eloquence. Becoming
a writer, he transforms the power of the spoken word into the ironic,
self-conscious, symbolic potential action of his improvisatory autobiography and Ellison's novel.

2

As he begins to write his story, Invisible Man is suspended
between identities. For equilibrium's sake, he clutches his old self:
"But I am an orator, a rabble-rouser — Am? I *was*, and perhaps shall
be again. Who knows?" (*IM*, p. 11). Unlike his speeches, which he
delivers in the world and presently reconstructs as a writer, his
narrative addresses no audience waiting to be moved to particular
action on a specific occasion. Nevertheless, he closes the prologue
with a writerly variation on call-and-response. "But what did *I* do
to be so blue?" he asks. "Bear with me" (*IM*, p. 12), he answers,
and implies that bearing witness to his tale could make readers
participate in a continuing common story. Between the prologue and
the epilogue, readers enter Invisible Man's mind as he struggles
through his speeches, and at other times are present as members of
his audiences. As witnesses, we seek to mediate between Invisible
Man and his listeners, and so his tale prepares us, too, to take
responsibility for our common fate as Americans.

Freedom, an old apparitional slave woman tells Invisible Man,
"ain't nothing but knowing how to say what I got up in my head"
(*IM*, p. 9). Often, eloquence bursts upon Invisible Man in unexpected,
small personal encounters with characters whose living stream of
speech feeds the great river of the American language. Such moments
of eloquence are affirmations of self, citizenship, and potential national community. But Invisible Man is too self-absorbed in his career
to build a framework of leadership from his encounters with Peter
Wheatstraw, Mary Rambo, Tod Clifton, Brother Tarp, and others.

Retrospectively, however, he punctuates his passage from orator to writer, innocence to experience and knowledge with a self-conscious, self-critical, and, at the same time, improvisational recreation of five of his speeches.

The appearance and reality of eloquence coexist uneasily throughout Invisible Man's autobiography. As a young man, his reputation for eloquence rests on an old-fashioned set-piece on uplift and humility that he writes, memorizes, and delivers when he graduates from the Negro high school. From his writer's subsequent vantage point, Invisible Man recalls that even then he did not believe that "humility was the secret, indeed, the very essence of progress." "How could I," he asks, "remembering my grandfather?—I only believed that it worked" (*IM*, p. 14). In his former life, the will to believe returns when he repeats his speech for "the town's leading white citizens." But their agenda is not his. "Told that since I was to be there anyway I might as well take part in the battle royal to be fought by some of my schoolmates as part of the entertainment" (*IM*, pp. 14-15), Invisible Man undergoes initiation into the code of white supremacy in a succession of terrifying, degrading, humiliating rituals. Don't believe any high-faluting praise—especially ours—is the message; your place is the same as that of all other Negroes—at the bottom. As a potential leader of your people, you especially are at the mercy of our money and power. During the battle royal, Invisible Man fights pain and defeat with visions of an oratorical triumph: "I wanted to deliver my speech more than anything else in the world, because I felt that only these men could judge truly my ability" (*IM*, p. 20). Judge it they do, but the white men judge Invisible Man and the testamental call-and-response form of African-American culture according to the stereotypes of minstrel entertainment.

In his speech, Invisible Man builds his edifice of African-American identity on an old American foundation stone: self-reliant individualism. Naive and ambitious, he does not understand that in this context he cannot answer Emerson's call for the "simple genuine self against the whole world."[10] On the contrary, he inhabits a world of slippery surfaces, sudden depths, and strange forms, a world in which an invisible man needs a trickster's mask, a stance of improvisatory double-consciousness if he is to succeed. Half-wittingly, he invokes a tradition. "In those pre-invisible days I visualized myself as a potential Booker T. Washington" (*IM*, p. 15), and his oration steals its meat from Washington's 1895 Atlanta Exposition Address. But he confuses legend with historical actuality, and he has no idea of the contingent relation of language to context, audience, and action. Somehow he cannot imagine that *he*, a young African-American aspiring to racial leadership, would receive a radically different response from "the town's leading white men" than he had from his fellow Negroes. Nor does it occur to him that in their apparent enthusiasm for his praise of humility, the black townspeople may have been putting him on, yessing that naively opportunistic former self of his to death and destruction, or perhaps, like his grandfather, yessing him toward conformity as an ironic tactic of survival.

Although he borrows his words, Invisible Man fails to investigate their rhetorical context. Booker T. Washington possessed more influence than any of the small-town white men Invisible Man addresses at the smoker. That influence was useful and seemingly without menace to whites. In short, Booker T. Washington was somebody, and the leading white citizens of his day knew it. Because of his standing with Negroes and perhaps even more with the northern industrialists and philanthropists the new South needed to advance its economic development, Washington was invited to address the 1895 Exposition. Moreover, there was a certain eloquence about Washington's Address. He rooted the speech in the fallow ground of the Exposition organizers' decision to allow southern Negroes to represent their accomplishments since Emancipation in a separate exhibit. Again and again Washington rested his belief in the mutual progress of the races upon the Exposition—shrewdly if somewhat self-servingly he pointed to the invitation issued to him as evidence of social uplift and progress. Though kept separate from one another, both white and Negro citizens were included in the audience. Clearly, Washington's presence and some of his words moved many of his race to pride, though doubtless some of these same people resented his apparent acquiescence to segregation and social and political inequality. He pleased white southern and northern establishments because his words came so close to an endorsement of their program. At the same time, near the end of the Address Washington urged "a determination to administer absolute justice."[11] As a performer, he slipped some strong words into the occasional breaks of his call for accommodation. Washington's oratorical effectiveness stemmed from his painstaking knowledge of American race relations and from his disciplined dedication to what W. E. B. Du Bois called the "gospel of Work and Money."[12]

Invisible Man is a nobody, and his reenactment of Washington's words parodies the original occasion. In addition, the smoker's ritual initiation of the next generation into the rules of southern society underlines the failure of Washington's program. "We mean to do right by you," one of the white men tells Invisible Man after his slip of "social equality" for "social responsibility," "but you've got to know your place at all times" (*IM*, p. 25). The white men mock Invisible Man when he utters a word of "three or more syllables" to teach him that his words are necessarily without power. But about language they are wrong; there is a power in words even on captive occasions. After all, the audience's ridicule releases Invisible Man's deep, long-denied, and unacknowledged thoughts in the charged phrase, "social equality." With those two unconsciously intentional words, Invisible Man says *no* to the audience's attempt to make him a mechanical orator and *yes* to the principle of equality affirmed by his grandfather, though seemingly denied, and seemingly affirmed by Thomas Jefferson and the other founders, though denied by certain specific provisions the framers built into the Constitution and the American legal code.

In this episode, Invisible Man's set-piece is strained to the breaking point by the cruelty of the audience and its abuse of call-and-response. These leading citizens recall Br'er Fox and the other animals in the "Tar Baby" tale. Had they let Invisible Man alone, they would have immobilized the pathetic carcass of his language. Instead, their sadism summons a single eloquent phrase—"social equality"—eloquent because it expresses the capacity of American first principles to emerge in the rhetorical open even on the most degrading occasions. Eloquent, too, because, for an instant, Invisible Man has publicly avowed and "*yelled* a phrase I had often seen denounced in newspaper editorials, heard debated in private" (*IM*, p. 24, my italics). Doing so, he juxtaposes two traditions: the official white southern written word and the unofficial black southern spoken word.[13] But neither Invisible Man nor his white audience allows his intrusive words to disrupt the social equilibrium. Desperately, each reverts to a corrupt facade of order upheld by ritual. Only briefly do chaos and the possibilities of extemporaneous form unite in the word, and this is due to Invisible Man's subsequent narrative ability to perform with both the written and the spoken word.

3

The state college for Negroes is a training ground for young men and women aspiring to be leaders of their race. During his time there, Invisible Man encounters several masters of the spoken word. But hearing is not yet thinking for him; he is too mesmerized by words as words to interpret their context. And he does not grasp the nexus between fixed and fluid elements crucial to oral performance. Namely, improvisation is at once incidental and essential to Jim Trueblood's tale and, for that matter, Homer Barbee's Founders' Day sermon; each man delivers an oral set-piece embellishing an original story with significant details for the sake of his audience. Trueblood plays the trickster aware that, like the rednecks in the county sheriff's office, the rich white trustee from the North is liable to reward a black sharecropper's tale of incest, properly told. Barbee, the blind black minister, preaches a sermon so spellbinding that his audience, especially the northern trustees, believes that President Bledsoe's ruthless, manipulative, shrewdly masked personal power carries on a mythic past of magic, mystery, and miracle.[14]

In his confrontation with President Bledsoe, Invisible Man continues to miss the relationship between the spoken and the written word. He hears Bledsoe threaten "to have every Negro in the county hanging on tree limbs by morning" (*IM*, p. 110), and still puts his fate and his faith in words written in a letter he has not seen—a letter he keeps invisible, at Bledsoe's instruction, until it silences him. Up North, unemployed and an outcast, "the more resentful [he] became, the more [his] old urge to make speeches returned" (*IM*, p. 197). Then, perplexed by an eviction he witnesses on the streets of Harlem, he hears more than he sees:

> "Sho, we ought to stop 'em," another man said, "but ain't that much nerve in the whole bunch."
> "There's plenty nerve," the slender man said. "All they need is

someone to set it off. All they need is a leader. You mean *you* don't have the nerve." (*IM*, p. 203)

In these spoken words Invisible Man hears a call for the missing leader. He looks but still does not see until, hearing old Mrs. Provo's voice, he sees that her things reveal his history, too, from the FREE PAPERS of 1859 to a yellowing newspaper clipping announcing Marcus Garvey's deportation in 1927. In an epiphany Invisible Man sees the ancestral past littered on the street. He witnesses the refusal of Mrs. Provo's request to go inside for a last prayer. In response, the crowd sways toward action — "To hell with all this talk, let's rush the bastard." Invisible Man experiences a rush of ambivalent energy, for the very renunciation of language affirms the power of the word. "I was both afraid and angry, repelled and fascinated. I both wanted it and feared the consequences, was outraged and angered at what I saw and yet surged with fear" (*IM*, p. 208) at the chaos and danger of violence. Instead, he pursues symbolic, verbal action. Instinctively, he pushes his way forward, "talking rapidly without thought but out of my clashing emotions" (*IM*, p. 209), as if the act of speech would give coherence to his thoughts.

As public discourse, Invisible Man's eviction speech seems an absurdity, for it affirms the reverse of what is happening. In it he improvises *against* the crowd's potential for action. He begins saying *no* to the crowd by saying *yes*. "We're a law-abiding people and a slow-to-anger people," he calls out. Perhaps because his words contradict the people's mood, his speech briefly has the effect he desires. "They stopped, listening. Even the white man was stilled" (*IM*, p. 209). But the performance stalls because Invisible Man proposes no alternative action to the angry crowd, and this failure of improvisation marks the limits of his eloquence. Because his initial gesture possesses some of the electricity of action, his speech produces an effect antithetical to his intention. Once again he fails to intuit or analyze his context, fails to grasp that his audience resents its reputation as a law-abiding, slow-to-anger group. Therefore an ironic collaboration occurs between Invisible Man and his audience. Accommodate, he urges, perhaps again echoing Booker T. Washington's southern strategy, but his words remind these northern Negroes of why they came north, remind them of injustice endured passively too long. They interrupt his speech not to encourage him, as members of a congregation might, but to silence him because his speech threatens to rob them of bold action. In effect, Invisible Man and his audience reverse call-and-response. Although he fears their point of view, he adapts and changes his pitch. He must, if he wishes to keep on talking—and words are essential to a leader's identity.

For instance, trying to make a case for a southern Negro school principal who turned over a fugitive to "the forces of law and order," he yields the point when a woman angrily contradicts him:

> "He was a handkerchief-headed rat!" a woman screamed, her voice boiling with contempt.
> "Yes, you're right. He was wise and cowardly, but what about us? What are we to do?" I yelled, suddenly thrilled by the response. "Look at him," I cried.
> "Yes, just look at him!" an old fellow in a derby called out as though answering a preacher in church. (*IM*, pp. 209-10)

Even though the woman's response derides his anecdote and his point of view, he performs two quick modulations that exhibit his native gifts. He agrees with the antagonistic woman, softens and complicates her violent rhetoric, then abruptly refocuses on old Primus Provo's predicament. His recall of Provo summons an affirmative response, and Invisible Man resumes his earlier attempt to tell the story of African-American history by breathing significance into the inanimate personal effects and household possessions strewn along the curb. For a time his words rechannel the people's energy into reflection as he seeks a middle ground between caution and recklessness. But he finds none and instead plays off the audience's belligerent response to his stalling: " 'Dispossessed'? That's a good word, 'Dispossessed.' " But he has no nonviolent option left except to challenge the Marshall: "How about it, Mr. Law? Do we get our fifteen minutes worth of Jesus?" (*IM*, p. 211).

Invisible Man fails to hold the moment in suspension for two reasons: first, because those carrying out the eviction order are closed to possibility, and second, because the crowd has in mind a preconceived response to the situation. "Where do we go?" he asks, and first one, then another and another answer by rushing past him. Throughout his speech they have been ready to overpower the cops and repossess the apartment. Finally, aroused by his words, they overcome the restraint implicit in his rhetorical question. Intriguingly, Invisible Man does not sulk. He does not run off. He lends his voice to their action: " 'We're dispossessed,' I sang at the top of my voice, 'dispossessed and we want to pray. Let's go in and pray. Let's have a big prayer meeting. But we'll need some chairs to sit in . . . rest upon as we kneel. We'll need some chairs!' " (*IM*, p. 213). Invisible Man's rhythm and repetition transcend the literal meaning of his words. He stays because these people have been a participatory audience and because he has become implicated in their action. By improvising he participates, "no longer struggling against or thinking about the nature of my action" (*IM*, p. 213). At every point, he follows the lead of his audience. He wanted to calm them and assert his right to leadership; instead, he stirs them up and they literally push him out of the way. Again, the power of words is not static, stable, or containable; when spoken, words can lead to contingent, unanticipated, unsought consequences different from the speaker's intention and his version of their meaning. In love with the idea of eloquence, Invisible Man follows the people in a response explicitly denied but implicitly affirmed by his words.

At a submerged level, Invisible Man understands his essentially passive role in the people's action. Others, however, do not. Brother Jack, a witness to the performance, recruits Invisible Man for the Brotherhood organization because he has use for the young man's vagrant as yet unfocused, uncontextualized capacity for eloquence. But he misunderstands what has happened. "You aroused them so quickly to action," he tells Invisible Man. "With a few words you had them involved in action" (*IM*, p. 219). Jack's explanation misreads the complex, contingent relationship between audience and performer. Because of his collectivist, scientific ideology, he refuses to recognize that a personal, emotional bond galvanizes Invisible Man and the other black individuals into a sense of community. To Jack, Invisible Man is nothing more or less than a black *voice* worthy only to serve the Brotherhood's program. "You shall be the new Booker T. Washington, but even greater than he" (*IM*, p. 233), he tells Invisible Man, defining him historically before he writes down a new name for him. For his part, Invisible Man resolves to have "one of us, in at the beginning of something big"; and besides he thinks, "if I refused to join them where would I go—to a job as porter at the railroad station? *At least here was a chance to speak"* (*IM*, p. 234, my italics). As elsewhere, he defines his freedom and ambition in terms of public speaking but leaves others to define language, leadership, and power.

4

When Invisible Man makes his first speech for the Brotherhood, he believes his words capable of fusing his interests with those of his race and the organization.[15] Approaching the microphone, he sees as one audience the Brotherhood committee on the stage and the crowd sitting in the Harlem arena. The unfamiliar microphone enables him to forge a bond with his audience and generate the theme of his speech. "It looks like the steel skull of a man! Do you think he died of dispossession?" (*IM*, p. 250). In the best improvisatory tradition, he makes the microphone a complementary, almost totemic, instrument, and so turns a potentially disabling mechanical difficulty into an occasion for contact. The response from the audience—"We with you, Brother. You pitch 'em we catch em!"—confirms his sense of power with words and kinship with those who listen to him. "That was all I needed," he remembers: "I'd made a contact, and it was as though his voice was that of them all" (*IM*, p. 258). In a widening circle of reciprocity, speaker and listener testify for each other, and together they speak for the entire audience.

Currents of energy now flow toward Invisible Man. Charged, he looks to the audience as a congregation, a community with shared values and objectives. The people's responses compensate for his feeble command of Brotherhood literature. "I couldn't remember the correct words and phrases from the pamphlets," but the voice from the crowd, like the evicted couple's possessions, connects him with his past. "I had to fall back upon tradition and since it was a political meeting, I selected one of the political techniques that I'd heard so often at home: The old, down-to-earth, I'm-sick-and-tired-of-the-way-they've-been-treating-us approach" (*IM*, pp. 258-59). He recognizes eloquence as his sole coin, but eloquence without any *particular* ideology or program. Here, as so often happens in the novel, Invisible Man draws on both American and African-American traditions. No doubt, he has heard the populist oratory of white southern politicians, a few of whom appealed to the black poor even during the decades of disenfranchisement. But Invisible Man also borrows from "the Negro church, wherein," Ellison recalls in "Remembering Richard Wright," "you heard the lingering accents of nineteenth century rhetoric with its emphasis upon freedom and individual responsibility; a rhetorical style which gave us Lincoln, Harriet Tubman, Harriet Beecher Stowe and other abolition-preaching Beechers. Which gave us Frederick Douglass and John Jasper and many other eloquent and heroic Negroes whose spirit still moves among us through the contributions which they made to the flexibility, the music and idealism of the American language."[16] Thematically, too, the speech's trajectory moves from politics to personality, with dispossession the bridge between two imperatives: identity and equality.

Throughout, Invisible Man employs call-and-response. He testifies to his and his audience's complicity in their dispossession through images and metaphors of vision. Soon, however, he exhausts the political theme and, in the midst of applause, "realized that the flow of words had stopped" (IM, pp. 260-61). So far he has been using his voice to summon a vision suitable for almost any group, any occasion, and perfectly compatible, he thinks, with this rally and its mixed audience. Now though, emptied of the familiar, he must improvise a new story to go with the devices of the oral tradition. But how, since he has no program of action, no promise of revolution, no specific vision of a different society? All he has is an existence verified by the response of the audience. Therefore, Invisible Man modulates from a vague political rhetoric into a confessional voice. His emerging, "more human" identity, he tells them, awaits their confirmation.

Oratory yields to storytelling. Encouraged by another response in the form of a gentle personal question, he comes home rhetorically and declares himself "a new citizen of the country of your vision" (IM, p. 262). But the listeners' vision flows from his words, and the speech's formulaic ending transforms dispossession into a spontaneous, briefly powerful kinship, incipiently political and perhaps racial, as well as strongly personal. Call-and-response turns I and you into we, as Invisible Man names his audience the "PATRIOTS

AND CITIZENS OF TOMORROW'S WORLD" (*IM*, p. 262). He strains eloquence to the limit, puts his identity on the line, and persuasively, safely, vaguely asserts the potentiality of action. But he does so outside the Brotherhood's scientific framework and political program. He generates the preliminary electricity of action by virtue of his sudden authority as an articulate presence and personality able to perform so that he and his audience, for an instant, become one.

Afterward, Invisible Man learns that his speech and technique displease most of the Brotherhood committee. Brother Jack approves because he thinks the people have coalesced and are therefore " 'just waiting to be told what to do' " (*IM*, p. 263). But the pure ideologues resist Jack's non sequitur and accuse Invisible Man of a " 'wild, hysterical, politically irresponsible and dangerous' " speech antithetical to the Brotherhood's ideology. Both miss the point, though the critics have the better of the argument. The audience was moved because of Invisible Man's creation of an identity in response to its participatory voices. Although that moment passes, any action in the future also depends on participation; because, as the ideologues recognize better than Jack, the contact point between Invisible Man and the audience has been defiance of externally imposed authority.

In a self-conscious meditation later that night, Invisible Man assesses what happened to him during the speech. The person who emerged and the voice that spoke strike him as strangers, intruders — perhaps in the way Ellison formerly considered Invisible Man's "taunting, disembodied voice" an act of intrusion. "What had come out was completely uncalculated, as though another self within me had taken over and held forth." He finds his technique radically changed; "no one who had known me at college would have recognized the speech" (*IM*, p. 267). Later, when Invisible Man takes his cue from confidence man, B. P. Rinehart, identity changes according to disguises of dress and appearance; here, self corresponds to the guises of speech. "I *was* someone new," he muses, struck by the paradox, "even though I had spoken in a very old-fashioned way" (*IM*, p. 267). Until the eviction speech and his performance in the arena, Invisible Man identifies eloquence with oratorical set-pieces whose formalized delivery is intended to shut the gates of self — for both speaker and audience — against terrors of the unexpected, the tabooed. What he calls "very old-fashioned" approaches the testamental, participatory, rejuvenating forms of the oral tradition, the contemporary improvisations of jazz as well as the rhetoric of southern politicians and preachers. For eloquence depends on the speaker's expression of what is happening at the moment of performance—the ability to reveal his identity as it develops in response to the immediate audience and perhaps a larger implicit audience attuned to similar experience and traditions.

In this sense Invisible Man's newness emerges from his interplay with his audience. When he spoke of what was happening to him, he shed some of the old limits of self and story, because he was not supposed to reveal his story. His identification, if not his identity, is newly invented, his new name written down by the Brotherhood, and his story is supposed to unfold under official conditions as controlled as those of a scientific experiment. But without verbal kinship with his audience, an improvisatory speaker loses the power of speech. "They had wanted me to succeed, and fortunately I had spoken for them and they had recognized my words. I belonged to them" (*IM*, p. 267). Invisible Man's conclusion signals the dangerous contingency of improvisation—a speaker's temptation to derive his identity from his audience. In the way he has done with individuals, Invisible Man embraces the audience's power to define his actions. "The audience was mixed, their claims broader than race. I would do whatever was necessary to serve them well." And he acknowledges a frightening prospect: "How else could I save myself from disintegration?" (*IM*, p. 267). Apparently, now, his coherence as a human being depends on service and on confirmation by those served.

Paradoxically, his analysis inclines him to hand others the right to judge his performance. He does not question or test his premise that he has "become more human" by virtue of his call-and-response improvisation with the audience. Instead, he affirms the mystery of words but, characteristically, subordinates the mystery to his personal agenda of ambition and success. "Here was a way to have a part in making the big decisions, of seeing through the mystery of how the country, the world, really operated. . . . I had only to work and learn and survive in order to go to the top" (*IM*, p. 268). The top is not the mountaintop; he wants to make it in American society and, like Bledsoe, will use others, black and white, to climb the mountain. At this point both eloquence and the country (the word and the world) are mysteries Invisible Man regards as keys to power. The pursuit of power is a secret kept uneasily by Invisible Man, since he has yet to build a bridge of words and action between self and American democratic ideals. Equally important, he has yet to penetrate the ambiguities involved in the pursuit of an African-American political agenda and the theory and practice, the power relationships, of American politics. Unlike Booker T. Washington, the historical archetype of this section of the novel, Invisible Man lacks a political program. Unlike the cautious and prepared Washington, who always knew who he was, for Invisible Man eloquence has become solely the art of improvisation. He forgets the counsel of his former literature teacher: "Our task is that of making ourselves individuals" (*IM*, p. 268). Obsessed with making *it*, he resists the knowledge that his cultural identity and his words need to become more than nervous reflexes if he is to find his way home through the labyrinth of American society.

5

After Invisible Man becomes the chief spokesman of the Harlem District, Brother Tarp gives him a portrait of Frederick Douglass. Douglass "belongs to all of us," Tarp tells him, and Douglass replaces Booker T. Washington as the ancestral model of African-American eloquence and leadership. As a leader, Invisible Man rallies the community behind the Brotherhood agenda. Soon he feels his "old self" slipping out of touch with "the new public self that spoke for the Brotherhood" (*IM*, p. 287), but he responds to this danger by rekindling his urge to personal power. The Brotherhood "was the one organization in the whole country in which I could reach the very top and I meant to get there" (*IM*, pp. 286, 287). His words recall the metaphors of "sittin' on high" and "de rulin' chair" in *Their Eyes Were Watching God*. Like Janie Crawford, Invisible Man eventually—in his case he involuntarily and unceremoniously descends—rejects such simplistic, hierarchical notions of success and self-fulfillment. But for a long time, he clings to the texts of Booker T. Washington and Benjamin Franklin.[17] He vows to climb "a mountain of words," and confesses his belief that "there was a magic in spoken words." He focuses on Douglass, not as Tarp has done, as a leader of and for the people, but as an archetype of individual success—a fellow orator who "had talked his way from slavery to a government ministry" (*IM*, p. 288). He notes that Douglass, too, had "taken another name" but does not mention Douglass's eloquence as a writer, or his ability to use autobiographical narratives to complement the rhetoric of his speeches.[18]

Preoccupied with personal destiny, Invisible Man forgets that Douglass's power was bound up with the personal, racial, national cause of freedom and justice. Besides, Douglass used the force of his words and personality to change the thinking of powerful individuals and organizations. He persuaded others to his articulate vision and moved them to action, whereas Invisible Man seems to encourage the Brotherhood to manipulate him. For instance, accused of having a personality cult, he is suspended from his leadership position in Harlem and sent "to lecture downtown on the Woman Question." In an arrogant parting shot, Brother Jack tells him, "My pamphlet, 'On the Woman Question in the United States' will be your guide" (*IM*, pp. 306, 307). Invisible Man's assignment stirs memories of Douglass speaking for women's rights. Without his eloquent speech to the 1848 Seneca Falls Convention, the resolution endorsing votes for women would almost certainly have failed, and he spoke to a women's rights group in Washington, D.C., on the day he died. Douglass did none of these things—or little else in his life—as a consequence of someone's orders. Like Abraham Lincoln, who was both ally and adversary, colleague and equal in the struggle for democracy, he lived out Emerson's imperative that the orator be a general whose "speech must be just ahead of the assembly, ahead of the whole human race, or it is superfluous."[19] But Invisible Man ignores Douglass's fraternal example and leaves Harlem without a word of explanation or farewell to Brother Clifton, Brother Tarp, or anyone else who has helped him.

Summoned back to Harlem by the committee months later, he finds Clifton vanished and the Brotherhood operation nearly defunct. "There had been, to my surprise," he notes in the bloodless, euphemistic language of the party line, "a switch in emphasis from local issues to those more national and international in scope, and it was felt that for the moment the interests of Harlem were not of first importance" (*IM*, p. 324). He fails to interpret Clifton's departure as a response to the Brotherhood's betrayal of political principle and his (Invisible Man's) betrayal of fraternal principle. Only when he happens on Clifton performing an ironic minstrel show with paper-maché Sambo dolls does Invisible Man realize that others see him as the Brotherhood's ventriloquist's dummy—"he'll kill your depression and your dispossession" (*IM*, p. 327). Humiliated into inarticulate fury, Invisible Man watches in silence as Clifton is gunned down by a white policeman. Back in Harlem, denied access to the Brotherhood committee, Invisible Man acts from "personal responsibility" and organizes a public funeral.

As he looks down from the speaker's platform, amazed at the enormous turnout, he asks two silent, related questions. "Did it signify love or politicized hate? And could politics ever be an expression of love?" (*IM*, p. 341). Rooted in his own muddled motives, his questions nevertheless reach out toward that American and African-American conviction that an individual's deepest personal beliefs and experience are somehow bound up with the political life of the nation. When he looks out and sees faces in the crowd, Invisible Man realizes that for these people politics is an expression of love in the complex sense identified elsewhere by Ellison as "that condition of man's being at home in the world which is called love and which we term democracy" (*SA*, p. 106). In this context Invisible Man seeks fraternity and community, if not democracy. Unexpectedly, he hears the sudden solo voice of an old man raised in "Many a Thousand Gone" and suddenly understands that for these people love intensifies the engagement with the world that becomes inevitably political. To this man and those who hear him in the burning heat, Tod Clifton is more than an individual. He was an individual man, yes, and to be praised for his step, his quick hands, his love for his people expressed in his style as much as his politics. But now he has become one of the many thousands gone, the victims of racial injustice. And so they mourn him doubly in the testamental tradition. The "old plaintive, masculine voice" of the singer, "stumbling in the silence at first alone," is answered by someone on a euphonium horn. The painful, lovely duet leads more and more people in a collective improvisatory expression of grief, struggle, and transformation.

Invisible Man muses enviously on the old man's power to move the people and his own apparent lack of eloquence. "It was as though," he reflects, "the song had been there all the time and he knew it and aroused it; and I knew that I had known it too and had failed to release it out of a vague, nameless shame or fear. But he had known it and aroused it" (*IM*, p. 342). This man has no narrow political or personal stake in the funeral. His act of voice becomes a citizen's fraternal call answered in kind by the crowd. Whatever the past defeats and continuing obstacles, he and they aspire to being at home in the world. And at last Invisible Man shares the kinship, aware that the song goes on within him, too, and that its words and performance "had touched something deeper than protest or religion" (*IM*, p. 342).

Invisible Man feels "deepened by that *something* for which the theory of Brotherhood had given me no name" (*IM*, p. 342, my italics). His *something* is deliberately, necessarily vague, expressively so; perhaps like the *somehow* in Lincoln's Second Inaugural, the word assumes palpability in this context. "All knew," Lincoln said as the Civil War was ending, "that this interest was somehow, the cause of the war." Lincoln bore witness to his and his fellow citizens' consciousness that underneath the arguments and statistics, the explanations and rationalizations, underneath logic and language, too, the question of slavery and the fate of the African-American provided an uncategorical, irreducible, decisive, and, in some sense, mysterious test for democracy. For Lincoln, language and action expressed equally a private and public commitment to love and politics. Likewise, in Harlem's Mount Morris Park, Invisible Man and all who hear the song are moved by feelings deeper than that "old longing, resigned, transcendent emotion" summoned by "the same old slave-borne words" (*IM*, p. 342). The rendition of "Many a Thousand Gone" arises from present circumstance and past experience. The song joins the people as listeners and participants who know that in the midst of life and death the struggle for freedom goes on. It continues through expressions of personality that lead people to stop, to think and feel, and to see the end and the beginning of things in the life around them. Some tangle of kindred thought and emotion, some new responsiveness, leads Invisible Man to accept grudgingly, if not to affirm the place of inarticulateness, the word groped for, felt but not yet found, the word as sign of the speaker's inability to penetrate and solve the mysteries of experience.

Strangely, Invisible Man's inarticulate response flows from the tones of the song. "I had no words," he remembers, and when he does speak, his words sound harsh, as if resisting the need to respond to the call of the song. "What are you waiting for me to tell you?" he shouts, and follows with a bitter riff that leads into his ironic refrain: "Go home." But he does not fool the people; they know from his tone that something else is happening. And they listen to his denial of eloquence in an appropriate way. "They were listening intently, and as though looking not at me, but at the pattern of my voice upon the air" (*IM*, p. 343). What matters more than his words is the rising and falling, fluid pattern of his voice—his articulate/ inarticulate struggle to form connections between his identity and theirs. "Go home," he repeats over and over, but, really, they are home at this moment in their park. Still, "they gave no sign," so he tells them the story of Clifton's life and death—his murder. As he speaks, he feels desperately empty and inarticulate, almost nauseous over his unwitting but terribly consequential betrayal of Clifton and his audience, the people of Harlem. "It wasn't political," he thinks, but he is wrong. He does not know it, but his speech improvises on the song, theirs and his. It answers the question about politics and love in concrete terms, public and private, biographical and auto-biographical. Clifton's work flowed from love and so does the people's presence. Invisible Man's speech, shouted with no microphone for support, becomes political exactly because he sees Clifton now as someone he could not formerly love because of his narrow ambitions.

His words recreate Clifton as part of the community's inner and outer life, someone who, if he could speak, would utter words fusing love and politics. "Tell them," he says using Clifton's rhythm and style, "to get out of the box and to teach the cops to forget that rhyme. Tell them to teach them that when they call you *nigger* to make a rhyme with *trigger* it makes the gun backfire" (*IM*, p. 346). Yet Invisible Man curiously exhorts his audience to fold up its tent and "go home, keep cool, stay safe away from the sun" (*IM*, p. 346): the last things they will do. Once again, the effect of Invisible Man's words differs from what he thinks he has produced. "I stood looking at the crowd with a sense of failure. I had let it get away from me, had been unable to bring in the political issues" (*IM*, p. 356). His mind's logic lags behind the actual energy of his words. Granted, he does not leave the people in a fighting mood according to the precepts of classical oratory. Better, for his political purposes, he leaves them with smouldering thoughts of how closely they (and he) are bound up with Clifton's "plunge outside of history" (*IM*, p. 331). Something is going on, moved by Invisible Man's speech, in which he merges the rhetoric and technique of a preacher with those of a savvy contemporary storyteller. Silenced by his own on-again-off-again performance, Invisible Man for the first time sees an audience in its own reality, distinct from his identity, his agenda. Most important, "as I took one last look I saw not a crowd, but the set faces of individual men and women" (*IM*, p. 347). Somewhere in a corner of his mind, he realizes that the people may be temporarily in hibernation, a point he does not reach until the narrative's events are over, a state of being he then defines as "a covert preparation for a more overt action" (*IM*, p. 11). The words of the old song and his improvised speech move the people to a determined, anticipatory silence. Though understood, the lesson remains unspoken: To have "social responsibility," you have got to be willing and able to take "personal responsibility," just as earlier it is implied that true "social responsibility" flows from the condition of "social equality." To become a community, individual men and women must be "capable of their own action" (*IM*, p. 414).

6

As he writes, Invisible Man's vision of the crowd as individuals turns into an important revelation, but immediately after the funeral he does not grasp the reversal that once again makes him follow the lead of the people. He creeps along, "confused and listless moving through crowds that seemed to boil along in a kind of mist." Resisting the people's palpable and impalpable fluidity, Invisible Man fusses: "plans had to be made; the crowd's emotion had to be organized" (*IM*, p. 347). Meanwhile, the Brotherhood committee is furious at his twin improvisations of funeral and speech. In a meeting Brother Jack mocks Invisible Man's explanatory words— "'on your personal re-spon-si-bility.'" His parody of call-and-response recalls the smoker where the white men demand jeeringly that Invisible Man repeat the phrase "social responsibility." Jack's categories deny the transforming energy that flows between speaker and audience during a true improvisation. His ideology divides consciousness from language, language from action, and denies an orator full access to those he nourishes and is nourished by.

In a passionate response to Jack's accusations, Invisible Man affirms the complexity and autonomy of his people: "The Brotherhood isn't the Negro people; no organization is" (*IM*, p. 353). Consequently, he testifies to (and embodies) a context wherein his mind and the people's are activated and revealed by their voices. Listen some Saturday damn near anywhere in Harlem, he tells them — "A whole unrecorded history is spoken there, Brother" — and then he advances toward an American vernacular destination. Experience, Emerson's companion to eloquence, is now Invisible Man's territory: "I stand on what I see and feel and on what I've heard, and what I know" (*IM*, p. 356). Nonetheless, Invisible Man continues to affirm his Brotherhood life on the ground that, despite its hypocrisies and outrages, "it was the only historically meaningful life that I could live" (*IM*, p. 361). Only when his private tutor reveals the secret party line does Invisible Man become, after his grandfather's example, "a traitor" and "a spy in the enemy's country" (*IM*, p. 13). "It's impossible not to take advantage of the people," Brother Hambro informs him. "The trick is to take advantage of them in their own best interest" (*IM*, p. 381). Hearing this Bledsonian cynicism, Invisible Man reels alone and stunned into the street: first in reverie and later in the act of writing, he becomes able "to articulate the issues which tortured [him]" (*IM*, p. xviii). Because he is still unaware that the people's capacity to speak an eloquent "unrecorded history" implies a capacity for action, Invisible Man seeks some "firm ground for action that would lead them onto the plane of history." But the people have been standing their ground on the *plains* of history longer than he knows, and how *absurd*, to use one of his favorite words, is the idea that he "would have to move them without [himself] being moved" (*IM*, p. 383).

Certainly, he slips and slides while seeking a foothold on his "mountain of words." To find one, he seizes on a newfound ability "to look around corners" and accept all of his "separate experiences," no matter how foolish or bizarre. "They were me; they defined me. I was my experiences and my experiences were me, and no blind men, no matter how powerful they became, even if they conquered the world, could take that, or change one single itch, taunt, laugh, cry, scar, ache, rage or pain of it" (*IM*, p. 383). This eloquent riff becomes public only when he writes it down later and it is read. Yet in its private form it prepares him for his climactic encounter with the world, a reality he now acknowledges as more important than Brotherhood and other narrow categories of perception and experience.

Suddenly but inevitably, those "set faces of individual men and women" who had listened silently to his funeral speech a few days before release their anger and passion in wild, riotous actions, some individual, some collective. Rushing uptown, Invisible Man experiences an old reflex to lead somehow, but once in Harlem he is happy to melt into the occasion. Hit by a bullet, he is stunned into "a sudden and brilliant [and dangerous] suspension of time" (*IM*, p. 404), before he is rescued by some men he has never seen before (or even imagined). They seize the chance to burn down the tenement in which they have lived their unnoticed lives. For Invisible Man, this action and the manner of its execution stand as the most revealing political and personal experience in the novel. As Dupre, Scofield, and others prepare their work, Invisible Man is struck by Dupre's simple, direct, spontaneous exercise of leadership. "And let's have some organization," he says, in words that parody the Brotherhood's posturing about leaders and the people, and demonstrate how effective leadership emerges from a particular context. The egos of Scofield and his companion become one with the flow of the action.

Caught in this rhythm, Invisible Man carries a bucket of coal oil. Characteristically, he broods: "What was the meaning of it all? What should I think of it, *do* about it?" (*IM*, p. 410). But his observer's pose dissolves into a participatory response to the moment. "And now," he remembers as he relives the experience, "I was seized with a sense of exultation. They've done it, I thought. They organized it and carried it through alone; the decision their own and their own action. Capable of their own action" (*IM*, p. 414). He is illuminated and transformed. Suddenly a participant, he grabs a bucket of kerosene and hurls it into a burning room. For the first time, he expresses his urge toward eloquence in action, not words, and becomes one with his deed.

Almost immediately, another chance experience reforms his personality and rejuvenates him. Words are the catalyst, this time spoken by individuals he does not know, people whose lives he has held of little account. He overhears a man tell a woman, "If it become a sho' nough race riot I want to be here where there'll be some fighting back." With terrific, unexpected force, "the words struck like bullets fired close range, blasting my satisfaction to earth." Another crazy reversal occurs on this night of chaos, for words overpower Invisible Man's consciousness as the real bullet failed to do to his flesh. "It was as though the uttered word had given meaning to the night, almost as though it had created it" (*IM*, p. 417), he remembers, and now, as then, the word arouses his mind and imagination. When the man's words explode "against the loud, riotous air," Invisible Man constructs an interpretation of the events he has been witnessing and experiencing. To fight without guns is suicide, he thinks, and, as the scale of the Brotherhood's manipulation, machination, and complicity sinks in, he imagines the outcome as mass murder, perhaps planned by the committee.

At length, he has the climactic encounter of the night and the narrative—a final contest with his nemesis, Ras the Exhorter, now Ras the Destroyer, as that rabble-rouser's leadership also turns from words to deeds. Coincidentally yet predictably and inexorably, Invisible Man crosses the path of Ras's inflamed band of Black Nationalist followers. His sunglasses broken and therefore his Rinehart disguise shattered, he discovers new meaning and potentiality in the signs of previous experience. Brother Tarp's leg chain becomes brass knuckles and the locked and laden briefcase a club, but most of all, Invisible Man acts with a calm sureness that comes from "a new sense of self." Reflexes of consciousness, language, and action flow as one: "I knew suddenly what I had to do, knew it even before it shaped itself completely in my mind" (*IM*, p. 420). Yet first, he sticks to his habit of trying to be effective with articulate, improvisational words in the form of a speech.

If the context were different, his uttered words might be eloquent, that is, persuasive and consequential. In a dramatic reversal, he implicates the Brotherhood in a scheme to manipulate blacks to participate in the developing race riot for the organization's propaganda advantage. But Invisible Man's interpretation and exhortation are contrary to Ras's lust for violence, his determination to use the riot for his own ends. "Grab him," Ras commands, and instinctively, "without thinking," Invisible Man fuses a word—"No"—with "a desperate oratorical gesture of disagreement and defiance." He wrenches Ras's spear free, "gripping it mid-shaft, point forward," and spells out simply and powerfully the meaning behind the chaos of this crazy night:

> "They want this to happen," I said. "They planned it. They want the mobs to come uptown with machine guns and rifles. They want the streets to flow with blood; your blood, black blood and white blood, so that they can turn your death and sorrow and defeat into propaganda. It's simple, you've known it a long time. It goes, 'Use a nigger to catch a nigger.' Well, they used it to catch you and now they're using Ras to do away with me and to prepare your sacrifice. Don't you see it? Isn't it clear?" (*IM*, p. 421)

Invisible Man's use of call-and-response is contingent, and the effect varies according to the different contexts of his spoken and written words. Now, in the continuing present of his narrative act, the words form an eloquent truth that reverberates in the world. But on that chaotic night in the past, his words inspire only Ras's call for a murderous act. " 'Hang the lying traitor,' Ras shouted. 'What are you waiting for?' " (*IM*, p. 421). "Wait," Invisible Man cries and stops, as if struck dumb. For the first time he feels and understands the contingencies of language and the limits of eloquence. "I had no words and no eloquence" (*IM*, p. 422), he thinks then, and in the narrative present writes how he performed the negating and affirming act of ceasing to speak. On the page, the words he has spoken are direct, stunning, and convincing, but as spoken words they lack transforming power because no bond of consciousness exists any longer with his audience. Performance and creation, improvisation and eloquence—leadership, he recognizes at last—depend on readiness, responsiveness, and fluidity by both speaker and audience. If either becomes antagonistic, there can be no true call-and-response; without the possibility of love, there is only the politics of hate.

Then and now his words backfire. But they also reverberate in a self-revelation experienced that night and made eloquently, forcefully articulate during the time he performs (and Ellison composes) the narrative. He is and was, he realizes, "no hero, but short and dark with only a certain eloquence and a bottomless capacity for being a fool to mark me from the rest." *Hearing* who he is, he sees his audience, too: "saw them, recognized them at last as those whom I had failed and of whom I was not, just now, a leader, though leading them, running ahead of them, only in the stripping away of my illusionment" (*IM*, p. 422). As Ellison thirty years later tells us would be the case with such an underground African-American *character*, Invisible Man at the moment of self-recognition affirms the momentary, reverse English quality of his leadership in a voice audibly "less angry than ironic" (*IM*, p. xvii). In an exemplary verbal act, he peels the disguising, distorting rhetoric from the edifice of his personality. But his audience does not follow. And why should it, on an instant's notice, since in the past he has put eloquence in the service of illusions—his, his listeners', and, worse, his (and their) manipulators'?

Now, for an unbearably, necessarily long instant between his last spoken word and his violent preemptive gesture, Invisible Man looks at death and listens to its voice. Would death at the hands of his listeners instruct them about their true identity? Yes, he decides stoically, it might "perhaps move them one fraction of a bloody step closer to a definition of who they were and of what I was and had been." "But," he goes on in a swerving reversal, "the definition would have been too narrow." He is right: "it was better to live out one's own absurdity than to die for that of others, whether for Ras's or Jack's" (*IM*, p. 422). Besides, from his interior monologue radiate words that resonate with the riddle of nationhood and the paradox of individual citizenship. "The beautiful absurdity of their American identity and mine" is now his text, and these words might well be the novel's epigraph. But at the time of this experience, eloquence fails because there is no way for Invisible Man to break the pattern of conflict.

"A cry on the perilous edge of the fight," Emerson demanded from any orator who aspired to eloquence, "or let him be silent."[20] Aided by his meditation, Invisible Man conjures silence into action. He improvises a violent, eloquent gesture. He throws the spear back at Ras, and unlike his words, the weapon finds its mark. It penetrates Ras's cheeks and locks his jaws, silencing him. But as he flees, Invisible Man pines after the healing power of the spoken word. He wishes he could lay down his improvised weapons of briefcase and leg iron and say to his pursuers: "Look men, give me a break, we're all black folks together" (*IM*, p. 423). But it's no good, and he knows it. Invisible Man cannot successfully invoke the theme of African-American solidarity with Ras's men. How can he when just now he has made their leader another of the "many a thousand gone"? For the moment, Invisible Man will have to be satisfied with "silence, exile, and cunning"[21]—the weapons of James Joyce's Stephen Dedalus, another man destined to be his own father—if he is to have a chance to pursue eloquence underground in the form and voice of the written word.

"The beautiful absurdity of [our] American identity": Invisible Man hears his proposition enacted as soon as he eludes Ras's gang and before he descends into a manhole to avoid a pair of murderous whites. Then, he overhears two black men describe Ras's antics. They do not see him in Black Nationalist or African tribal terms. Instead, they identify him with vernacular American culture, with that archetypal white cowboy hero, the Lone Ranger; for good measure, one of the men riffs that Ras's *black* "hoss shot up the street like Heigho, the goddamn Silver" (*IM*, p. 426). Because two black men he has never seen before discover an American identity common to both Ras and the Lone Ranger, Invisible Man changes his mind, as he has had to do so many times after chance encounters with eloquent, unknown African-Americans. Indignant, he nevertheless allows this perspective, which *he* never could have imagined, to penetrate his mind. Yes, Ras's performance is *funny* as these street characters suggest in their rich, irreverent, defiant vernacular. It is also dangerous as Invisible Man realized before he put a violent end to that performance. And if there is tragedy here, it does not undermine Invisible Man's will to meet life in its mad, endlessly various guises and disguises. In the midst of everything—pain and loss, love and hate, politics and propaganda—a rich act of vernacular speech urges Invisible Man to challenge what Ellison calls the "apparent forms of reality" (SA, p. 114).

7

It remains for Invisible Man to replace the "apparent forms of reality" with a visible form of his own. He realizes that he "had been used as a tool" (*IM*, p. 426), and that in his case the tool was the spoken word. Rightly, he now fears dispossession of voice. In his underground nightmare at the close of the narrative proper, he dreams that Jack and other adversaries castrate him and hang his testicles "*beneath the apex of the curving arch of the bridge*" overhead (*IM*, p. 430). His sexual parts stand for all of those illusions that have nourished his false identities. The nightmare ends when "the bridge seemed to move off to where I could not see, striding like a robot, an iron man, whose iron legs clanged doomfully as it moved." Invisible Man's illusions crank the bridge into an enormous robot endowed with motion and an insensate, terrifying, quasi voice. "*No, no, we must stop him*" (*IM*, p. 431), he shouts to no one and then awakens to the desolate silence of his underground dwelling.

In the epilogue Invisible Man puzzles out the terms of his nightmare. How can he say "we," for instance? Alone and underground, cut off from responsive human contact, how can he warn against his apparition of conformity's totalitarian technological soul? In an improvisational response to the story he has just written down, he tries to tell what is happening now that he has changed his vocation from orator to writer, especially "what was happening when your eyes were looking through" (*IM*, p. 439). His performance as a writer testifies to his past failure as a rabble-rouser, a leader, and a speaker. But even as he meditates on failures of eloquence with the spoken word, he achieves eloquence as a writer by relying on an urgent but unintimidating conversational style. The epilogue is not merely meditation; in it Invisible Man forges a style by responding to what he imagines are his readers' (listeners' too, imaginatively) observations on his and his country's evolving identity. He intends all of this as an example to his readers. They (really we), if moved and persuaded by his views of selfhood and nationhood, are free to improvise a response. We may, in diverse ways, combine creation and performance in many individual complex acts that follow from his author's act of leadership. These are some of the possibilities he articulates when he suggests in his last words, and asks us to confirm, that he speaks for us.

Invisible Man complicates the possibilities of eloquence because he is conscious of his inchoate identity as a writer. He does not forsake its existence in the world—how could he when his just concluded narrative bursts with eloquent instances of the spoken word? How could he when the goal of his narrative has been freedom from the shackles of illusion, self-preoccupation, and isolation? Seeing that the act of narrative is bound up with the "rich babel" (SA, p. 112) of American oral expression, Invisible Man aspires to eloquence in his new profession (not career) as a writer. In that vocation, the techniques of spoken eloquence and the related forms of jazz and storytelling are exemplary points of reference for narrative. As a writer, Invisible Man continues to be a performer. He addresses his audience directly with the pronoun, *you*, as he has not done since the prologue, where he made his defiant demand for attention. But now *you* seems more fraternal and intimate than aggressive and impersonal, even if ironically so, for now his irony seeks a positive, participatory response from readers.

As a performer, Invisible Man has been changed by the narrative act, by writing down his story, especially by symbolically reperforming his speeches and by the earlier experience of living that story and giving those speeches. Writing puts him in touch with his former performing voice, excites a more complex, inclusive sense of identity, and connects him responsively to the world. So much so that he leaves open the possibility that the "socially responsible" role he will soon emerge to try may involve the repursuit of eloquence through the spoken word. And, indeed, his just completed memoir is a writer's act of social responsibility, a recognition that "American society cannot define the role of the individual, or at least not that of the *responsible* individual" (GT, p. 49).

In the epilogue the act of writing is informing and anticipatory because it requires so much self-revelation. For this reason, Invisible Man's narrative of invisibility is an act of profound visibility. And the visibility of his words on the page hastens his decision to reenter the world. Moreover, he does not exaggerate the pleasures of the written word. "So why do I write," he asks, "torturing myself to put it down?" Because writing's disciplined contest with self moves his will closer to action. "Without the possibility of action, all knowledge comes to one labeled 'file and forget,' and I can neither file nor forget" (*IM*, p. 437). Whereas throughout his time as an orator, he used acts of speech to restrain his audience's urge to action, now the act of writing commits him to action. The first consequence of his new position is a resolve "to at least tell a few people about it" (*IM*, p. 437)—about his journey to experience and knowledge, about the possibility and necessity of action. Like Emerson's *writing* on eloquence—like Douglass, Lincoln, and Twain, Emerson was a preeminent public performer who infused the written with the spoken word—Invisible Man's epilogue calls his potential participatory audience to action.

Invisible Man's career as a failed orator teaches him that he must speak to us, his audience, in order to speak *for* us. And he returns to that condition of eloquence in the profoundly rhetorical question with which he ends: "Who knows but that, on the lower frequencies, I speak for you?" A writer's communication with his audience— citizens, some of whom may also be other writers—may be an act of leadership. But, because of the nature of literature, narrative leadership is a symbolic act. Invisible Man, having set himself free, encourages his readers to take similar action. He does not attempt, as he has done presumptuously and blindly so many times, to lead his audience but to make contact on an equal individual basis. Everyone has a life to lead, a story to tell, but not necessarily a narrative to write. The last depends on craft and circumstances, personality, chance, and will, yet Invisible Man's question implicates every citizen in Ellison's call for a novel "fashioned as a raft of hope, perception and entertainment that might help keep us afloat as we [try] to negotiate the snags and whirlpools that mark our nation's vascillating course toward and away from the democratic ideal" (*IM*, p. xix). In the end Invisible Man and Ellison float toward eloquence and the "possibility of action" on their respective narrative rafts of memoir and novel.

For his part, Invisible Man acknowledges and spells out the transforming effects of the act of narrative. As was the case with his speeches, his initial intention differs from the effect of his words. "Here I've set out to throw my anger into the world's face, but now that I've tried to put it all down the old fascination with playing a role returns, and I'm drawn upward again" (*IM*, p. 437). But the act of writing complicates and changes his idea of performance. His written words turn him back to social action as his spoken words propelled his audiences. The act of writing, "of trying to put it all down," sharpens his awareness of diversity and complexity, possibility and limitation, and leads him to accept the burden of love. "I have to love," he writes, "so I approach it [life] through division. So I denounce and I defend and I hate and I love" (*IM*, p. 438). At the level of conjunction and relationship, *and* replaces *but* as the rhythm and meaning of his words signal reengagement with the world.

In his essays, Ralph Ellison proposes a reading of American fiction rooted in the idea and practice of democracy. What Invisible Man calls division is, in Ellison's view, essential if one is to understand and participate fully in American life, socially and culturally as well as politically. In "Twentieth Century Fiction and the Black Mask of Humanity," an essay written in 1946 when he was struggling with *Invisible Man*, Ellison asks why contemporary American fiction had failed to create "characters possessing the emotional, psychological and intellectual complexity which would allow them to possess and articulate a truly democratic world view?" (*SA*, p. 37). This is less a question than an assertion of the task Ellison sets for characters and narrators alike. Invisible Man's arduous self-reconstruction forces him to recognize the ambiguity and contradiction as well as the possibilities inherent in the "principle on which the country was built" (*IM*, p. 433), its many violations, and in his own contrary and complementary impulses toward love and politics. In the epilogue the pursuit of narrative becomes the Declaration's pursuit of happiness as Invisible Man calls eloquently for reconsideration of the rights and responsibilities of democratic citizenship.

Formally, too, Ellison's commitment to an American improvisatory vernacular rescues Invisible Man: namely, the epilogue's embodiment of an open, responsive, literary text. Call-and-response turns the dialectic of words into Invisible Man's resolve to act, to emerge from his underground solitary confinement to play "a socially responsible role." Together, his experience and narrative confirm the concept of eloquence. Invisible Man's failure as an orator and would-be African-American leader and his slow, painfully self-critical comprehension of that failure have "taught [him] something of the cost of being an individual who aspires to conscious eloquence" (*SA*, p. 117). And so he enacts a favorite Ellison proposition: that a work of art "is a social action in itself" (*SA*, p. 137). This in no way exalts the word over the world. Rather, it declares allegiance to both language and action, and calls for collaboration between writer, narrator, and reader, between oral and literary techniques and traditions, between performance and composition.

For Ralph Ellison, the struggle with form is bound up with America. He is fascinated by his country and affirms its principles and possibilities in complicated, mysterious, tender, satiric, vulnerable, and multifaceted ways. Then and now, he refuses to leave definition of the nation to those who misunderstand or underestimate the richness, complexity, and possibility inherent in its vernacular culture. Therefore, Ellison chooses to write a patriotic novel, but on his terms. "My problem," he has written, "is to affirm while resisting."[22] And he condemns and renounces many of his country's practices; this, too, is the essence of the patriot's role. As an American novelist and a Negro, he strives to influence the novel in somewhat the same way that the civil rights movement of the 1950s and 1960s set out to change the social and political character of American society. Who knows, to paraphrase Invisible Man's last lingering question, but on the "lower frequencies," Ellison's articulate, intellectual passion informed the struggles of the 1950s and 1960s? Who knows but that *Invisible Man* was a cultural catalyst for some of the energy and achievement of the civil rights movement?

Certainly, few values were more unfashionable among American intellectuals during the late 1940s and early 1950s than patriotism. For expressions of that attitude and tone, Ellison looked to the nineteenth century and discovered a sense of national complexity and responsibility, an experimental attitude appropriate to the metamorphoses taking place in *Invisible Man*. There, he declares, "the moral imperatives of American life that are implicit in the Declaration of Independence, the Constitution, and the Bill of Rights were a part of both the individual consciousness and the conscience of those writers who created what we consider our classic novels— Hawthorne, Melville, James, and Twain" (*GT*, p. 248).[23] Yet Ellison could not simply return to the aesthetic terms of the nineteenth-century novel when for him "every serious novel is, beyond its immediate thematic preoccupations, *a discussion of the craft*," and when "more than any other literary form the novel is obsessed with the impact of change upon personality" (*GT*, pp. 240-41, 244, my italics)—and with the impact of social change upon literary form. Nor could he merely innovate because for him form for form's sake renounces the novelist's responsibilities to society. "The novel," he insists throughout the 1950s, "is bound up with the notion of nationhood" (*GT*, p. 242).

When Ellison contends that "the interests of art and democracy converge," and when he connects "the development of conscious, articulate citizens" to "the creation of conscious, articulate characters," he makes inextricable the evolving twin experiments of democracy and the novel. In his view "resonant compositional centers" of fiction express the complexity of both the novel and American democratic society (*IM*, pp. xviii, xix). For him the novelist's individual imagination responds to the flux of American life. According to Ellison's 1982 introduction, Invisible Man already existed as a very real, as yet unimagined version of the "conscious, articulate citizen." Ellison did not so much invent him as fill in his character from the grain of his voice. And this is exactly Ellison's point about American society: there are countless articulate but invisible men and women in the nation's complex underground who profess "a certain necessary faith in human possibility before the next unknown" (*GT*, p. 319). Similar voices, yet to be identified and given palpable form in American fiction, excite Ellison's faith in the possibility of expressing that special American fluidity of class, culture, and personality. These variations on a volatile, seething, largely unheard and ignored eloquence spur Invisible Man's call for collaboration with Ellison and with us, his kin, at his narrative's end.

Finally, because of his symbolic performance in the epilogue, Invisible Man merges social and personal impulses in "a single complex act" of narrative. When he writes *you*, he refers to Ellison as well as to potential and actual readers—after all, Ellison was his initial audience. In some sense each sets the other free. What began as an act of "antagonistic cooperation" (*SA*, p. 143) ends as a sympathetic, continuing dialectical act. Like the reader, Ellison is enjoined to talk back to Invisible Man. And he does. Moreover, his author's act of response builds on an earlier idea about the protean nature of fiction. Back in 1946, Ellison argued for the novel's potential as a social action and form catalytic to the continuing experiment of American democracy. "Once introduced into society," he wrote, "the work of art begins to pulsate with those meanings, emotions, ideas *brought to it by its audience* and over which the artist has but limited control" (*SA*, p. 38, my italics). Now, more than three decades later, Ellison strengthens his novelist's bill of rights with an amendment: the writer, before and after his act of composition, is audience to his work and has the same rights and responsibilities as the rest of us—equally and individually, in the name of eloquence and action, in the name of citizenship.

NOTES

1. Ralph Ellison, *Invisible Man* (1952; rpt., with author's introduction, New York: Random House, 1982), p. 439. This volume will be cited hereafter as *IM*.

2. Ralph Ellison, *Shadow and Act* (New York: Random House, 1964), p. 143. This volume will be cited hereafter as *SA*.

3. Ralph Ellison, *Going to the Territory* (New York: Random House, 1986), p. 59.

4. Invisible Man refers to *Notes from Underground* at the beginning of his prologue and revises and revoices Dostoevski's narrator's perspective to express his African-American voice and condition. Unlike Dostoevski, Ellison does not intervene and write an ironic footnote as apologia for his character/narrator. Invisible Man consciously plays off Dostoevski and his underground man to imply that he will go to both traditions of the vernacular, literary and folk, to become a writer in what Ellison repeatedly calls this "crazy country."

5. For Ellison's further comment on his view of Negro leadership at the time of writing *Invisible Man*, see *Going to the Territory*, pp. 44, 45, 59, 60, 62, 63, 125-33, 144, 317, 318.

6. Both Larry Neal and Albert Murray have found evidence of musical form in *Invisible Man*. In "Ellison's Zoot Suit," *Ralph Ellison: A Collection of Critical Essays*, ed. John Hersey (Englewood Cliffs: Prentice-Hall, 1974), Neal argues that from the entrance of Louis Armstrong's "Black and Blue" in the prologue, "the subsequent narrative and all of the action which follows can be read as one long blues solo" (p. 71). And in *The Omni-Americans* (New York: Outerbridge, 1970), Murray claims that "Ellison

had taken an everyday twelve-bar blues tune . . . and scored it for full orchestra" (p. 167). Likewise, in his biography, *The Craft of Ralph Ellison* (Cambridge, Mass.: Harvard University Press, 1980), ch. 5, pp. 78-104, Robert G. O'Meally discusses jazz and folk songs in *Invisible Man*.

7. Ishmael Reed, Quincy Troupe, and Steve Cannon, "The Essential Ellison: An Interview," *Y'Bird* 1, no. 1 (1978), 132.

8. *The Journals and Miscellaneous Notebooks of Ralph Waldo Emerson*, Vol. IX, 1843-1847, ed. Ralph H. Orth and Alfred Ferguson (Cambridge, Mass.: Belknap Press, 1971), pp. 425-26, my italics.

9. Ellison discusses the impact of Kenneth Burke's "The Rhetoric of Hitler's Battle" and his own notion of "symbolic action" in the *Y'Bird* interview, "The Essential Ellison," pp. 148, 156.

10. Quoted by R. W. B. Lewis, *The American Adam* (Chicago: University of Chicago Press, 1955), p. 6.

11. Booker T. Washington, *Up from Slavery* (New York: A. L. Burt, 1901), p. 224.

12. See W. E. B. Du Bois's discussion of Washington in "Of Mr. Booker T. Washington and Others," *The Souls of Black Folk: Essays and Sketches* (1903; rpt., New York: Fawcett Publications, 1961), p. 48.

13. And in the South, opposition to Washington was voiced almost at once. A few months after Washington delivered his Atlanta Address, a young black scholar named John Hope told a Nashville audience in public repudiation of Washington's stance: "Now, catch your breath, for I am going to use an adjective: I am going to say we demand social equality. In this republic, we shall be less than freemen, if we have a whit less than that which thrift, education, and honor afford other freemen." Quoted by Edgar A. Toppin in *A Biographical History of Blacks in America since 1528* (New York: David McKay, 1971), p. 165.

14. From his student days at Tuskegee in the mid-1930s, Ellison was fascinated by T. S. Eliot's and James Joyce's use of "ancient myth and ritual." "But," he commented in a *Paris Review* interview, "it took me a few years to realize that the myths and rites which we find functioning in our everyday lives could be used in the same way" (*SA*, p. 174).

15. In his long account of the Third National Negro Congress, "A Congress Jim Crow Didn't Attend," *New Masses* (May 14, 1940), pp. 5-8, Ellison makes some fascinating observations on the different styles and perspectives of those aspiring to Negro leadership from the left. This and other Ellison articles for *New Masses* confirm his long-standing interest in the question of Negro leadership in the United States.

16. Ellison, "Remembering Richard Wright," *Going to the Territory*, pp. 208-9. This volume will be cited hereafter as GT.

17. For a good discussion of Douglass's complex role in *Invisible Man* and Invisible Man's misunderstanding of Douglass's vocation as a writer, see Robert B. Stepto's *From Behind the Veil: A Study of Afro-American Narrative* (Urbana: University of Illinois Press, 1979), pp. 172-75, 185-90. Stepto's argument hinges on the idea that a number of African-American narratives are polar works of immersion or ascent. In the sense that he authors his autobiography, Invisible Man's account of his past misconception of Douglass reveals his comprehension of Douglass's achievement as a writer. Douglass also tried his hand at fiction, and there, too, as Stepto argues in "Storytelling in Early Afro-American Fiction: Frederick Douglass's 'The Heroic Slave,' " *Georgia Review* 36, no. 2 (Summer 1982), 355-68, pursued what Stepto calls the "quest for freedom and literacy."

18. Like Invisible Man, Frederick Douglass first spoke his story and then wrote it, in his case in three successive, evolving autobiographies: *Narrative of the Life of Frederick Douglass, An American Slave, Written by Himself* (1845); *My Bondage and My Freedom* (1855); and *The Life and Times of Frederick Douglass* (1892).

19. Emerson, *Journals and Miscellaneous Notebooks*, pp. 425-26.

20. Ibid., p. 426.

21. James Joyce, *A Portrait of the Artist as a Young Man* (1916; rpt., New York: Viking, 1964), p. 247.

22. Letter from Ralph Ellison to the author, Aug. 12, 1983. For further discussion of the importance of history and the pursuit of democratic fiction in Ellison's work, see my "Chaos, Complexity, and Possibility: The Historical Frequencies of Ralph Waldo Ellison," *Black American Literature Forum* 11, no. 4 (Winter 1977), rpt. with revisions in *Chant of Saints*, ed. Michael S. Harper and Robert B. Stepto (Urbana: University of Illinois Press, 1979), pp. 33-52, and in *Speaking for You: Ralph Ellison's Cultural Vision*, ed. Kimberly Benston, in press, and also see my "Democracy and the Pursuit of Narrative," *Carleton Miscellany* 18, no. 3 (Winter 1980), 51-68.

23. Ellison was reading Henry James's fiction extensively when he began to write *Invisible Man*, and acknowledges a debt to the aesthetic and moral complexity with which James pursued the "American" theme. Yet Ellison found James largely deaf to the democratic commitment to "make the illiterate and inarticulate eloquent enough so that the educated and more favorably situated will recognize wisdom and honor and charity, heroism and capacity for love when found in humble speech and dress" (*GT*, p. 273). For Ellison's discussion of James, see also *GT*, pp. 249-54, 262-73, 313-16. Daniel Duke made a number of helpful comments on the importance of the relationship between speaker and audience to democratic eloquence.

CHAPTER 6

A Moveable Form: The Loose End Blues of *The Autobiography of Miss Jane Pittman*

1

Perhaps tired of hearing the hound dogs baying after his novel-in-progress, Ralph Ellison leads them to the briar patch where *Invisible Man* was born and bred. His introduction to the 30th Anniversary Edition advances the position that "every serious novel is, beyond its immediate thematic preoccupations, a discussion of the craft, a conquest of the form, and a conflict with its difficulties; a pursuit of its felicities and beauty."[1] For a new generation of readers, Ellison, in effect, has the first and the last word, because his introduction responds to Invisible Man's closing words by telling the story of their first improbable, unpromising meeting. Like his novel and Invisible Man's memoir, Ellison's introduction explores the impact of oral performance on the writer's narrative art. And when Ernest J. Gaines writes *The Autobiography of Miss Jane Pittman*, some twenty years after *Invisible Man*, he, too, frames his storyteller's tale with an introduction. Gaines carries the framing device a step further: his introduction is inseparably part of the novel, and it is written by a young black history teacher who tape-records Miss Jane telling her story.

As a writer, Gaines feels the burden of imbuing his fiction with the immediacy of the spoken word. "Now maybe what I need to do," he tells one interviewer, "is sit in a chair on a stage and just tell people stories rather than try to write them. I wish I could do that. I wish I could be paid just to sit around and tell stories, and forget the writing stuff." Yet he knows that Charles Dickens, Mark Twain, and other platform storytellers first reached their audience through the written word. "But, unfortunately, I am a writer," Gaines continues in tones recalling Ellison's phrase for the demands of craft—"that same pain, that same pleasure"[2]—"and I must communicate with the written word."[3] As Gaines talks about writing, you hear the arduous, self-wrenching, self-creating transition he has made to the writer's vocation. You feel the pull of the past (and present) oral tradition of the old folks whose voices and stories Gaines heard and absorbed as a boy in Louisiana, and, after he arrived in California as a teenager in the late 1940s, vowed he would get on paper.

Clearly, he prefers to give up little or nothing of the heritage he remembers so vividly: "Sometimes they would sew on quilts and mattresses *while they talked;* other times they would shell peas and beans *while they talked.* Sometimes they would just sit there smoking pipes, chewing pompee, or drinking coffee *while they talked.* I, being the oldest child, was made to stay close by and serve them coffee or water or whatever else they needed. In winter, they moved from the porch and sat beside the fireplace and drank coffee—and sometimes a little homemade brew—*while they talked.*"[4] "One gets the flow,"[5] Michael S. Harper has written of Gaines's work, and it is not surprising to hear Gaines say that "once I develop a character and hear his voice, I can let him tell the story."[6] Speech is Gaines's gift, and he reoralizes the written word with the old immediacy of oral storytelling.

"Usually," he repeats, "I think of myself as a storyteller. I would like for readers to look at a person telling the story from the first person point of view as someone actually telling them a story at that time."[7] In his fiction "that time" is often a condition similar to Gertrude Stein's continuing present, a double-conscious time of things happening and perceived happening, simultaneously. This sense of present time derives from the oral tradition and the immediate contact that existed between accomplished storytellers and their audience. For Gaines, the stories he has heard and those he creates revivify a world of kinship ties based as much on reciprocal speaking and listening as on blood. This is why his stories are often told from the perspective and in the voice of someone who participates in or initiates the action as well as tells it. As Gaines develops a character, conventions of seeing and knowing yield to a prior necessity. For although Gaines writes words on the page, he changes seeing-is-believing into hearing-is-believing. According to his speech-driven *donnée* of fiction, for the writer to be free, his characters must be free, and an independent, individual voice is the first test of freedom.

For Gaines and his characters, writing and storytelling are acts of remembrance, creation, and performance that sometimes lead to acts of change. His characters witness, experience, and sometimes promote change, yet their idiom changes little. Speech stabilizes their lives and helps them find the courage to participate in the changes coming in what one of them calls "the scheme of things."[8] Gaines's time in Louisiana — 1933-48 — precedes the turning point in southern experience when a social order, defined and sustained by the officially sanctioned relations between blacks and whites, was about to be disturbed. His fiction mediates two complementary facts of life: first, that very little changes in his remote parish between the Civil War and his departure after World War II; and, second, that even rural Louisiana could not resist the racial upheaval of the 1950s and 1960s. But a social, political, and economic order as powerful and long-lived as the deep South's peonage system does not crumble overnight.

"The past ain't dead," Gaines is fond of paraphrasing William Faulkner, "it ain't even passed."[9] So, too, the voices of the living and the dead from Gaines's past possess and quicken his memory. In oral performances of the kind he witnessed down in the quarters, people presented themselves and their stories as their ancestors did in slavery days. But only through the artifice of the written word can Gaines introduce strangers to his Louisiana world. Paradoxically, he shifts from speech to print, from oral storytelling to fiction so that readers may hear his people's voices and experience imaginatively their oral culture. But writing involves performance, too, although the action is of a different, more interior kind. Writing is a solitary struggle, sometimes painful, sometimes exhilarating. With luck and skill, you move from talking to yourself to conversation with your characters and, later perhaps, with readers. In writing as well as speech, voice articulates the self and the self's capacity for form and eloquence. The link between form and voice explains why Gaines listens until he hears and recognizes his character's voice, then, convinced of the character's individuality, allows him to tell the story.

"My writing is strongest when I do that,"[10] Gaines says referring to the flash point when he yields the storytelling voice to his character. He seeks what Kate Chopin, whose fiction is also full of the sensuous feel of Louisiana sun, sky, and speech, calls that point of moral awareness when one is "beginning to realize her position in the universe as a human being, and to recognize her relations as an individual to the world within and about her."[11] Gaines's first-person narrators come into possession of storytelling voices, but in *The Autobiography of Miss Jane Pittman* Gaines discovers his form in the oral tradition of call-and-response between storyteller and audience. Until then, his narrators, though audible to readers, and other characters, lack the immediate audience enjoyed by oral storytellers. Jim Kelly, narrator in *Of Love and Dust*, and the narrators of the *Bloodline* stories, including the ten successive individual voices in "Just Like a Tree," tell Gaines's stories in interior voices. In an interview Gaines compares Kelly with Nick Carraway, F. Scott Fitzgerald's participant-narrator in *The Great Gatsby*. "I needed a guy who could communicate with different people. I needed a guy who could communicate with Bon Bon, the white overseer, with Aunt Margaret, with Marcus."[12] Like Carraway, Kelly hears parts of the story from other characters and incorporates them into his narrative. Yet Kelly has no audience directly in mind and, unlike Carraway, does not tell of writing down his words.

Likewise, the stories in *Bloodline* are not told in a dramatic context. No one appears to be present except the character, and the stories seem to unfold entirely inside the narrator's mind. But they are told with an accuracy of idiom, an authenticity of voice, and an economy of form worthy of Gaines's approving phrase—"*That's writing.*"[13] Moreover, Gaines arranges the stories in a progression so that six-year-old Sonny in "A Long Day in November," eight-year-old James in "The Sky Is Grey," and nineteen-year-old Proctor of "Three Men" shape attitudes toward experience because of their exposure to an increasingly complex and challenging gamut of voices. In the title story Felix, the seventy-year-old narrator, is true to his experience and the speech of the others, black and white, living on the plantation. Because he respects the truth and those who embody it, his voice has an enabling, sarcastic yet loving power. In some sense the story Felix tells reenacts the Civil War—blood against blood—and, clearly, the old questions of union and equality, democracy and kinship are still at stake. Here, and in much of Gaines's fiction, the essential connections between people of both races imply a common fate— whether fortunate or not is unclear. But it is clear that the destiny of each will be determined by both. For the time being, the transitional time of the story, Felix's stoic, truthful, compassionate voice allows him to show the antagonists to each other as kin; by blood and birth, yes, but equally through contingent, voluntary acts of telling and listening, through the acknowledgment of unofficial history and tradition, through the mix of voice lines.

Throughout *Bloodline* Gaines makes written speech of the characters' voices. His narrators talk to themselves, out loud perhaps as they remember and prepare their stories. But Gaines makes the stories public, blending their voices with his, his with theirs. In "Just Like a Tree," the last story in the collection, he comes closer to the traditional performance of oral storytelling. A sequence of ten voices moves the action forward in time. One after another, children, adults, old people, men and women, black and one white, southern, and an irreverent, somewhat callous northern black man tell the story in a medley. "I wanted people around to give their own personal views," Gaines says. "And of course the sound of the language. I like the sound of individuality," he adds. "I want sounds, different sounds, different angles, as when you set up a camera."[14] Gaines's montage of voices flows according to cinematic and also musical form. Elsewhere he tells of listening to Moussorsky's *Pictures at an Exhibition* "daily and daily and daily"[15] to get the feel of different sounds passing into one another in the same space.

The form of "Just Like a Tree" expresses interiority. The multiple voices are not telling successive parts of the same story to each other or, apparently, to anyone else. Gaines composes their interior monologues into "a single story from different angles."[16] But if you listen hard, you hear some of these voices straining to break into speech, to converse with each other. Looking at Aunt Fe, whose daughter has come to take her North because of bombings near her home, Leola responds inwardly as if she is talking directly to the others. "How can she be joyful, *I ask you*, how can she be?" (*B*, p. 226, my italics). Chris, too, is articulate within because he imagines that he communicates with others: "Watch out, I think to myself, here come another lie. People, he just getting started" (*B*, p. 238.) Moreover, Aunt Clo, the central voice in the tale, speaks a parable based thematically on the old spiritual of the story's title and formally on the oral pattern of call-and-response. Weatherbeaten, unvictorious, undefeated, abiding, Aunt Clo reverberates the ages, and her successive *yous* implicate everyone in the struggle for dignity that goes on inside and outside Gaines's fiction. Aunt Clo, Aunt Fe, and many others in their generation never stopped telling the truth or blessing the efforts of the young. Through all the days of defeat, their voices kept self articulate and strong within, and in speech confirmed the people's connection with one another and the world beyond.

2

Telling your story is a way of shaping your life, and therefore a struggle with the form of experience and imagination. *Bloodline* prepares for change in the social order through personal changes. Its narrators bide their time and intensify the possibilities of their lives as individuals in a threatened black community. Gaines follows *Bloodline*'s limited, immediate, temporal and social scale with *The Autobiography of Miss Jane Pittman* whose voice and story lines work back to the Civil War and forward to the continuing present where, before her death, Jane Pittman puts her eloquence to work for change—a small heroic action, perhaps unanticipated when she begins to tell her story, but an act that her mastery over storytelling and experience makes her ready to perform. *The Autobiography of Miss Jane Pittman* begins with a call for storytelling. Jane responds, and before she is done, history and circumstance also call. Here, too, she responds and changes storytelling from a secondary to a primary act. Her voice, her life, her story, and her last civil rights action fuse with her people; individually and together, they influence "the scheme of things" in the quarters and, through the history teacher's good offices, the world beyond.

Gaines is explicit about the imaginary but authentic act of public performance that drives *The Autobiography of Miss Jane Pittman*. His novel depends on the artifice and actuality of communal storytelling among black people in the quarters. Miss Jane's voice belongs also to the community whose members help her by listening and contributing to the task of storytelling. To this Gaines adds a contemporary variation on the call-and-response of oral storytelling. A young man who has left to teach history returns to get Miss Jane's voice and story on tape and in print. Like Gaines, he finds his professional work hindered because Jane and her story are missing from the books. Gaines's frame flows from his experience and the experience of many in his race in the decades after World War II. This was a time of migration away from the rural South for many young blacks, and the question addressed is how folk traditions are to be carried on by those who leave. Gaines's teacher holds dear his cultural kinship ties with Miss Jane; he comes back determined to preserve her story and her voice through the technology at his disposal: a portable tape recorder. This is a contemporary variation on an oral tradition going back to slavery and hundreds of years before to the tribal cultures of West Africa. Coming generations of students will learn Miss Jane's story as it is retold and interpreted by their teachers. Also hearing her voice, they will hear her story as she told it, experiencing for themselves something of the power of her presence.

In *The Autobiography of Miss Jane Pittman* Gaines wanted more than the feel of voices. He wanted the novel's *donnée* to be a complex performance of oral storytelling. Like the characters whose voices he puts on paper, especially the young history teacher, Gaines arrives at his eventual form only after a long hard struggle. "I wanted to continue from 'Just Like a Tree'—where a group of people tell the life story of a single woman," Gaines characterizes his original intention. "The story was to begin on the day that she was buried— the old people who had followed her body to the cemetery would later gather on the porch of a lady who had never walked in her life, and there they would start talking."[17] Everyone would be a storyteller, and from the start the audience would be a congregation performing the essential community work of culture. "At first," Gaines notes, "a group of people were going to tell about this one person's life, and through telling of this one person's life, they were going to cover a hundred years of history, superstitions, religion, philosophy, folk tales, lies."[18] But after a year Gaines discarded this form of multiple voices, multiple points of view. "I had fallen in love with my little character," he admits, telling a little of his story, "and I thought she could tell the story of her life much better than anyone else."[19] As a craftsman, Gaines questions the authenticity of his initial multiple-voice storytelling. "After I'd written it like that one time, it was untrue, so I broke it down to one person telling the story, the individual herself telling the story."[20] Thus, *A Short Biography of Miss Jane Pittman* becomes *The Autobiography of Miss Jane Pittman.*

"All I could do was act as her editor," Gaines says playfully of his relationship with Miss Jane Pittman, "never her advisor."[21] But he turns over the editorial function to the history teacher. In the introduction *the editor* tells how Jane Pittman's story becomes the community's before and after her death. His account reenacts complexities of African-American storytelling going back to the time when slave tales were told on request to outsiders—whites like Joel Chandler Harris and blacks with some claim to membership in the community but who, like Zora Neale Hurston, had a professional interest in having the stories told. Because the young teacher apparently has grown up in or near the quarters, he understands the old slave saying: "Everything I tells you am the truth, but they's plenty I can't tell you."[22] There is plenty missing from the books he uses to teach history, so he is determined to expand what is told and the audience it is told to. So the history teacher takes the lead and tells his story. He tells of his sometimes blundering struggle for Miss Jane's story. His account reinforces oral storytelling as a vital, functional everyday habit and also as a ritual occasionally of sacred significance in African-American culture.

Before the history teacher can be an editor with the taped spoken and the transcribed written word, he has to overcome Miss Jane's resistance. He begins conversationally as if to suggest that a certain familiarity, even intimacy characterizes his initial tug-of-war with Miss Jane. His tone heeds the need for patience and persistence and hints that sometimes calls for stories and oral performances are rejected because the feel is wrong.[23] "I had been trying," he tells us, perhaps to encourage readers to become friends with his and Miss Jane's story, "to get Miss Jane Pittman to tell me the story of her life for several years now, but each time I asked her she told me there was no story to tell."[24] Admitting his past failures, he recreates his successful call to Miss Jane:

> When school closed for the summer in 1962 I went back to the plantation where she lived. I told her I wanted her story before school opened in September, and I would not take no for an answer.
> "You won't?" she said.
> "No, ma'am."
> "Then I reckon I better say something," she said. (*AMJP*, p. vii)

This particular call is answered because instead of trying to persuade Miss Jane, the young man moves her by the urgency of personality and presence for which his call stands. This time his call puts service to others above his individual destiny or desires.

For her part, Jane's response signifies that she is willing to tell her story both for the sake of her race and because, like her namesake Janie in *Their Eyes Were Watching God*, she is full of "that oldest human longing—self-revelation."[25] But she realizes that those who have stood by her and protected her, older black people like Mary Hodges, resent the young man's intrusion. "You don't have to say a thing," Mary butts in as soon as Miss Jane responds to the teacher's call. He has chosen not to live among them, and for strict constructionists like Mary that puts him outside the community's circle of storytelling; therefore, she cannot bear for Jane to give him her story or even her attention. Mary worries that he may use Jane for his personal ends and distort the meaning of her life; she may also think he violates the spirit of privacy and tact so essential to the balance between individual and community.

All the same, Miss Jane decides to tell her story. She knows it has significance. She is pleased, even flattered by the young man's interest and wants to include him and the folks from the quarters as a double participatory audience. She shrewdly understands that her performance can help unify black Americans of different backgrounds, ages, and agendas. To avoid having Mary go off in a huff, Miss Jane lays back and allows her to enter the conversation seemingly in the guise of a mediator. In reality, Jane is completely, though subtly, in command; already she shows a preference for collaborative authorship by allowing Mary to stand in, though not speak for her.

> "What you want know about Miss Jane for?" Mary said.

"I teach history," I said. "I'm sure her life's story can help me explain things to my students."

"What's wrong with them books you already got?" Mary said.

"Miss Jane is not in them," I said. (*AMJP*, p. viii)

Once Mary participates, the good manners reinforced by call-and-response compel her to remain involved, even though Jane's decision—"When you want start?" (*AMJP*, p. viii)—goes against her advice.

As soon as the teacher begins to interview Miss Jane, it is apparent that her sense of time and form differs drastically from his. He works from a schedule and sets a deadline of September 1962 for completion of the interviews. Jane tells her story as she lives her life—according to her time. She also chafes at his format. The one-on-one, question-and-answer technique of his "interviews" compromises Miss Jane's habit of free-flowing, asymmetrical storytelling, and seems merely an ironic, attenuated version of call-and-response. But Miss Jane's resistance is indirect. Reminiscent of folk strategies going back to slavery, she keeps her counsel and chooses the refuge of forgetfulness. "I don't know whether she was doing this purposely or not," the editor writes later on, "but suddenly she could not remember anything any more" (*AMJP*, p. viii). Outmaneuvered, the teacher adapts to a context Jane is comfortable with—the improvisatory, participatory storytelling of the oral tradition.

In a characteristically small, incremental way, Miss Jane's forgetting is a catalytic act. For the teacher catches on and acknowledges his rescue, more than hers, by the community's spontaneous participation. The form becomes deeply communal because when Jane stops talking, "someone else would always pick up the narration," and when this happens, Jane remains involved, "listening until she got ready to talk again" (*AMJP*, p. ix). Her individuality flows from her relationship to the community. Even though she is the primary storyteller and hers the lead or calling voice, she knows no one person contains the past anymore than one individual can narrate reliably and fully the race's present situation or future prospect. All the same, Jane feels free to disagree with what is said by those she has invited to participate. At those times, "the other person would not contradict her, because, after all, this was her story" (*AMJP*, p.

ix). In the terms of call-and-response, the other person has his say, and Jane's objection reasserts her responsibility. Perhaps as an example to the history teacher, as well as a courtesy to Miss Jane, the other old people let the contradictions stand. In this context, everyone is a participant, including the young history teacher and interviewer. He, too, changes, and changes more than the rest. Once the old folks initiate him into their tradition of storytelling, he speaks of the *narrative* rather than the *interview*. He enters gingerly the territory of fiction and imagination.

Nevertheless, he remains stubborn about the discipline of history. He holds fast to the tar baby of conventional logic and chronology until Jane and the others chase him into the briar patch of contingency and improvisation. "Miss Jane," he complains, "would talk about one thing one day and the next day she would talk about something else totally different" (*AMJP*, p. ix). Jane's breaks offend his commitment to arbitrary continuity. He does not hear her digressions as progressions. But when he objects, Mary intervenes in defense of Jane's sense of timing and selection—her authority as storyteller. " 'What's wrong with that? You don't like that part?' I would say, 'Yes, but—' Mary would say, 'But what?' I would say, 'I just want to tie up all the loose ends.' Mary would say, 'Well, you don't tie up all the loose ends all the time. And if you got to change her way of telling it, you tell it youself' " (*AMJP*, p. ix). In effect, Jane opens the teacher's closed circuit interview to a narrative form in which others' words splice hers precisely because she is confident and collaborative in her craft. Her form respects forgetfulness, discontinuity, digression; in short, her storytelling is faithful to the chaos of consciousness and experience. Like narrative, the work of history never strays very far from the chaos beyond the pale of frail, imposed order. History tells the story of all the attempts to make known what has happened in the past. History, Miss Jane teaches the teacher indirectly, and Mary tells him explicitly, is not clean, tidy, or pat. Like the human condition it speaks of, history is dirty, messy, chaotic, intuitive, and mysterious. History is possibility. History begins with loose ends and to loose ends returns, like the human dust that inspires it.

For Miss Jane the form of storytelling keeps things open, undecided, unconcluded—*loose*, to return to the word given different values by the teacher and Mary. The teacher's subsequent comments show that he applies Miss Jane's lesson to his editorial narrative work. He distinguishes his written narrative from Miss Jane's spoken tale and accepts responsibility for his principle of selection and his editorial decisions. He recognizes that he "could not possibly put down on paper everything that Miss Jane and the others said on tape during those eight or nine months." Keeping to the spirit of the oral performance he has witnessed and participated in, he tries "not to write everything, but in essence everything that was said." That essence is inclusive; it is both his and Miss Jane's. He puts Miss Jane's language on paper: "Her selection of words, the rhythm of her speech" (*AMJP*, p. ix). Most important, after Miss Jane's death he keeps her form alive by conversing with "many of the people whom she had tallked about. I told them about the tape and I asked could I talk to them sometime" (*AMJP*, p. x). Jane's still audible voice and story provide an introduction to people who otherwise might regard his questions with suspicion.

The history teacher approaches people who were not part of the original performance partly to authenticate what he has on tape and partly to help him with his secondary editorial act of storytelling. As he does so, he displays a new combination of scrupulosity about historical method and openness to storytelling's contingencies. He reconstructs accurately the substance and spirit of the responses to his queries—so much so that his approach resembles Zora Neale Hurston's fieldwork and writing as an anthropologist. His willingness to shed the mask of professional objectivity and regard his work as his story, too, leads those he questions to open up and makes him respectful and alert to their testimony. "Almost everyone, both black and white, said I could. Some of them wanted to hear the tape, or part of it, before they made any comments. After hearing the tape they refused to say anything. Others laughed and said not everything on the tape was absolutely correct. Still, others were glad to give information without listening to the tape at all, and in most cases much of what they said was pretty close to what Miss Jane had said before" (*AMJP*, p. x).

You could call his account the "Loose End Blues." "Many," "almost," "both black and white," "some," "others," "not everything," "in most cases": these words verify Miss Jane's story in the act of qualifying it. Not everyone sees or hears things the same way. The teacher's language confirms the importance of Jane Pittman's spoken history precisely because it is hers, because no one else sees her story exactly as she sees it. Such complexity is or ought to be a principle of history, written, spoken, and taught in a nation founded on equality and diversity whose coins are stamped with the motto *E pluribus unum*. As an editor, the teacher fulfills his historian's vocation. Initiated by Miss Jane, Mary, Pap, and others of the oral school, he teaches his students and the wider audience of his countrymen and -women the method along with the facts of history.

At last, the teacher is true to his oral historian's editorial task, to Miss Jane's role as storyteller for her people, and to her community's participatory act of witness. As an imaginary contemporary historian, the editor does for historiography what Gaines does for the novel; he uses the oral tradition to advance the narrative possibilities of history. "Miss Jane's story is all of their stories, and their stories are Miss Jane's" (*AMJP*, p. x). Their presence and participation turn Gaines's original "folk biography" into a "folk autobiography" — Jane's, the quarters', the history teacher's, his students', and if, like him, we are now ready to live with loose ends, ours, too.

3

Jane Pittman's voice secures the novel. The editor, following the form and flow of Miss Jane's life and African-American history, divides the story into four successive books. "The War Years" and "Reconstruction" take the action from a memorable day during the Civil War when Jane, then called by the slave name, Ticey, seizes a name of her choice, to some ten or twelve years into the twentieth century. "The Plantation" carries the story up to the mid- or late 1930s in a narrowed landscape. Finally, "The Quarters" focuses on the black folks' own world and tells of Jane's experience up to and perhaps including part of the time she tells her story. During the first three books, the editor punctuates Jane's tale by making short-titled chapters of her reminiscences. Miss Jane was never so self-conscious or prosaic as some of the titles, but mostly the editor chooses a word or a phrase spoken by Jane. But by the time Miss Jane reaches "The Quarters" on her narrative journey, even such minor distractions as titles fall away before the increasingly urgent and immediate, though still discursive, conversational sound of her voice. "The Quarters" marks the fusing of Jane's storytelling with her participation in the civil rights struggle, an act perhaps bound up with the young black history teacher's repeated calls for her story.

Jane's opening words create temporal and spatial immediacy. "It was a day something like right now," she begins, fusing the past with the present moment, "dry, hot, and dusty, dusty." Her story is almost a song. "It might a' been July, I'm not too sure, but it was July or August. Burning up, I won't ever forget" (*AMJP*, p. 3), she says, and you can feel her stop to catch her breath. As a storyteller, Miss Jane embellishes her tale with details experienced by her and her audience at the moment of performance. She also testifies to the intensely pragmatic quality of her memory. I might not remember the month, she tells us, but I will never forget that it was hot. Her memory rises from sensuous experience; over and over again she roots her moral being in stubbornly particular, elemental, objective phenomena.

In "The War Years" Miss Jane reveals that she is an accomplished storyteller confident of her improvisational form and timing. "Don't worry, I'll come to Ned later," she tells all of her different audiences. "Yes, Lord, I'll come to him later" (*AMJP*, p. 17). Her time is as important as the chronology of enormous public events that intersect with her life. She holds her audience by her expert mimicking performances of colorful characters, each with the rich speech of a distinct voice. She does "Secesh" soldiers and Yankee soldiers, her mistress, a hapless and dangerous slow wit who tries to steal her name and her virtue, the remarkable Big Laura whose murder is a loss to the story, and a "red red" man whose yarn of geography rivals the tall tales of Mark Twain. Jane hears, too: "heard nigger," she tells little Ned, and her accurate ear leads to a meal and a good night's sleep instead of a beating and maybe death.

Occasionally, in an understated way Jane tells of her necessary apprenticeship as a storyteller during her dangerous, foolhardy, fruitlessly courageous search for Ohio. Like Huck Finn, Jane learns that survival depends on telling a story convincingly and colorfully. She learns that there is strength in the wit and charm of words. But in the present moment of her storytelling with the teacher and others in the quarters, she passes quickly from one episode to the next. Her reason has to do with strategy, not loss of memory.[26] "I can tell you all the things we went through that week," she says with a careful modulation into the present tense, "but they don't matter." Not because they are unimportant but "because they wasn't no different from the things we went through them first three or four days" (*AMJP*, pp. 54-55). She's mastered the representative anecdote and in her eloquence persuades us that what she leaves out is really there in her (and potentially our) imagination.

Miss Jane reserves the right to editorialize, and when she does, she speaks in images, rarely abstractions. On these occasions she expects rigorous acts of memory from her audience. For instance, when she gives the meaning of Ned Douglass's life and death near the end of Book II, she revoices and revises imagery her former mistress used to commemorate the slave-bound Confederate South: "He died at the end of the other century and the beginning of this century. He shed his precious blood for them. I remember my old mistress when she saw the young Secesh soldiers saying: 'The precious blood of the South, the precious blood of the South.' Well, there on that river bank is the precious dust of this South. And he is there for all to see" (*AMJP*, p. 113). Jane's words, her reperformance of Ned's eloquent last speech, and her entire story are living examples of what he fought for. Moreover, she celebrates him according to his reality in death — *precious dust*. But she repeats and expects us to remember the burning words spoken by her mistress a hundred years ago. She uses them to note the folly of a construct like *the* South. She overcomes the old false words by affirming the ground under her feet and renaming it, with its dust and bones, as *this* South. Jane knows that her act of speech is necessary to keep Ned Douglass vividly alive as an ancestor to those who would act for change in her time and beyond. She knows, too, that later in her story, Jimmy, Ned's successor and a contemporary leader, pays with his life. Dust is a fact and a word; Jane's voice makes it a metaphor for the earth's mediating role between the living and the dead.

In "The Plantation" the dominant focus is not temporal but spatial as Jane comes closer to home. She addresses her audience by the familiar *you* more and more often; increasingly, she shifts into the present tense. In particular, she speaks directly to her listeners about matters on which she would like a last word before her story and her life are over. If she had her way, she and we would talk to the rivers and trees forever. "But when you talk to an oak tree that's been here all these years, and knows more than you'll ever know, it's not craziness; it's just the nobility you respect" (*AMJP*, p. 146). Instead of bristling at being called crazy, Jane includes her audience in her behavior; in effect, she dares any doubting Thomas in the crowd to come away empty from talking to the rivers and the trees. Levees and concrete spillways are inventions that one day will be "long dead, too, but the water will never die. That same water the Indians used to believe in will run free again." As if to acknowledge her mortality and affirm her audience's continuity with the elements of nature, she ends on an intimate, defiant note of challenge: "You just wait and see" (*AMJP*, p. 148).

On disputed issues of the historical record, like Huey Long's assassination, Miss Jane can be downright quarrelsome and petulant. Indeed, in the next to last book, she swings impatiently from large to small matters. She seems divided between her commitment to tell the story of a hundred years and her urge to come home to the quarters and relate with familiarity, intimacy, and love the climactic story of Jimmy Aaron. She prepares shrewdly for her free-flowing storytelling in "The Quarters" by ending "The Plantation" with a version of the Tee Bob–Mary Agnes story told by her white friend, Jules Raynard. Listening to Raynard spin a Faulknerian yarn of implacable fate, Jane interrupts, showing her skepticism:

> "But ain't this specalatin?" I said.
> "It would be specalatin' if two white people was sitting here talking," Jules Raynard said, looking round. But he couldn't look round too far; his weight didn't allow that.
> "But it's us?" I said.
> "And that makes it gospel truth," he said.
> "Then what happened?" I said. (*AMJP*, p. 192)

He tells her his version, and though the reconstruction is plausible, it is still, as Miss Jane suggests, "specalatin." When she responds, it is clear that Raynard desires only confirmation of his story and not Jane's own ideas about why what happened happened. She ends the conversation with a simple good night, and though Raynard may not know it, Jane's audience senses she has not had her say. That say will not be ineffectual, somewhat romantic speculation about a tragic finality. Rather, her say will embody the actuality of overcoming the old destructive rules of race in favor of a new letter and spirit of human possibility. To have that say, Jane cuts immediately to her home ground and tells a story no one else can tell.

4

As both a masterful storyteller and a private person, Miss Jane understands that performing your autobiography is not the same as telling stories. This distinction may be one reason she avoids telling her story for so long. For that matter, many of the storytelling sessions that make up the first three books consist of related virtuoso oral set-pieces that could be gathered in a volume called *The Collected Tales of Miss Jane Pittman*. Sometimes these are Jane's meditations: on history, as in the tragic end of Reconstruction ("A Flicker of Light; and Again Darkness"); on religion, in her account of spiritual illumination ("The Travels of Miss Jane Pittman"); on nature, as in the folly of man's attempts to have dominion over the universe ("Of Men and Rivers"). At other times Jane reconstructs someone else's words, gestures, and story. But in the "Quarters," her voice is consistently personal, even intimate, her story fluid and resilient yet absolutely determined in its destination. Jane's more and more intensely integral, improvisatory form moves the editor to dispense entirely with chapters and titles. Like water from one of her rivers, Jane's words flow freely, separated occasionally by space on the page. These intervals signify pauses in her speech. They give her time to catch her breath and her audience a chance to sift its thoughts and perhaps speak what is unspoken.

The fullness of her time and space arrive when, in her eighties, Miss Jane moves back down to the quarters from Samson house. The editor follows her lead naming the last book of her narrative "The Quarters," as if he is truly home, too. The book is about leadership and deliverance, so Jane summons biblical folk tones and the rhythms of prophecy, derived from the spirituals and sermons. "People's always looking for someone to come lead them," she begins: "Go to the Old Testament; go to the New. They did it in slavery; after the war they did it; they did it in the hard times that people want call Reconstruction; they did it in the Depression—another hard times; and they doing it now" (*AMJP*, p. 197). Like a prophetess who lives to see what she foretells, Miss Jane places her testimony in a continuous tradition. And like an experienced, eloquent storyteller, Miss Jane fuses the thing told—the passage to leadership and action—with the process of telling it. She nurtures her audience's awareness slowly and inexorably as if, like leadership, awareness is a natural force growing and evolving in its own time according to its special rhythm.

Jane also deliberately holds back the leader's identity for awhile. For her purposes, his individual qualities are important chiefly insofar as they advance or retard his metamorphosis into "the One," the potential contemporary leader sought by the people in the quarters. "Anytime a child is born, the old people look in his face and ask him if he's the One" (*AMJP*, p. 197). This scrutiny of the newborn is more the pursuit of a leader than a response to someone's already evident, predetermined destiny. "People and time bring forth leaders" (*AMJP*, p. 226), Jane later tells an impatient Jimmy Aaron, and, in his case, the people nurture him in paradoxical ways. On the one hand, they make sure he hears and absorbs their stories, their folklore, and their history; they also encourage him to master the written word so he can write their letters. But they communicate his status as "the One" implicitly, intuitively, silently. "No, no, no," Jane assures those listening to her, "we never told it to him like I'm telling it to you now; we just looked at him hard" (*AMJP*, p. 206). The people are rigorous and even puritanical in their demands on Jimmy. They know they are preparing him to call on them to participate in dangerous acts of change in the future.

Jimmy's roots are in the quarters. But his influence, like the leaves and branches of the tree in the old spiritual, reaches out to all African-Americans and all people who are nourished by courage in the struggle for justice. In her performance Miss Jane relies on the rhythms of call-and-response and sees that storytelling "is in itself a small though necessary action in the Negro struggle for freedom."[27] She changes an informal occasion into a ritual in which she bears formal witness to Jimmy's revelation and eventual martyrdom as "the

One." As one of those who calls him, she responds to his leadership and asks others to follow him, too. But she recounts all this gently enough so that those who either were not present or who, being present, chose not to respond now may be inspired to act bravely in another time or place. At the very least, her testamental references to her audience and its historical and/or imaginative experience seek a preliminary commitment of witness.

Over and over again in "The Quarters" Jane shifts pronouns using *you* as counterpoint to *I* and *they*, and as symbolic complement to *we*. Characteristically, she is scrupulous about the partial extent to which her *yous* expand the community. For example, of the old people's call to the newborn, she says: "No, they don't say it out loud like I'm saying it to you now." She respects the boundaries of her community and the differences among its members. She does not expect her storytelling to make her and her audience (readers, too) one. That would be antithetical to her love of unpredictable, different, spontaneous and, sometimes, even crazy human behavior. But she does try to help her audience, listeners and readers alike, to "just feel it" (*AMJP*, p. 197).

Sometimes *you* refers primarily to Jane's immediate, physically present audience, secondarily to the already identified subsequent audiences of the history teacher's students, and, finally, to unspecified others. "I write for the black youth of the South," Gaines has said echoing the teacher's sentiments, "and I write for the white youth of the South so they can better understand themselves."[28] Jane's observations on the perverse renewal of the plantation landscape call black and, especially, white southerners to awaken from moral complacency. She tells angrily how Robert Samson hands out land with black sharecroppers' cabins on it to greedy Cajuns with their plows. "That's why coming down here now, you see cane and corn where houses was twelve, fifteen years back." Even so, life goes on among black folks in these quarters, though few on the outside hear of it. "But they've had a many babies born here, and many old people have died here, *you hear me*" (*AMJP*, p. 204, my italics). Jane's audience from the quarters sees and feels these conditions, like she does, because of experience. But white folks nearby or passing through and black folks with little or no knowledge of the plantation's "scheme of things" might see fields of corn and cane and not know that a world is being plowed under without a trace.[29] Here, seeing and hearing become believing through the agency of Jane's emphatic mnemonic voice.

Enough of Jane's *yous* include everyone—"Of course, I want the world to read my work"[30]—to create an inclusive context of citizenship and responsibility. When Jane talks about Yoko's expulsion from the Samson place because her son marches in a Baton Rouge civil rights demonstration, she forces everyone to blink at the blinding chifforobe mirror on top of the departing wagonload of belongings. "It flashed on you, too, if you didn't get out the way" (*AMJP*, pp. 219-20), and she makes sure there is no hiding place. She brings anyone interested to church with her on 'Termination Sunday, but she contracts *you* to mean local black folks as she marks the differences between Jimmy's way of talking and the turgid speech of the "long-head boy" who comes with him to recruit her for a civil rights action. Soon again she expands *you* to include everyone now willing to walk with her to Bayonne as that segregated town existed not too long ago. "Do you know Bayonne at all?" she asks those unfamiliar with her parish, black and white, before she describes Jim Crow conditions. She fears that the official, degrading terms of her past— "White, yes; but nothing for colored" (*AMJP*, p. 228)—are becoming historically remote, unremembered by the teacher's students and by future generations of African-Americans, and unfelt by white Americans.

Her ensuing *yous* call white Americans to imaginative participation in the past and present lives of black southerners. Throughout "The Quarters" Jane's shifting *yous* keep everyone alert to the choices made with language as individuals perform life's many small, significant actions. Variously, she asks the vernacular question crucial to every person's unfolding, always emerging voice and story: "Who you for?" (*AMJP*, p. 228). Certainly, her complex use of *you* crosses every conceivable line between what one person experiences and another only imagines. "The white people had a fountain," she tells us, "one of them white fountains *you* have in most places. A shiny little thing to drink from, a shiny little knob to turn" (*AMJP*, p. 229, my italics). Then, *you* meant white, not black, but by the end of her story *you* includes both black and white. As we do not know yet but will discover when we go with her to Bayonne, Jane's concrete vivid description comes from direct experience. For she goes and drinks from that fountain despite a prohibition so vicious and violent that her Jimmy is murdered to preserve it not long before she tells her story.

Jane does not claim it, and the editor does not either, directly, but it is possible that Jimmy's murder and the people's action, undertaken before and carried through after his death, motivate her to tell her story from the summer of 1962 to early 1963. The young history teacher urges her to tell him her story "for several years" before 1962. Each time she declines. In "The Quarters" she dates Jimmy's last return some months after "that bus with the Freedom Riders had just been destroyed" (*AMJP*, p. 217), so he is killed close to the time the history teacher shows up again, "when school closed for the summer in 1962" (*AMJP*, p. vii). It is also possible that Jimmy's death and the integration of the drinking fountain happen during the eight or nine months it takes Jane to tell her story. Her sessions take place on-and-off, and it would be in character for her and, by her example, the editor to avoid the obvious temptation to dramatize Jimmy's killing. Probably, the events persuade Jane to tell her story because they confirm eloquently that any story of her life would be the urgent story of her people, from Ned Douglass to Jimmy, to all those gathered around her in the living moment of her storytelling.

Regardless of the date of Jimmy's murder, Jane marks the still intensely felt nearness of that time with a return to *I* and *we*. Her *yous* have invited anyone willing to be a witness into her real and symbolic congregation. Significantly, in an act restoring Big Laura's place in the lineage of leaders celebrated by her story, Jane tells of the young black women who inspire her while Jimmy is away serving his apprenticeship with the Reverend Martin Luther King and his lieutenants. Waiting for Jimmy, Miss Jane is rejuvenated by the heroic actions of Rosa Parks,[31] Autherine Lucy, and another unidentified young girl whose sacrifices for school integration go together with "the ribbon in her hair" and her "sweet little face" (*AMJP*, p. 216). Telling of Jimmy's return, Jane concentrates on recreating the quarters' actual response to his call for nonviolent action. Earlier she revoices his speech to the church on 'Termination Sunday. Now, telling of his visit to the church the following Sunday, the day before his murder, Jane voices, as if it were an act of consciousness in the present, the words in her mind while Jimmy speaks. "I sat there looking at Jimmy, thinking: Jimmy, Jimmy, Jimmy, Jimmy, Jimmy. It's not that they don't love you, Jimmy; it's not that they don't want believe in you; but they don't know what you talking about. You talk of freedom, Jimmy" (*AMJP*, p. 234). And she continues in a passage both loving and critical of her people, these reluctant black folks. However, she talks to Jimmy silently. The "black veil," "black quilts," "black curtains" she imagines covering the people's eyes, bodies, and windows muffle her voice, too, that Sunday morning.

As she reenters the historical moment, Jane realizes and accepts her kinship with the people's condition of silence and fear. "But, look at me acting high and mighty. Don't the black curtain hang over my window, don't the black veil cover my face? And maybe, now, because my arms too weak to push the quilt down the bed I tell myself I'm brave enough to go to Bayonne" (*AMJP*, p. 235). Because we know her courage and scrupulous honesty, her self-doubts strike an authentic chord. She also recapitulates and reconsiders her judgment of others. "How could I know?" she asks, aware that some in her audience may not know yet that her reading of the people as cowardly or unready was proven false that Monday morning; aware, too, that those who are from the quarters know the story ends differently from her expectation. Her admission that she was wrong extends her authority from the Bayonne demonstration to this moment of storytelling in the continuous present. Moreover, because black people now drink from the water fountain in Bayonne does not mean injustice is ended. The struggle goes on during and after the time when Miss Jane tells her story, and the presence of her voice and words on tape and on the page keeps open the urge toward change felt by those who hear and read her story.

In her reexperience of the night before Jimmy's murder, Miss Jane talks to her belongings, even calls her rocking chair and looking glass *you*. Her willingness to go with her idiosyncratic impulses and her sense of experience as open, of things never completely solved, lead to an intimate confiding tone of voice. "When you get to be a hundred and eight or a hundred and nine you forget what scared is" (*AMJP*, p. 241), she tells us, but how would we know? We do not, but again her *you* respects us enough to declare us witnessing, imaginative participants in her experience. She calls us to make her story ours, to collaborate. It is work, her *yous* insist, to hear a story. Who knows, to turn *Invisible Man*'s question into a refrain, but that you will be called on to tell your story? And when that happens, which of us will be ready to speak for Jane as truly as she speaks for us?

This is the consequence and the challenge of Miss Jane Pittman's storytelling. Nowhere are the letter and spirit of collaboration subtler or stronger than in the last words of her story. It is as if she draws her listeners and readers in close; at this point you and I have a chance to become the potential *we* implied by Jane's repeated, shifting, various *yous*. Like the people in the quarters the morning of the demonstration in Bayonne, we make the choice as individuals. Having achieved intimacy with her audience, Miss Jane finishes her tale in a manner reminiscent of the dry bleached bones of slave tales and spirituals. She speaks of I and we, calls the names of those who figure in her story's ending, and invites all of us to join her congregation of saints.[32] Her account includes both those who walk up the quarters toward the car going to Bayonne and those who, frightened that this defiant act will uproot them from their homes, remain behind. Those who go are frightened, too; and though this civil rights action is collective, each person who goes makes a tough, trembling, individual decision. "They was walking like every last one of them was by himself and any little noise could turn him around" (*AMJP*, p. 243). "Ain't gonna let nobody turn me around" is the refrain of an old freedom song from slavery days revivified by the civil rights movement, and in both contexts Jane knows how strenuous it is to live out the meaning of these words.

Meanwhile, she is scrupulously honest, as if only the truth frees her to recreate the struggle. "Probably half of the people was still down there," she remembers, distinguishing the swelling group of those who are going from the others who are not. But once Robert Samson drives up with news of Jimmy's murder and orders the people to go back to the quarters, the importance of this distinction between the two groups of black folks dissolves. Each and every black person becomes "all us," because under pressure, Robert sees black folks as a series of undifferentiated, unindividualized projections. "Go home," he says in a command, with a predicate and an absent, merely implied subject. But these black individuals coalesce as a people for

Jane, and she challenges Robert in her voice and their name. " 'You mean, get off, don't you?' I said." Robert refuses to take the bait. " 'I mean go on back home,' he said." But they are home, and Robert's small ambiguity is all one young man needs to declare his intention to commit an act of defiance.

> "I'm going to Bayonne, me," Strut's boy said.
> "I'll follow Alex," I said. (*AMJP*, p. 243).

Jane's word "follow" acknowledges Alex's spontaneous emergent leadership, and, in turn, he is moved to call all the black folks gathered in front of Robert Samson. " 'Them who want go to Bayonne, let's go to Bayonne,' Alex said. 'Let's go to Bayonne even if we got to come back here to nothing.' " Failing to face down Alex, Robert enlists Jane on the basis of common sense. " 'You know better,' Robert said to me," when *he* should know better than to speak those words to her. In response, Jane affirms Alex's call, not Robert's command, and she puts things in a historical spiritual context. " 'Just a little piece of him is dead,' I said. 'The rest of him is waiting for us in Bayonne. And I will go with Alex.' " Her declaration reminds the others gently, unintimidatingly that she has responsibilities to black people in and beyond these quarters. As storyteller, too, Miss Jane Pittman clings to the utterable truth. "Some of the people," she recounts—some of these are present as she tells her story—"backed away from me when I said this, but the braver ones started for the road" (*AMJP*, pp. 243-44).

To the end Jane's voice accepts kinship with every person in the quarters, even though some of them decide not to participate in the demonstration. Not only that, at the end Jane risks the pain and complexity of contact with Robert Samson. Her last words, under-stated as any highly charged experience tends to be in the telling, are a masterful expression of her life and story:

> Me and Robert looked at each other there a long time, then I went by him. (*AMJP*, p. 244)

As she tells her story, Jane's former action flows through her, and her voice, now an extension of that silent human contact she insists on, softens and unspeakably intensifies the confrontation. Jane affirms a bond of kinship and equality with Robert in the act of denying his authority. The meaning is simple and complex; the language so finely wrought that the grace, resistance, and courage of Jane's struggle beat the rhythm of continuity into her words. Her voice suspends time for her and Robert and for us before she sets it flowing again by her eloquent gesture. Because of her integrity in her moment of bodily action and her burning, purging honesty in her moment of storytelling, Jane's closing words are an implied call for engagement with the world.

Jane is not afraid that her act of acknowledgment diminishes the force of her voice for those young blacks who will be the tape's primary audience. She teaches them and the rest of us that gains achieved through action that necessarily divides people may be worth winning only if the human bond remains unbroken. From the introduction we know that Jane Pittman returns to the Samson plantation after Bayonne. We know that Robert does not throw those who demonstrate off his place. He, too, responds to Jane's call. We know that she dies in this landscape made home by blood and bones and breath. Meanwhile, her voice continues to ascend in response to the call of a new generation as, previously, her body and spirit rose up in response to Jimmy's call. Her voice calls all to become kin. Through the offices of the editor's and Gaines's form Jane Pittman's voice reaches the printed page in a free flight from the African-American oral tradition. There, in the open spaces between the written words, we hear that voice speaking and calling still.

5

I wanted to smell that Louisiana earth, feel that Louisiana sun, sit under the shade of one of those Louisiana oaks, search for pecans in that Louisiana grass in one of those Louisiana yards next to one of those Louisiana bayous, not far from a Louisiana river. *I wanted to see on paper* those Louisiana black children walking to school on cold days while yellow Louisiana busses passed them by. *I wanted to see on paper* those black parents going to work before the sun came up and coming back home to look after their children after the sun went down. *I wanted to see on paper* the true reason why those black fathers left home — not because they were trifling or shiftless — but because they were tired of putting up with certain conditions. *I wanted to see on paper* the small country churches (schools during the week), and I wanted to hear those simple religious songs, those simple prayers—that devotion. (It was Faulkner, I think, who said that if God were to stay alive in the country, the blacks would have to keep Him so.) And I wanted to hear that Louisiana dialect—that combination of English, Creole, Cajun, Black. For me there's no more beautiful sound anywhere—unless, of course—you take exceptional pride in "proper" French or "proper" English. I wanted to read about the true relationship between whites and blacks—about the people that I had known.[33]

When Ernest Gaines confesses his love for the Louisiana of his experience, he simultaneously declares his craft. He brings into existence the world of his fiction, and creates his characters from the Louisiana dust. Through the act of writing Gaines reexperiences the landscape on a primary sensuous level. His repeated incantations of the word Louisiana transport him to the place; once there, he puts on paper the historical but alterable society that exists in the midst of nature's abiding reality. And the instrument behind the passage of the spoken word to the page is the writer's healing human voice. Like his storyteller, Miss Jane Pittman, and his editor, the young history teacher, Gaines breaks down the barriers between his voice and the voices of his people, his characters. He has heard them all and, writing, hears them still, talking, living their lives, and telling their stories. As a writer for his people, Gaines keeps faith with the oral tradition—a tradition of responsibility and change, and, despite violent opposition, a tradition of citizenship. In turn, his novel's spirit of call-and-response invites readers to pick up the loose ends, join in the storytelling, and, like Miss Jane Pittman, come home.

NOTES

1. Ralph Ellison, *Going to the Territory* (New York: Random House, 1986), pp. 240-41.

2. Ralph Ellison, "That Same Pain, That Same Pleasure: An Interview," *Shadow and Act* (New York: Random House, 1964), pp. 3-24.

3. Ernest J. Gaines quoted in " 'This Louisiana Thing That Drives Me': An Interview with Ernest J. Gaines," by Charles H. Rowell, *Callaloo* 1, no. 3 (May 1978), 41. This special issue of *Callaloo* deserves mention also because it includes both "Miss Jane and I" and "Home: A Photo-Essay" by Ernest J. Gaines and an early excerpt from his novel-in-progress then

called *A Revenge of Old Men,* subsequently much revised and published in 1983 as *A Gathering of Old Men.*

4. Gaines, "Miss Jane and I," pp. 24-25, my italics.

5. Michael S. Harper, "Gains," *Images of Kin: New and Selected Poems* (Urbana: University of Illinois Press, 1977), p. 60.

6. *New York Times Book Review* (June 11, 1978), 13.

7. Gaines interview, *Callaloo,* p. 41.

8. Ernest J. Gaines, *Bloodline* (1968; rpt., New York: W. W. Norton, 1976), p. 134. This volume will be cited hereafter as *B.* For a discussion of the relation between voice and change, see my "Hearing Is Believing: The Landscape of Voice in Ernest Gaines's *Bloodline,*" *Callaloo* 7, no. 1 (Winter 1984), 86-112.

9. Gaines interview, *Callaloo,* p. 42.

10. *New York Times Book Review* (June 11, 1978), p. 13.

11. Kate Chopin, *The Awakening* (1899; rpt., New York: Capricorn Books, 1964), p. 33.

12. *Fiction!: Interviews with Northern California Novelists,* ed. Dan Tooker and Roger Hofheins (New York: Harcourt Brace Jovanovich/William Kaufmann, 1976), p. 95.

13. *New York Times Book Review* (June 11, 1978), p. 44, my italics.

14. Gaines interview, *Fiction!,* p. 95.

15. Ernest J. Gaines to the author in an unpublished interview in June 1974. As Moussorsky rendered the texture of one art form (painting) into another (music), so Gaines brings the texture and form of the oral tradition to life on the page.

16. Gaines interview, *Callaloo,* p. 34.

17. Ibid., pp. 35, 36.

18. Gaines interview, *Fiction!,* p. 89.

19. Gaines interview, *Callaloo,* p. 37.

20. Gaines interview, *Fiction!,* pp. 89-90.

21. Gaines interview, *Callaloo,* p. 37.

22. *Lay My Burden Down: A Folk History of Slavery,* ed. B. A. Bodkin (Chicago: University of Chicago Press, 1945), pp. ix, 271. On the differences between novel and film versions of *The Autobiography of Miss Jane Pittman,* see my "Image-Making: Tradition and the Two Versions of *The Autobiography of Miss Jane Pittman,*" *Chicago Review* 29, no. 2 (Autumn 1977), 45-62.

23. Dennis Tedlock, *The Spoken Word and the Work of Interpretation* (Philadelphia: University of Pennsylvania Press, 1983); see ch. 13, "Ethnography as Interaction: The Storyteller, the Audience, the Fieldworker, and the Machine," pp. 285-301.

24. Ernest J. Gaines, *The Autobiography of Miss Jane Pittman* (New York: Dial Press, 1971), p. vii. This volume will be cited hereafter as *AMJP*.

25. Zora Neale Hurston, *Their Eyes Were Watching God* (1937; rpt., Urbana: University of Illinois Press, 1978), p. 18.

26. Tedlock, *Spoken Word;* see his discussion of the Zuni storyteller, Andrew Peynetsa, particularly the episode of the bottle-necked gourd in his tale.

27. Ellison, *Shadow and Act*, p. 142.

28. Ernest J. Gaines to the author during a conversation on May 18, 1985, in Baton Rouge, La.

29. Gaines returns expansively to his theme of a world plowed under in *A Gathering of Old Men* (New York: Knopf, 1983), especially Johnny Paul's speech on p. 92.

30. Gaines interview, *Callaloo*, p. 50.

31. In the unpublished interview I did with Gaines in 1974, he commented that Rosa Parks's refusal to give up her seat was one of the "heroic acts of the twentieth century."

32. On the matter of who is eligible for membership in the black congregation of saints, and why, see "When de Saints Go Ma'ching Home" in *The Collected Poems of Sterling A. Brown* (New York: Harper and Row, 1980), pp. 26-30; see also Robert B. Stepto's "'When de Saints Go Ma'ching Home': Sterling Brown's Blueprint for a New Negro Poetry," *Kunapipi* 4, no. 1 (1982), 93-105.

33. Gaines, "Miss Jane and I," p. 28, my italics.

CHAPTER 7

The Hoop of Language: Politics and the Restoration of Voice in *Meridian*

1

"I have experienced a revolution," Alice Walker writes in 1973, "unfinished, without question, but one whose new order is everywhere on view in the South." Walker's experience of revolutionary change intensifies her preoccupation "with the spiritual survival, the survival *whole* of [her] people."[1] In *Meridian* Walker pursues the African-American subconscious through the inner voice of a young black woman. She confronts the desperation of the late 1960s and early 1970s when, despite the successes of the civil rights movement, Black Elk's words seemed a fitting epigraph for the chaos of America. "The nation's hoop is broken and scattered,"[2] he said, grieving over the violent end of his people's dream. On a preliminary page of *Meridian*, Walker uses Black Elk's words to announce the political and spiritual desolation that must be overcome in the lives of individuals and society. Symptomatically, for her generation, the hoop of language—that continuum of voice going back to slavery and embodied in fiction by *The Autobiography of Miss Jane Pittman*—was broken and scattered. During the 1960s, as James Alan McPherson notes in "Elbow Room," words "seemed to have become detached from emotion and no longer flowed to the rhythm of passion."[3] That is the condition Walker and her character seek to overcome in *Meridian* as, together, they work to restore language, self, and nation.

For Walker and Meridian, silence and solitude become an essential prologue to speech and social action. Like Invisible Man, though for different reasons and in a different context, Meridian suspends the pursuit of eloquence. Like Zora Neale Hurston, Walker is a friend to her character. But she does not tell the story in a frame directly associated with the oral tradition. For one thing, she knows that Meridian, though brave and eloquent, is too preoccupied with her survival and the struggle of the people she works among, to focus on telling her story. For another thing, Meridian goes in search of a loving political voice after she finds that revolutionary rhetoric is often a mask for hate and emptiness and that the debased political language of the late 1960s upholds the condition of violence, egotism, and injustice she and her radical contemporaries seek to overthrow. To heal her soul and restore the spirit of words, Meridian listens and responds to the voices of the dead, particularly those black and Native American ancestors who haunt Walker's Georgia as they did Jean Toomer's. Consequently, the story unfolds gradually through visions and in remembered snatches of song and speech stitched together by Meridian's meditative political voice. And for her part, Alice Walker's pursuit of intimacy with her readers begins in her relationship with Meridian.

Meridian Hill is "an exemplary, flawed revolutionary"[4] for her time. In the tradition of runaway slaves who became conductors on the underground railroad, she believes that "escape for the body and freedom for the soul [go] together."[5] Therefore, according to Walker, she is a "revolutionary worth following." As a novelist, Walker *follows* Meridian by taking her form from the labyrinth of Meridian's mind. "I wanted to do something like a crazy quilt, or like *Cane*," she says, "something that works on the mind in different patterns." Or "like a collage," she adds, "like the work of one of my favorite artists, Romare Bearden."[6] Like the gifted, often unknown black women who design and sew crazy quilts and like Toomer and, especially, Bearden, Walker's technique is "eloquent of the sharp breaks, leaps in consciousness, distortion, paradoxes, reversals, telescoping of time and surreal blending of styles, values, hopes and dreams which characterize much of Negro American history."[7] Walker's discontinuous, apparently incongruous voices fuse personal, racial, and national history with myth so that, as Calvin Tomkins observes of Bearden's *Odysseus Collages*, "the images that he chooses and the manner in which he places them create vibrations, waves that carry us into regions not *visited but remembered,* dimly or vividly, from previous experience with the myth."[8] In *Meridian's* case the myth is the myth of deliverance. True rescue, as Meridian Hill's story demonstrates, lies within those reaches of self beyond the babel of fashionably militant tongues.

To Meridian voice is a blessing and call-and-response an act performed in kinship with what is sacred to self, others, and the world. While those around her demand *correct* responses, she struggles to know the *right* response to dilemmas of personal and political experience. The ascent aspired to in Walker's title and Meridian's name requires a long painful descent into what Zora Neale Hurston calls the "infinity of conscious pain."[9] Although the effort alienates her from her contemporaries and brings her to the brink of madness and death, Meridian practices a politics that is "an expression of love" and not "politicized hate." Like her forebears in history and fiction, Meridian learns to tell false voices from true ones. She begins at home with her own voice. Like her rhetorically militant contemporaries, Meridian knows the tricks of speech, the *retrick* of a glib, false call-and-response. But to her, possession of a true personal voice is bound up with the creation of an authentic public and political voice. Like Janie Crawford, Meridian distinguishes true from false texts in her intimate life, and like Invisible Man and Miss Jane Pittman, she pursues connections between her inmost individual identity and her responsibility as a citizen.

2

Like Ellison in *Invisible Man,* Walker makes the chronology of her novel's opening mostly a matter of consciousness. She follows Meridian's mind back and forth through time in response to what is happening in the immediate present. But the historical narrative moment anticipates the nation's Bicentennial and leads Meridian to reconsider the old and new meaning of America's fate as a revolutionary society. Namely, Truman Held, Meridian's former civil rights coworker and briefly, *abortively,* her lover, interrupts work on his Bicentennial statue of Crispus Attucks and drives all night from New York to Georgia to see Meridian. Their encounter prompts her to reexperience the significance of language for personality and politics. In their conversation Meridian tries to persuade Truman to open the interior of his mind and memory:

> "I know you grieve by running away. By pretending you were never there."
> "When things are finished it is best to leave."
> "And pretend they were never started."
> "Yes."
> "But that's not possible." (*M*, pp. 13-14)

Ironically, Truman's affirmation closes out dialogue, whereas Meridian's denial calls for consciousness in which the past informs the present moment.

Truman's silence is evasive, but in her reverie Meridian reenacts the principle of open consciousness learned the hard way nearly ten years before. Truman's clichés, characteristic of many emotional lives in his generation, remind Meridian of similar political evasions from the chaotic years of the late 1960s. In her mind she hears the two direct, apparently simple, self-evident questions posed by some black radical comrades in a former time of "extreme violence, against black dissidents, of the federal government and police" (*M*, p. 15), when the officially sanctioned policies of the state seemed to partake of politicized hate. To join the self-proclaimed revolutionaries Meridian must answer *yes* to both questions. She affirms easily and at once her "willingness to die for the Revolution." But she cannot answer the second question: "Will you kill for the Revolution?" Not because she necessarily opposes revolutionary violence, but because instinctively and viscerally, without the intimacy of language and experience that allowed Janie Crawford's "tongue" to be in her "friend's mouf,"[10] "Meridian's tongue could not manage" (*M*, p. 14).

Unlike the others, she cannot answer simply as an individual and a contemporary because for her social and political change is bound up with love and with the witnessing, participatory form that belongs to a true community. All the same, like her fellow radicals, Meridian views America as a society in extreme crisis, racially and otherwise, and she is disturbed by her interior dissent from their call. She looks for flaws in herself, not in the vague, unrooted, arrogant phrase, *the* revolution. Consequently, civil war breaks out within her, personified by "a small voice that screamed: 'Something's missing in me. Something's *missing'* " (*M*, p.14). Meridian is not a coward, far from it, but for her speech is action, the word her sacred bond with herself and her people, her history and theirs. She wishes she could join her contemporaries' call to arms. But because she takes them and their talk of revolution seriously, Meridian meditates on the question at hand in a silent call-and-response of the soul.

While Meridian struggles for the *right* response, the others wait impatiently for the *correct* response. In the break between their call and her response, Meridian discovers why her voice resists her comrades' expectations. Her inability to declare that she will kill for the revolution grows out of experiences in *her* past and the images and voices inside her from *the* African-American past. In her silence she is "not holding on to something from the past, but *held* by something in the past" (*M*, p. 14). Unlike many of her contemporaries, Meridian does not surrender to that easily manipulated instantaneity in which "television became the repository of memory" (*M*, p. 21). Instead, her memory mediates between her interrogation in the present situation and those "old black men in the South who, caught by surprise in the eye of a camera, never shifted their position but looked directly back." For these men, whose breed Jean Toomer found in Georgia and Ernest Gaines in Louisiana, courage was a condition of being, a silent autonomy in response to the temptation to present a synthetic face to the world. Never easy, their stoicism hints at an inner ease and confidence, and their eloquent silence encourages Meridian to trust her refusal to speak in a pandering voice. In her mind she also sees and hears "young girls singing in a country choir, their hair shining with brushings and grease, their voices the voices of angels"; girls like these inspired Miss Jane Pittman with their bravery. Like Toomer, Meridian believes "she could actually *hear*" the singers' souls (*M*, p. 14). These images and voices embody Meridian's conscious, reciprocal relationship with the past. She cannot imagine killing except in collaboration with those humane black Americans whose lives are the comfort of her soul. For her sake and theirs, she speculates about the cultural consequences of violent politics in an inner voice of moral imagination: "If they committed murder—and to her even revolutionary murder was murder—what would the music be like?" (*M*, p. 15).

As she feels the hostile silence of her interlocutors, Meridian descends to another painful level of being. Here, too, she struggles against the loss of love she associates with failing to respond to the wishes of others. In her reverie she again sits in church "drunk as usual with the wonderful music, the voices themselves almost making the words of the songs meaningless." She basks in her father's sweet voice while resisting his wooing of death. But her mother, like the "revolutionary cadre" of the 1960s, demands Meridian's unconditional surrender to authority. In this case authority is not political or spiritual but narrowly religious. Seeing her daughter's tears, Mrs. Hill presses her to "acknowledge Him as our Master." Then as now, Meridian "sat mute, watching her friends walking past her bench, accepting Christ, acknowledging God as their Master" (*M*, p. 16). As a consequence, she loses her mother's love but loves her mother in return because of her feeling that it is "death not to love one's mother." To survive, she lives with her mother's scorn as she will bear the rejection of her radical contemporaries rather than barter her soul for a conditional love.

Called back to the present "from a decidedly unrevolutionary past," Meridian struggles to overcome the paradoxical conflict between politics and personality. Her contemporaries, she realizes, "made her ashamed of the past, and yet all of them had shared it," whereas she keeps faith with the sustaining personal warmth of the past as a touchstone of contemporary politics. But she does not reject her comrades; "she felt she loved them," even though "love was not what they wanted, it was not what they needed" (*M*, p. 17). As she does with her mother (and also the young men who pursue her sexually), Meridian tries not to offend or alienate, even if she cannot please. Using the familiar pattern of call-and-response, she seeks common ground in the chaos and violence of American life. Slowly, she becomes the lead voice, and the others join her call believing she is about to announce her willingness to "kill for the Revolution":

"I know I want what is best for black people."
"That's what we all want!"
"I know there must be a revolution. . . ."

"Damn straight!"
"I know violence *is* as American as cherry pie!"
"Rap on!"
"I know nonviolence has failed." (*M*, p. 18)

Meridian understands the struggle and the lingo. She has marched and been abused, beaten, and jailed, and she has gone back out on the line. She knows how to speak to her contemporaries and for them — so much so that they answer her rhythmic, repetitive *I knows* with one voice.

Her words invoke the simplicities of the current situation, but her pause implies its complexities as well as her refusal to enter the country of false eloquence. But Meridian's audience rejects the intimate, contemplative note her brief silence brings to the dialogue. They seek capitulation from her, not conversation with her. But their failure to let her respond individually to the collective call — "Then you will kill for the Revolution, not just die for it?" (*M*, p. 18) — chases her back to the private region of her mind. "I don't know" she says, and her truthful answers to this and subsequent questions make her an outcast. She is the victim of psychological political aggression reminiscent of Janie Starks's wifely experience in *Their Eyes Were Watching God*: "Mah own mind had tuh be squeezed and crowded out tuh make room for yours in me."[11] Yet Meridian is not entirely a casualty. When a former friend among the revolutionaries asks her condescendingly, "What will you do? Where will you go?" Meridian keeps faith with those images and voices that persist in the depths of her mind as companions to her identity:

"I'll go back to the people, live among them like Civil Rights workers used to do."
"You're not serious?"
"Yes," she said. "I am serious." (*M*, p. 18)

Unlike the others, because of her past (and her self-restoring sense of *the* past), Meridian cannot even pretend to disconnect political work from personal experience, particularly her surrender of her child and the related loss of her mother as psychological kin. Now in a simple courageous voice Meridian tells this hostile audience her choice: a life and politics committed to love and creation instead of hate and violence. She still does not know definitely whether or not she should or could kill for the revolution or for any other cause. But she does know that her answer must be her people's answer, and she cannot discover either in New York. (In her glossary Walker gives *southern* as a rare meaning for meridian, and Meridian is the name of the Mississippi town in which the murdered black civil rights worker, James Cheney, grew up and was buried in 1964.) Like Jean Toomer who went to Georgia seeking a loving artistic voice, Meridian goes south in quest of a loving political voice, rooted in her life and the people's—what Robert Hayden, in his poem for Frederick Douglass, calls "this beautiful and terrible . . . needful thing" of freedom. But Meridian alters Hayden's idea of "lives grown out of [Douglass's] life."[12] Her new life will grow from the people, provided she is able "to see them, to be with them, to understand them *and herself*," while, true to her vision, they become next of kin "who now fed her and tolerated her and also, in a fashion, *cared* about her" (*M*, p. 19, my italics).

As Walker tells of Meridian's gradual personal revolution, her voice achieves a muted simplicity and eloquence. Her relationship with Meridian, like the people's, is sometimes tentative and always respectful of difference and otherness. Like a friend, she follows Meridian, sometimes up close in participation, and at other times from a distance in acts of witness, while Meridian digs out her story in response to her life's slow revolutionary trajectory after the sudden fits and starts of the 1960s. For although revolutions sometimes culminate in explosions, lasting change is prepared for gradually by grubby actions like those Meridian performs in one little southern town after another. And true revolutions are never finished; like Meridian's life and story, they illustrate an elliptical pattern of continual change.

In her form Walker experiments with the idea of revolution. Her narrative follows a meridian along which Meridian's "mind-voice directs the flow of thought and action."[13] By choice, Meridian lacks a platform and an audience, but as she absorbs the other characters' voices, they, too, become threads in the crazy quilt of the novel. Because so many of her characters, especially those of Meridian's generation, live in fragments, Walker's narrative collage is often deliberately attenuated, as if she were guiding readers through individual and national labyrinths. Nevertheless, *Meridian* is a meditation on wholeness and as such Walker's confession of faith. Its embrace of silence as a nest for speech protests against and overthrows false voices as the first act toward restoration of the word and the creation of genuine dialogue. By shunning the traditional office of storyteller, Walker, like Meridian, invites the "rest of them" (and us) to participate in a generation's unfinished personal and political work.

3

Jarringly, almost violently, Walker fires a succession of names at her readers in the no-man's land between Meridian's life in the present and her reconstruction of the past:

MEDGAR EVERS/JOHN F. KENNEDY/MALCOM X/
MARTIN LUTHER KING/ROBERT KENNEDY/CHE
GUEVARA/PATRICE LUMUMBA/GEORGE JACKSON/
CYNTHIA WESLEY/ADDIE MAE COLLINS/DENISE
MCNAIR/CAROLE ROBERTSON/VIOLA LIUZZO. (*M*, p. 21)

Like sounds from an automatic rifle, the slashes signify the political assassinations that open, close, and recapitulate the 1960s. The last five names belong to "those [four] black girls /blown up/ in that Alabama church"[14] in 1963 and a northern white woman shot to death while driving civil rights workers back to Selma after the march to Montgomery in 1965. All were private persons whose names Walker restores to consciousness. Others, too, are victims of violence, and in *Meridian* Walker explores the relationship between voice-lessness and the extremes of violence often visited on women and children. And among the young women in the novel an urge to violence sometimes shuts out the healing, sustaining presences from the past and leads to self-destructive acts performed in response to false inner voices.

The story of Wile Chile illustrates the obstacles in the way of Meridian's search for a usable voice. Apparently nameless, articulate only with curses, and visibly pregnant, Wile Chile embodies "how alone woman is, because of her body."[15] After Wile Chile is run over and killed by a speeder, the young women at Saxon College realize instinctively and inarticulately that their fate is bound up with hers. But in their rage at the president's refusal to let them use the college

chapel for the funeral, they turn on Sojourner, their protectress—
"the largest magnolia tree in the country," an abiding, animate,
magical maternal presence. Except for Meridian, the young women
no longer remember or care that their ancestors in slavery "claimed
the tree could talk, make music, was sacred to birds," and that "in
its branches, a hiding slave could not be seen" (*M*, pp. 31, 34). They
forget that the tree shields their lovemaking from detection and, as
a ritual ground, offers them solace and strength to offset their vulnerability as women.

Powerless, the young women strike against a living presence signifying womanly power as far back as slavery. For as Meridian learns
and shares, the Sojourner tree owes its magnificence to the severed
tongue of the slave woman, Louvinie—a master storyteller "whose
[family's] sole responsibility was the weaving of intricate tales with
which to entrap people who hoped to get away with murder" (*M*,
p. 31). In America, Louvinie's audience consists of the young Saxon
children who "adored her." The last story she is able to tell reverses
the familiar terms of slavery. In it, as written down later by one of
the older Saxon girls, a very black African man captures "little white
children," buries them alive up to their necks, and allows pet snakes
to make them playthings. This and perhaps other of Louvinie's "new
American stories" express her anger at captivity and also draw a
moral and political lesson for the next generation of slaveholders.
But the older Saxons fail to tell Louvinie that the youngest member
of her audience, "an only son, suffered from an abnormally small
and flimsy heart" (*M*, p. 32). In the midst of her tale, the boy has
a fatal heart attack, and as punishment, "Louvinie's tongue was
clipped out at the root" (*M*, p. 35). Mutely, she pleads for her tongue
lest the singer in her soul be lost forever. Then she ministers to her
severed tongue until, during the magically black sun of an eclipse,
she buries it beneath "a scrawny magnolia tree" that eventually
outgrows all the others even before her death. Among the Saxon
students in the 1960s only Meridian understands that Sojourner is
the living agent of Louvinie's voice and story—the dead slave's gift
of life and eloquence to the black women who come after her.
Spiritually, Meridian recognizes, Louvinie refuses to accept powerlessness or voicelessness, even though she is a slave who cannot speak.
Louvinie's Sojourner tree also commemorates Sojourner Truth, an

escaped slave who defied those white women who tried to deny her right to speak and whose eloquent call-and-response ("And a'n't I a woman?"[16]) electrified the 1853 Akron women's rights convention; like Louvinie, her mystical, earthy, sibylline voice exemplifies the struggle for wholeness. In her young womanhood, Meridian, too, like Hurston's Janie Crawford under the pear tree, experiences a oneness that is both cosmic and individual, imaginative and deeply sensuous.

But the young black women fail to respond to Meridian's lone dissenting voice. Though she "begged them to dismantle the president's house instead, in a fury of confusion and frustration they worked all night, and chopped and sawed down, level to the ground, that mighty, ancient, sheltering music tree" (*M*, p. 38). True to the story of Louvinie's tongue, the severed tree does not die. From the lives and stories of Louvinie and Sojourner Truth and the immense, intimate presence of the great blooming maternal tree comes a legacy of responsbility in response to oppression and injustice. Bred of the "fury of confusion and frustration," the students' act nevertheless signifies potentiality waiting to be rethought, revoiced, and refocused before personal or social revolution can occur. For when they cut down the Sojourner, these young women turn their anger against themselves and the black maternal tradition. Otherwise, they would have assaulted the literally forbidding authority of the president's house (his patriarchal tree).

For her part, Meridian's ability to speak truly follows from her willingness to identify her mother's false words and still love the person who brought her into the world. As she meditates on her childhood after the Sojourner is cut down, she hears her mother's old unsettling question. "Conscious always of a feeling of guilt, even as a child," Meridian confides in her mother; but in response "her mother would only ask: 'Have you stolen anything?' " (*M*, p. 39). In the past these words seemed mechanical, cruel, and immobilizing, but subsequently, when she reconsiders her mother's life, Meridian concludes that "it was for stealing her mother's serenity, for shattering her mother's emerging self that [she] felt guilty from the very first, though she was unable to understand how this could possibly be her fault." Her creativity "refused expression" because of her conviction that marriage and motherhood meant that "her *personal* life was over," Meridian's mother fights "a war against those to whom she could not express her anger or shout, 'It's not fair.' " But like the young women who chop down the Sojourner tree, Mrs. Hill displaces her anger. She uses a false voice and hands on values that have stifled her life. She speaks for her society and, in an act of perverse social allegiance, tells her daughter "things she herself did not believe" (*M*, pp. 40, 41, my italics).

For a while Meridian acts out her mother's distorted, determinist view of a black woman's fate. "Be sweet" is her mother's only sexual counsel, and because Meridian does not know the words are intended as "a euphemism for 'Keep your panties up and your dress down' " (*M*, p. 53), she ends up pregnant and married to a man she neither loves nor desires. Following her son's birth, she dreams "of ways to murder him" (*M*, p. 63). A year later when Meridian gives up her child to accept a scholarship to college, her mother tells her only "some kind of monster" would not want her child, "and no daughter of mine is a monster, surely" (*M*, p. 85). Characteristically, Mrs. Hill intimidates Meridian with an apologia for her life: " 'I have six children,' she continued self-righteously, 'though I never wanted to have any, and I have raised every one myself.' " To which Meridian's friend Delores responds flippantly: "You probably could have done the same thing in slavery" (*M*, p. 86). But as soon as Meridian is away from home, these words trouble her, for she knows that in slavery her mother "would not, automatically, have been allowed to keep [her children], because they would not have belonged to her but to the white person who 'owned' them all" (*M*, p. 87). Meridian's honesty replaces her mother's mutually wounding, compliant rationalizations, but she pays a terrible price. At times of strain, as she works to become a serious productive student, she hears a subterranean voice.

"Why don't you die? Why not kill yourself?" the voice asks in another of those questions that lead Meridian to reconsider the terms of her existence. Meridian recognizes this as truly and terribly "her own voice": "It was talking to her, and it was full of hate." Part of her calls for annihilation as a punishment for her failure to "live up to the standard of motherhood that had gone before" (*M*, p. 88). She overcomes the urge to suicide in the same way she overcame her previous impulse to kill her son. Then, after her husband left her and their child, the murder of four people, three of them children, at the local civil rights headquarters prompted Meridian to volunteer. Now, in her second year at Saxon, she joins the Atlanta Movement and chooses dangerous, nonviolent political action over Saxon's finishing school distractions and the turmoil of her mind. Rather than lose her life in a battle with her voice, she pursues a life of her own through participation in the civil rights struggle. In extremis, Meridian once again chooses the evolving wider world over the call to violence issued by the false voice in her heart. She recognizes that an absolutely final act of self-preoccupation like suicide is a paltry response to the universe around her and the world of feeling within.

In silent opposition to her voice of self-hate, she remembers moments of ecstatic oneness experienced beneath the Sojourner tree and, before that, at the Sacred Serpent, an Indian burial ground held in a trust of reverent ownership by her father but seized by the government and turned into a tourist attraction that, "now that it belonged to the public, was of course not open to Colored" (*M*, p. 48). As she knows the Sojourner partly through remnants of Louvinie's voice and story, she learned to revere the Sacred Serpent through stories told about her passionate great-grandmother, Feather Mae. Then, in Meridian's time, she and her father also experience ecstasy at the Sacred Serpent. But they have different responses to the experience. For him "the body seemed to drop away, and only the spirit lived, set free in the world. But she was not convinced. It seemed to her that it was a way the living sought to *expand the consciousness of being alive*, there where the ground about them was filled with the dead" (*M*, p. 51, my italics). Ecstasy confirms Meridian's belief in the possibility of fusing body and soul, life and death, in a way that intensifies experience. For her self-respect is bound up with respect for the ancestral presences that inhabit the earth and her consciousness. Moreover, the possibility of personal and sexual wholeness is confirmed by the presence of both the sheltering African-American maternal tree and the equally sheltering Native American paternal serpent. "Minuteness and hugeness"; "sorrow and ecstasy": these words are touchstones to memories of being and feeling that signify Meridian's communion with both African-American and Native American layers of the past in her consciousness.[17] Her continuing awakening fortifies her against extrinsic correspondences to the ragged, violent, maddening fragments of her consciousness. For now in her "waking moments" everywhere in Atlanta she witnesses a patchwork nightmare of violence against black children and old women, "their humility of a lifetime doing them no good." Even more terrifying, she sees interior lives ravaged into blankness: "She saw young black men of great spiritual beauty changed overnight into men who valued nothing" (*M*, p. 92).

Meridian also suffers. In her inner civil war she is "too driven to notice" that her hair is falling out or that "her vision sometimes blurred." But the parts of her being do not secede from the whole; somehow, she will live or die an indivisible woman. Meanwhile, as her body responds to the call of her mind's guilt, she feels another factor of stress, a new tension that is more unpredictable, volatile, and incalculable than the others she has experienced in personal and political life. "Besides," she thinks and Walker writes, as if the emotion were an afterthought in the maelstrom of Meridian's consciousness, "she was in love with Truman" (*M*, p. 94).

Walker's understatement conveys her generation's casual understanding of passion and, therefore, calls attention to the danger Meridian faces as a woman. Two years earlier Meridian worked with Truman on voter registration in her hometown. There, attacked by white officers of the law, she breaks her disciplined silence only with a cry in her mind, "and the scream was Truman's name." She is *held* by him then, but not in the grip of sexual passion; rather, her interior voice utters a birth pang for both of them. "What she meant by it was that they were at a time and a place in history that forced the trivial to fall away—and they were absolutely together" (*M*, p. 80). But although Meridian believed the trivial to have fallen away, the *personal* lives of those in the movement were often marked by stereotypes of the previous decade, the 1950s. Black and white students challenge segregation in the separate but unequal public arena of American society, yet their relations as men and women follow old patterns of male dominance and female subservience and sometimes victimization. Namely, when Meridian acts on the basis of an intensely passionate attachment to Truman, she discovers that he is essentially a *true man* still held by unreconstructed urges to power within the old dispensation.

Now, years later, Meridian works through painful memories. For her soul's sake, she does not forget her former too easy acceptance of Truman on his terms as "the conquering prince." Formerly, she imagined him having personal qualities commensurate with the courage he showed in the civil rights movement. But, in truth, Truman, with his French phrases and princely Ethiopian robe, acts as though his political commitment entitles him to be selfish, shallow, and self-indulgent in his private life as a man. For one thing, Truman construes his voice to be dominant and authoritative and misreads Meridian's subtle, simple statements as evidence of inexperience. On one occasion their divergent language prefigures the bitter, tragic consequences of the relationship.

> "Let's not go to the party," he pleaded. "Let's go back to the apartment. Everybody else is here, we'll be alone. I want you."
> "I love you," she said.
> "And we're going to the party, right?" Truman sat up and ran his fingers through his hair.
> "But do you understand?" Meridian asked. "I'm not a prude. Afraid, yes, but not a prude. One day soon we'll be together."
> "You're so young," said Truman, getting out and adjusting his robe. "I wish I could make you feel how beautiful it would be with me."
> "I feel it, I feel it!" cried Meridian taking his hand and walking up the street." (*M*, p. 100)

Truman interprets Meridian's unembarrassed declaration of love as merely a refusal. When she sends out more promise signals, Truman does not hear them, and he does not draw her out as a friend would by asking gently for her story. Instead, he stereotypes her and ignores her point about fear and love, her implied warning about the contingency of passion. At once inside and outside the moment, Meridian responds both to Truman and to her previous painful, empty, and *consequential* sexual experience. Her last words and her gesture of taking his hand promise intimacy in love and discourse, but at the party Truman pursues one of the seductive, white exchange students from the North. At the end of the evening when he takes Meridian home and she invites him in, he declines: " 'Maybe tomorrow night,' he said, stifling a yawn" (*M*, p. 102), in smug, callous disregard for *her* sexual need.

Later on, Truman and Meridian consummate their passion but still do not have a true conversation. "Come here, woman, I missed you," he declares on that occasion, but his command is fatuous and unnecessary, "since she was already lying, like a beached fish, across his lap" (*M*, p. 110). From Meridian's point of view, they do not make love; rather, "they fucked (she consciously thought of it as that)." Nevertheless, their sexual encounter, though casual for him, is consequential and traumatic for her. Afterward, "she remembered that he had not worn a condom—the only means of contraception she knew" (*M*, p. 111). She mentions none of this to Truman, and when she returns from the bathroom, he is gone, again without words or gesture. In their private lives neither Truman nor Meridian confronts the other as directly or effectively as they do in the public context of the civil rights movement—Truman because his macho solipsism makes him oblivious to Meridian; Meridian because her upbringing leads her to accept responsibility for sexual consequences as a woman's lot. She does not tell him she is pregnant; in the meantime he returns to the white exchange students. She decides to have an abortion and in an act of grief and rage at the doctor's coarse, criminal proposition has her tubes tied in self-punishment. Like the students who cut down the Sojourner, Meridian turns her anger against her own life-giving potential.

Months later, after the exchange students have left, Truman tries to resume things. Characteristically, his language betrays his assumption that his attention confers identity on Meridian. "Stone fox," he calls her, and "African woman." At first, she responds with an astonished, taut but uncombative civility. But he will not leave her alone. Grotesquely, he cites their sexual encounter as evidence of his prowess and his power to liberate her. "I can make you come," he blurts out. "I almost did it that time, didn't I?" As he continues, Meridian, perhaps remembering the undertaker's assistant from her girlhood, who seemed to fuck with a pornography of voice, "turned away, shame for him, for what he was revealing, making her sick" (*M*, p. 113).

As a last resort Meridian asks Truman to respect her privacy and be silent:

> "It's over. Let it stay."
> But he looked at her with eyes of new discovery.
> "You're *beautiful*," he whispered worshipfully. Then he said, urgently, "*Have* my beautiful black babies." (*M*, p. 113)

His voice puts language in the service of monstrous illusions. Invaded to the quick, Meridian abandons speech as an agent of communication. Truman is no longer someone she can listen or talk to; conversation is out of the question because he does not grant her even a minimal freedom from his narcissistic fantasies. At last, in direct action expressing her experience and identity as a human being and a black woman, she hits him with her book bag again and again in a refrain of wordless protest. This encounter is at once futile, fatal, and, finally, enabling: futile, because of Truman's shallowness, false pride, and hypocrisy, his failure to grasp or accept the responsibility that goes with being human; fatal, because as a man he exercises a certain power over other lives, especially women; and enabling because Meridian's instinctively violent response is therapeutic and restoring. Seeing and hearing that her words fail to penetrate Truman, she turns her anger outward silently and effectively. Taking her own advice, she retaliates against Truman's distorted masculine assertion of power. She will no longer allow the tree of her life and voice to be diminished by the words or actions of Truman or anyone else.

4

Meridian's extrinsic act of womanly self-assertion leads to interior rejuvenation and reconciliation. Without warning, as she is about to graduate, she experiences "blue spells" of body and soul. Characteristically, she does not talk about her condition but in the privacy of her mind "felt as if a warm, strong light bore her up and that she was a beloved part of the universe" (*M*, p. 117). Formerly, Meridian's feelings of benevolent oneness came in response to powerful, unfathomable natural presences like the Sacred Serpent or the Sojourner; now she is transported by a serene energy in her own being. Ecstasy's promise is illumination and intimacy, its cost frailty and illness. To heal her soul, Meridian risks her body. Because her mother is not there, she does the work of reconciliation with Miss Winter, a teacher from her hometown whose insistence on teaching jazz and spirituals and blues earns her the enmity of the college administration and marks her as one of those courageous black women from Meridian's childhood who were always "imitating Harriet Tub-man—escaping to become something unheard of" (*M*, p. 105).

As Miss Winter tends her, Meridian remembers an earlier occasion when the older woman intervened on her behalf. At a high school oratorical competition, "Meridian was reciting a speech that extolled the virtues of the Constitution and praised the superiority of The American Way of Life." In the middle of the speech she stops, seemingly because of a memory lapse but in reality, as she tries to explain to her mother, because "for the first time she really listened to what she was saying, knew she didn't believe it, and was so distracted by the revelation that she could not make the rest of her speech" (*M*, p. 120). Her mother does not listen; instead, she tells her daughter to trust in God. Coming upon Meridian, Miss Winter tells her, in effect, to trust her voice's impulse to halt a speech false to her sense of the truth. "It's the same one they made me learn when I was here," she tells Meridian, "and it's no more true now than it was then" (*M*, p. 120). To Meridian, then and now, Miss Winter, though single and childless, belongs to the tradition of nour-ishing, nurturing black women; she, too, has an identity in relation to African-American maternal history. Namely, her healing presence inspires Meridian's vision of her mother's place in the African-Amer-ican maternal lineage. "Mrs. Hill," Meridian now acknowledges, "had persisted in bringing them all (the children, the husband, the family, the race) to a point far beyond where she, in her mother's place, would have stopped" (*M*, p. 121). For the first time Meridian sees her mother as a *giant* in an impersonal historical way rather than in the child's accustomed sense of her parent as a magnified, remote but intensely personal presence. Almost despite her conscious intention, Mrs. Hill carries on the tradition she has not fully under-stood or accepted but has absorbed from her great-great-grandmother who three times stole back her sold-away children; from her great-grandmother who painted such lovely, arresting decorations on barns she was able to buy her family's freedom; and from her mother who at night trudged off to do others' washing so she could send her daughter to school.

Meridian does not tell this story of her maternal history to Miss Winter. But when she dreams that her mother is about to drop her into the sea—perhaps the equivalent of Mrs. Hill forcing Meridian to sink or swim alone in womanly matters of survival—Miss Winter comes forward and lovingly performs the motherly office:

> "Mama, I love you. Let me go," she whispered, licking the salt from her mother's black arms.
> Instinctively, as if Meridian were her own child, Miss Winter answered, close to her ear on the pillow, "I forgive you." (*M*, p. 123)

Unlike Janie in *Their Eyes Were Watching God*, who becomes autonomous only after she realizes that she hates her grandmother, Meridian breaks free only when she feels and declares her love for her mother. That bond, which she chooses freely in her time and place, allows her to call on her dream image of her mother to let her go. And Miss Winter responds in a voice able to mediate between Meridian and Mrs. Hill. She completes the ritual of exorcism that Mrs. Hill could not do with her daughter. Danger is bound up with intimacy, the dream implies, and having voiced love for her mother, Meridian prepares to enter the world on her terms. At stake is her place in the continuum of black women's struggle.

But as so often happens, Meridian's new kinship with her mother's generation costs her the allegiance of a contemporary. For at the moment of Meridian's reemergence, her friend and roommate, Anne-Marion, denies her. "I cannot afford to love you," she tells Meridian in an act of cruel calculation, and in her unearned surety passes absolute historical judgment. "Like the idea of suffering itself, you are obsolete" (*M*, p. 124). But despite her spoken renunciation, Anne-Marion cannot write off Meridian. On the contrary, after Meridian goes back South in disgrace with the cadre of polemical revolutionaries, Anne-Marion "discovered herself writing letters to her, making inquiries month after month to find out which town she lived in and to which address she should send her letters." She writes "out of guilt and denial and rage" (*M*, p. 124), but she writes. She begins to accept responsibility for the painful, shared story unfolding somewhere inside her and the others as well as Meridian. Somehow she knows that her act of denial actually affirms and sustains them both. Like that great music tree, the Sojourner, Meridian is strong enough to absorb the blows. Nevertheless, Meridian responds to Anne-Marion with silence, but it is the rich silence of potential responsiveness and collaboration. For she knows that in her generation the spoken word is still tethered to ideology, the written word too self-reflexively therapeutic to restore a reciprocal personal and political communication. Through her silence and her solitary life of action Meridian prepares a nest for the scarcely alive voices of her generation, a secret refuge where they can listen to the spirit of the word.

5

Meanwhile the promise of personality and politics turns into triviality and pathology in the lives of the characters and the nation. Truman marries Lynne Rabinowitz, "the last of the exchange students," but their vicarious, prurient motives doom the relationship and signal a general condition of emptiness. For Lynne, "the black people of the South were Art" (*M*, p. 128), and Truman gravitates toward the white exchange students because, in addition to fulfilling a long-tabooed sexuality, "they read *The New York Times*" (*M*, p. 141). Even before their young daughter, Camara, is sexually assaulted and murdered, Truman and Lynne separately look to Meridian for solace and strength. With her as a moral guide, they slowly come to see themselves and others in the world as individuals who happen to be black or white, male or female, not incidentally or deterministically but consequentially and dynamically. This acknowledgment of human personality leads to reconsideration of what it means to be black or white, male or female, in contemporary America. Truman, for instance, revolves painfully toward a new identity as a man. But he needs Meridian to remind him that confessions are *useful*, rather than self-congratulatory, when they lead to reformulation of values. Thus, when Truman calls Meridian "the woman I should have married and didn't," her scrupulously responsive voice corrects him. " 'Should have *loved*, and didn't', she murmured" (*M*, p. 138), and the truthful force of her words shrivels him in his formerly most prized and proudest place, namely, "he felt a shrinking, a retreating of his balls: He wanted her still, but would not have wanted (or been able) to make love to her" (*M*, p. 139). In order to be free and a friend to Meridian or any other woman Truman must purge his predatory, proprietary sexuality, and his *temporary* incapacity seems bound up with his need to create a whole personality.

His first act of liberation involves hearing Meridian's "voice of instruction" (*M*, p. 140). With her help he reconstructs his past repugnance at the discovery that she has had a son and given him up. He examines his values and motives impersonally, for his sake and not any longer from a hope that turning over a new leaf will win him Meridian. In Truman's and Lynne's lives politics has been an expression of desire, not love, and their desire comes more from exigent, desperate need than from any spontaneous overflow of self. Theirs is a sexuality reinforcing incompleteness rather than tending toward wholeness. For them and others politics debases sexuality, and sexuality distorts political impulse. Private and public experience are reversed with disastrous, destructive consequences. In Lynne's case, although "she often warned herself" that "I will pay for this" because "it is probably a sin to think of a people as Art," she fails to heed her inner moral voice. "And yet," Walker and Meridian testify, "she would stand perfectly still and the sight of a fat black woman singing to herself in a tattered yellow dress, her voice rich and full of yearning, was always—God forgive her, black folks forgive her—the same weepy miracle that Art always was for her" (*M*, p. 128). Walker's interjection repeats the old imperative and adds a new one. Black folks need to forgive Lynne; God cannot do it, and she cannot do it by herself.

Lynne, to overcome her glibness of spirit, needs to understand the human agency of black people. Gradually, she learns to speak in a voice compatible with her experience. As a northern white woman abstractly worshipful of black American *images,* she marries one black man, is raped by another, his friend, and in pathetic, misdirected retaliation sleeps around, taunting black women with her long-tabooed sexuality. Later, in her slow passage to companionability and intimacy with Meridian, Lynne works through secondhand idioms to a language genuinely hers. At times she speaks in tones "affecting a Southern belle accent" (*M*, p. 149); at others a hostile imitation of black American speech: "So get up on me, nigger" (*M*, p. 151). Helped by Meridian's generous patience, Lynne reviews her life more in silence than in speech until at last she and Meridian understand each other and talk, "intimately, like sisters" (*M*, p. 176).

Before this breakthrough, Lynne frees herself from many illusions and stereotypes about black men and white women and, implicitly, black women, too. From her naive and sinister view of black folks as Art, she comes to regard them as varied, variable human beings whose responses to experience differ from both her dreams and her nightmares. For example, she is amazed to be the object of Tommy Odd's resentment when he loses an arm to a racist sniper's bullet. She misinterprets his calculation and hate when he shows up determined to possess her *by any means necessary*. Because of her sentimental ideology about black people, she is unprepared for the pathological form of his desolation. Grotesquely, as he is quick to sense, she pities him his blackness—"the one thing that gives me some consolation in this stupid world, and she thinks she has to make up for it out of the bountifulness of her pussy" (*M*, p. 166). Odds is cruel, his spirit hard and sharp as a razor, and he penetrates her because in her simultaneously self-denying, self-aggrandizing pity, she fails to take advantage of "a moment when she knew she could force him from her" (*M*, p. 160). Until much later, Lynne substitutes false pity for apprehension of another person's actuality. Odds acts out his sickness, not hers, and his is not about being black. But Lynne has not confronted her Jewish family and background; instead, she runs away into the arms of her ideas about black people. Her problem is vicariousness. She seizes simple, fixed, final versions of reality because of her predicament, not the African-American condition.

The day after her rape the simple manly voice of Altuna Jones rescues Lynne from her embrace of bestial stereotypes. Returning uninvited, Odds instructs Altuna and two other adolescent black boys on how to explore the "conquered territory" of Lynne's body: " 'Tits,' he said, flicking them with his fingers, 'ass' " (*M*, p. 161). As the boys turn away, terrified, from Odds's cold pornographic voice, Lynne peoples her mind with vicious images of gang rape. Although the boys' faces look "horrified," Lynne denies their sympathetic human response and for a moment convinces herself that they "were no longer her friends" and that "the sight of her naked would turn them into savages." But like so many southern black people, whose images Meridian sees clearly and sustainingly, the three boys remain true to their (and Lynne's) human dignity. Like a defrocked priest, Odds continues his obscene rite. "Go on," he commands, "have some of it" (*M*, p. 162). With eloquent courage Altuna Jones responds to Odds's prurient call with words that repudiate Odds's assumptions and deny his psychological power. He knows from experience that

Odds's pronoun assaults the very basis of human personality. " 'It? *It?*' he said. 'What it you talking about? That ain't no *it*, that's Lynne' " (*M*, p. 162). Altuna improvises out of his inviolable being, and affirms Lynne's, his, and, therefore, everyone's individual right to life and liberty. Lynne is Lynne, he asserts. She is a person, a human being who is also a woman, who is also white.

Altuna's simple genuine words set a salutary example for what is beginning to happen in *Meridian*. For a long time Meridian alone of the former civil rights activists understands the intense conscious effort required for personal or political change. In the mostly poor black village of Chicokema, her interior life so closely resembles the people's condition that soon "she looked as if she belonged" (*M*, p. 143). Unlike others in her generation, Meridian, frail and sickly, her physical and psychological survival at stake, goes to the oldest African-American well: struggle. She recalls that in slavery her ancestors had to bear up under Sisyphean toil—and still kept soul as well as body together. Moreover, their energy overflowed into the spirituals, the tales, the sermons, the blues, and the amazing quilts whose intricate form inspires Meridian's design of self as well as Walker's narrative form.

Lynne, on the other hand, alienated from her experience and her tradition, resists change and projects her condition on the world. "Why did you come back down here?" she asks harshly in a voice echoing those who called on Meridian to kill for the revolution. "These people will always be the same," she continues. "You can't change them." Characteristically, Meridian revises the question and shoulders the burden. "But I can change," she answers, and reinforces her seriousness with a modest self-call: "I hope I will" (*M*, p. 152). In time, Lynne, too, answers the call to personal revolution. In Meridian's presence, she abandons her earlier view of African-Americans as works of Art. " 'Black folks aren't so special,' she said. 'I hate to admit it. But they're not' " (*M*, p. 185). From here she renounces another idea given force by the history of race and sex in the South. She sees that the peculiar power that in her worst moments she has cynically, bitterly dared to exploit—her status as the desired tabooed white woman—signifies pathology.

In interracial relationships the African-American often becomes the cynosure, the bearer of burdens, and finally the metaphor for freedom in the nation. Usually the apparent issue between black and white Americans is whether their friendship allows them to talk about race, but too often race refers only to being black in America. This compulsion evades the question of what it means and feels like to be white in this country. In a reversal consistent with Walker's crazy quilt form, Lynne and Meridian test their newly developing intimacy by considering white women. Appropriately, the two women reach this topic through Truman, the temporary middle term who is both a presence and an absence in their relationship.

> "No Truman isn't much, but he's *instructional*," said Lynne. "Besides," she continued, "nobody's perfect."
> "Except white women," said Meridian, and winked.
> "Yes," said Lynne, "but their time will come." (*M*, p. 185)

No more words are spoken between Lynne and Meridian and none need be in the pages of the novel. But words on any subject *could* now be spoken by them. When their lives touch again, they can resume talking with a certain earned, assured freedom and intimacy. For this exchange with its ironic-intimate tones of call-and-response settles past accounts and enables Lynne and Meridian to confront together the reversals of politics and sexuality so prominent in the lives of the women and men of their generation. To joke companionably about race and gender after everything they have gone through as women foretells a capacity to talk about anything, in a common voice expressive of what is happening to them singly and together in the unfolding of what Walker believes is one "immense story coming from a multitude of different perspectives."[18]

6

Earlier in her life (and later in the novel), Meridian comes back to the South to restore herself and relearn the work of politics. But soon, in April 1968, she experiences a devastating low point that makes her journey to the people a categorical imperative. At first, like the speaker in Anna Akhmatova's "Requiem," she is mere "witness to the common lot, survivor of that time, that place" (*M*, p. 185). She stands with the uninvited, unacknowledged black poor outside the funeral of Dr. Martin Luther King as, "following the casket on its mule-drawn cart," this "pitiable crowd of nobodies" spontaneously "began to sing a song the dead man had loved." The song testifies to the love of these poor for *their* Martin, but the invited dignitaries only follow "eagerly in genial mime" without inner voices of responsiveness. As the music fades from the air, Meridian hears the other, unloving voices of individuals, white and black, who converse loudly, trivially, ostentatiously. Soon "the call for Coca-Colas" replaces the poor people's song, and "there was a feeling of relief in the air, of liberation, that was repulsive." In response, Meridian turns "in shame, as if to the dead man himself," but she hears only "a skinny black boy tapping on an imaginary drum" pronounce an epitaph, not for King but in defense of this desolate American carnival. "We don't go on over death the way whiteys do," he tells a "white couple who hung guiltily to every word" (*M*, p. 190).

After witnessing this tradition-sundering act of self-parody, Meridian drops out of sight and hearing. Walker's break sends readers to their own inner space, and the next words are the sound of Meridian's voice, years later, filling a new page. The time is about 1975, the place Chicokema, the occasion her pursuit of the revolutionary question in her continuing conversation with Truman. Because hers is a life of commitment, Meridian pursues the relation among ideas, emotions, and actions with an impersonal, troubled seriousness foreign to Truman. Because Truman has long since abandoned politics for a hypocritical artistic career, to him "the discussion was academic, so he could state his points neatly" (*M*, p. 191). Nevertheless, Meridian suspends her disbelief and treats him fraternally as a serious person capable of an evolving dialogue.

> "I mean, I think that all of us who want the black and poor to have equal opportunities and goods in life will have to ask ourselves how we stand on killing, even if no one else ever does. Otherwise we will never know—in advance of our fighting—how much we are willing to give up."
>
> "Suppose you found out, without a doubt, that you could murder other people in a just cause, what would you do? Would you set about murdering them?"
>
> "Never alone," said Meridian. "Besides, revolution would not begin, do you think, with an act of murder—wars might begin in that way—but with teaching."

"Oh yes, *teaching*," said Truman, scornfully. (*M*, p. 192)

Like a jazz musician trying out a new melody, Meridian develops improvisationally those ideas arrived at earlier in her solitary mind. To her, politics and teaching are variations on the African-American pattern of call-and-response. Action, like speech, is dialogue. But ideas seem to enter Truman like the current from a life-support machine. "Revolution," he tells her, "was the theme of the sixties" (*M*, p. 192), although she is at that moment living a life of undramatic but palpable revolution. Because she is willing to learn from any corner, she takes Truman more seriously than he takes himself. "But don't you think the basic questions raised by King and Malcolm and the rest still exist? Don't you think people, somewhere deep inside, are still attempting to deal with them?" (*M*, p. 193).

Meridian's words are a confession of faith backed up by her life, but Truman holds his ground rigidly, if honestly. "No," he replies, and his response recalls Walter Cronkite's official refrain during the 1960s and 1970s. *That's the way it is*, July so and so, nineteen hundred and such and such he would say every night as if to soothe the citizenry against the chaotic facts of war and riot alluded to in the previous half-an-hour of news. At this point of apparent standoff between Meridian and Truman, Walker fills in the memory gap with an account of one of Meridian's political acts of change. Rather than comply with recent federal desegregation laws, the Chicokema town fathers close down the public pool and retreat to "private swimming pools in their own back yards" (*M*, p. 194). Consequently, each spring and fall a black child usually drowns in water drained off from the reservoir into the adjacent low-lying black neighborhood. The afflicted community grieves passively, apolitically until Meridian leads them into the town meeting. In silence she leaves the body of a bloated decomposing child next to the mayor's gavel. The people promise to "name the next girl child they had after her," but Meridian seizes the moment and instead makes "them promise they would learn, as their smallest resistance to the murder of their children, to use the vote." Like Meridian's contemporaries, the people fear they will be laughed at "because that is not radical" (*M*, p. 195). Characteristically, Walker and Meridian withhold news of the outcome until we have witnessed the prior experience that enabled Meridian to speak and act with the people. Later, we are told matter-of-factly that these people, like those in Miss Jane Pittman's quarters, act on their own behalf. No more poor black children drown in this way in this town for the simplest and most effective of reasons: black votes joined to black voices.

In the meantime Meridian overcomes Truman's glib responses with a thoughtful, meditative silence. In the interval before they resume talking, Walker invites us to come along as silent companions as she follows Meridian's earlier quest for a loving political voice. Two months after Martin Luther King's assassination, Meridian begins going to black churches. Each time she chooses a different one, because she is not looking for any single true black church but instead those diverse dwellings where black people make church and find the way home in Ralph Ellison's sense of fusing love and democracy. In one such place Meridian answers unexpectedly the novel's persisting question: "Will you kill for the Revolution?" (*M*, p. 14). She does not change the question but interprets its terms according to a fuller context than that imagined by the revolutionaries who framed the question in the North some years before. To do so she follows the lead of a congregation that adapts the traditional music and ritual of black Christianity to its immediate needs and experience.

As she hears the people sing, Meridian recognizes an old "once quite familiar song," but when the words fail to come back to her, she "soon realized it was the *melody* of the song she remembered, not the words because these words sounded quite new to her" (*M*, p. 198). She is right, the congregation finds new words for the old melodies and also makes up new songs Meridian does not associate with church. The melody is martial, she realizes, and in response, "found herself quoting Margaret Walker's 'For My People' ":

> Let the martial songs be written,
> let the dirges disappear. (*M*, p. 199)

The unsought, unexpected connection startles Meridian into an apprehension of what is happening to these people whose souls she thinks hold no surprises. Disoriented, she hears the young minister begin to preach in a voice and cadence "so dramatically like that of Martin Luther King's that at first Meridian thought his intention was to dupe or to mock" (*M*, p. 199). So far her response lacks a center of gravity. Unfamiliar with the experience prompting the songs and now the sermon, she distrusts the young minister's relation to Martin Luther King: She is amazed that a contemporary could have an unself-conscious, intimate, kinship with King in this remote place far from talk of revolution. In an act of tolerance she stifles an impulse "to laugh bitterly" at what she thinks is "the pompous imitative preacher" (*M*, p. 199), and enters the flow of his voice. To her surprise, his voice bears witness to the potential wholeness in his people's personal and political lives. Moreover, the congregation's response tells her that he does speak for them, that his voice is also theirs.

Caught up in the flow of call-and-response, Meridian's inner voice picks up the rhythm. Her repetitive "he told" communicates his (and her) conviction that words and deeds are kin. For the minister does not aim his criticism only at white folks; he demands that the individuals in his congregation work harder to meet their responsibilities to each other. Meridian changes her mind because the call-and-response between the minister and his congregation builds on Martin Luther King's work. Don't go to Vietnam, he tells the young men; don't let your young children fight your battles, he tells the parents. And "it struck Meridian that he was deliberately imitating King, that he and all his congregation *knew* he was consciously keeping that voice alive" as a force for change. And as Meridian listens more and more responsively, she hears "not his voice at all, but rather the voice of millions who could no longer speak" (*M*, p. 200). Then, hearing the voices around her, Meridian revises her idea, for these people speak repeatedly through the varied intonation of the different *ah-mens* they utter in response to the preacher's calls to action. The congregation speaks unsentimentally, militantly, and their voices reach Meridian with "a firm tone of 'We are fed up' " (*M*, p. 200).

They have cause to be fed up. One of their own has been murdered, martyred in the struggle for justice like Jimmy Aaron in *The Autobiography of Miss Jane Pittman*. Along with the other worshippers, Meridian yields to the grief of the boy's father, a "red-eyed man" so devastated he wonders to what extent love led to his son's violent death. Formerly, he "had thought that somehow, the power of his love alone (and how rare even he knew it was!) would save his son.

But his love—selfless, open, a kissing, touching love—had only made his son strong enough to resist everything that was not love." Convinced of "his own great value, he had set out to change the ways of the world his father feared." To his father's puzzlement, he embraced struggle and revolution. Now, the grieving father "did not allow closeness" even by his people who long to "open themselves totally to someone else's personal loss, if it was allowed them to do so" (*M*, p. 201). He cannot bear so intimate a response, but his faith in the people remains, and, when asked, he appears and speaks on *occasions* like the anniversary of his son's death. Aware of his continuing part in their struggle, the people know the red-eyed man cannot grieve alone and remain true to his love for his son and his son's love for him and the people. So the red-eyed man's three painful, somehow adequate and eloquent words—"My son died"—arouse the people. Their response flows into the work going on more determinedly than ever because of the unspeakable murder and brutality inflicted on the best and strongest among them. As a willing potential participant, Meridian bears witness to the practical healing power of the people's song and ceremony: "And then there rose the sweet music that received its inimitable *soul* from just such inarticulate grief as this, and a passing of the collection plate with the money going to the church's prison fund, and the preacher urged all those within his hearing to vote for black candidates on the twenty-third. And the service was over" (*M*, p. 202). She is now a participant and, therefore, her voice is faithful to the inner rhythms of their story. Here culture, especially music, humanizes politics—those small actions that intensify and change the lives of the people and their children. In this black church the deepest, most abiding human responses of love and grief express the meaning of revolution in African-American experience.[19]

Now, in a miniature of the novel's crazy quilt collage, the fragments Meridian witnesses come together. Lingering in church, she puts into inner words the promise she has heard the people make with their amens and their music. " 'Look' they were saying, 'we are slow to awaken to the notion that we are only as other women and men, and even slower to move in anger, but we are gathering ourselves to fight for and protect what your son fought for on behalf of us. If you will let us weave your story and your son's life and death into

what we already know—into the songs, the sermons, the brother
and sister—we will soon be so angry we cannot help but move.' "
As she imagines the people's voice, the words include her in the
community of struggle. " 'Understand this,' they were saying, 'the
church' (and Meridian knew they did not mean simply 'church,' as
in Baptist, Methodist or whatnot, but rather communal spirit, togetherness, righteous convergence), 'the music, the form of worship
that has always sustained us, the kind of ritual you share with us,
these are the ways to transformation that we know. We want to take
this with us as far as we can' " (*M*, p. 204). In this shared voice
Meridian hears the people's awareness of each other and of her as
if they have waited knowing always what she has just come to
understand: namely, that "the years in America had created them
One Life" (*M*, p. 204).

This context reveals an intrinsic community and a community in
flux, and because of this, Meridian is able to address the question
posed without music by her contemporaries: "Will you kill for the
Revolution?" But she answers in relation to the condition of love
and struggle she has just witnessed and participated in, and so she
roots the word and idea of "revolution" in the particular flow of the
people's experience. True to her personality, her answer is not absolute, rigid, or final but fluid, promissory, and evolving. And her
response moves in harmony with the simultaneously traditional and
contemporary landscape she travels through and briefly rests in:
"Under a large tree beside the road, crowded now with the cars
returning from church, she made a promise to the red-eyed man
herself: that yes, indeed she *would* kill before she allowed anyone
to murder his son again" (*M*, p. 204). True to her slowly evolving
self, Meridian continues to work out the relationship between personal and political responsibility. Despite "the new capacity to do
anything, including kill, for our freedom—beyond sporadic acts of
violence," she recognizes that "I am not yet at the point of being
able to kill anyone myself, nor—except for the false urgings that
come to me in periods of grief and rage—will I ever be" (*M*, p.
205). For her, scrupulosity is a condition of being. From time to time
she comforts her soul with her cherished identity as someone who
walks behind the "real" revolutionaries, those who do the "correct
thing" and "kill when killing is necessary" (*M*, p. 193). But she

balances the "correct thing" with the "right thing." When those who have killed cannot sing yet yearn desperately for music, she will come forward "and sing from memory songs they will need once more to hear." Thus, overcoming the false notes in her own soul, Meridian imagines revolutionary politics as work of the spirit and music as a recuperative political act. She becomes a mediating voice between revolution and the traditions true revolutionaries seek to empower through just and radical changes in the body politic. "For it is the song of the people, *transformed by the experience of each generation*, that holds them together, and if any part of it is lost the people suffer and are without soul" (*M*, pp. 205-6, my italics). Music, as the people in the church have shown her, is both a healing balm and a companion to action in these days and in days to come as it was in the days of slavery and also the civil rights movement of the 1950s and 1960s.[20] Rounded in song, the mouth of the people becomes a figure for the restored hoop of the nation.

These questions of politics and identity, culture and revolution continue to engage Meridian according to the flow of her experience. Encountering a "starving child" or "a grown person who could neither read nor write" (*M*, p. 206), she renews her silent promise to kill for the sake of justice. But that promise moves away from murder, simple or complex, and toward her presence in the nation as a revolutionary citizen. In her rage at the injustice of particular lives, she feels "of a resolute and relatively fearless character, which, sufficient in its calm acceptance of its own purpose, could bring the mightiest country to its knees" (*M*, p. 206). Clearly, her sense of potential power is more extravagant than that proclaimed by her militant contemporaries in the 1960s. Surely, too, she is "a little crazy"; she needs to be, and this passionate overflow of self, if experienced many times over by many different individuals, might be the beginning of a second American revolution. For while Truman Held makes "a statue of Crispus Attucks [the first American to die in the Revolution] for the Bicentennial" (*M*, p. 193), in a partly cynical, wholly self-serving gesture, and Anne-Marion writes pretty poetry and, like the others in her former group, does "nothing revolutionary" (*M*, p. 205), Meridian redefines the meaning of equality and the inalienable rights in her daily work and life. Hers is the spirit of public happiness John Adams believed led to the success of the original American Revolution, reexpressed in a politics of, by, and for the black poor of the South two hundred years later. As Walker's novel stands in contrast to Truman's statue as a work of art in the context of the Bicentennial, so, too, Meridian brings to the original American revolutionary impulse a politics of nourishment and nurturing—what Walker calls a *womanist* sensibility.[21]

7

During his stay with Meridian, Truman gradually hears her meditative internal voice and begins to listen for his own. He changes his thinking more because of an inner dialogue than because of any words spoken between them. He goes south still hoping to resolve his life and end the story in the old way by marrying Meridian. But in his presence she keeps on with her healing life of satisfying work and in that context offers him friendship based on doing things together in a spirit of equality.[22] Appropriately, now the pattern of call-and-response shifts from rhetoric to action. Meridian asks nothing from Truman, but in response to his new silent openness, she takes him along on her voter registration work. With him at her side, she visits a family belonging to the poorest of the black poor. The mother is dying; the father rolls old slimy newspapers into logs he sells to white folks "for a nickel apiece and to colored for only three pennies." Meridian tries to persuade the man (and his wife) to register, but without polemics or ideology, for she sees that action as true and meaningful only in the context of particular lives. For Meridian, voting habituates the exercise of voice. "It may be useless," she tells the man who, struggling to survive, calls voting a waste of time, a needless risk "if we don't own nothing." In response, Meridian disagrees gently and changes the terms of the dialogue: "Maybe it can be the beginning of the use of your voice. You have to get used to using your voice, you know. You start on simple things and move on" (*M*, p. 210). But the man rejects her call and bids her go elsewhere, to people with fewer urgencies, whose right to life, liberty, and the pursuit of happiness is more assured. Go among your contemporaries, he might have said, and his meaning is not lost on Meridian. True to her earlier affirmation of teaching as a spoken and unspoken dialogue rather than "a handing down of answers," she understands that in the act of expressing another position, the man uses his voice to tell her about the "simple things" at the core of his life.

"Okay," Meridian says, and walks away in undiscouraged, easy silence. Her timing and instinct combine with her values in an act of respect that is the most abiding form of democratic leadership. And Truman follows willingly. He does not protest nor assert his manly presence by arguing with the man. Meridian's voice and motion assure the man of her sincerity so strongly that when she and Truman return shortly with two bags of food, he accepts them for his son and ailing wife. He and Meridian communicate from respect as if each were saying to the other: You meet your responsibilities, and I'll meet mine. So it is no surprise when, after the man's wife dies, he shows up with *his* gifts: "six rabbits already skinned and ten newspaper logs." That's for the groceries he might have said but doesn't and from respect, because his gifts are from his hands. With no prodding, no exchange of words, the man testifies to the reciprocal power of his voice and Meridian's in another way. He performs a political act — "under the words WILL YOU BE BRAVE ENOUGH TO VOTE in Meridian's yellow pad he wrote his name in large black letters" (*M*, p. 210). He signs up not for Meridian but to enlarge the struggle he carries on in his life. Made in the spirit of mutual, offhand eloquence, the man's commitment is his and not dependent on Meridian's personal presence. Convinced by his experience, including his encounter with Meridian, that "the years in America had created them One Life" (*M*, p. 204), the man acts on the authority of experience: his signature is his voice.

Despite other successes, Walker resists turning *Meridian* into a series of small triumphs for voter registration. Instead, she touches realities that are beyond the power of change, conditions that illuminate almost unspeakable corners of the human heart. Meridian and Truman, she writes in acknowledgment of an intense mutual fate, "must go to the prison. And so they must. And so they must see the child who murdered her child, nothing new" (*M*, p. 217). The repetitions roll and break like waves, which, as they are about to flatten out, throw up a sudden spume of fear. The girl's voice penetrates Meridian and Truman so deeply that, when she asks "who, in the hell, are you?" they fall back on words of identification that they think shield their identities. "People who ask people to vote," they answer in an inadequate mutual voice. But the girl sees through their mask of fact: "If you all can't give me back my heart (she says suddenly, with venom), go the fuck away" (*M*, p. 218). They do, they have to, they go away with nothing, not words, not friendship, not even Meridian's burning lines of verse as consolation. There is no politics to compensate for this "fucking heart of stone," as Meridian names the soul behind the girl's insane but undeniably human voice. And there is little comfort, for the girl is not entirely an anomaly in the world of *Meridian*. Her murder of her child recalls the brutal murder of Truman and Lynne's six-year-old daughter, Camara, and also Meridian's former urges to kill her baby son. Deep in their separate selves Meridian and Truman are bonded by what they have seen and heard and suffered together. Truman feels *shame* but is not able to identify his emotion with his and Lynne's murdered daughter nor with his and Meridian's aborted baby of whose existence he has no conscious knowledge. Meridian writes a poem of forgiveness for Truman, for everyone, not least herself, and as she sleeps "that night with Truman's arms around her," his "dreams [escape] from his lips to make a moaning, crying song." Truman's involuntary song foretells his evolving sensibility; soon he begins "to experience moments with Meridian when he felt intensely maternal" (*M*, p. 219).

At the end of *Meridian* everything whirls with the motion of change. Meridian and Truman "settle accounts," and at some indeterminate later time Truman declares a brotherly love for his wife, Lynne. "I don't want to do anything but provide for you and be your friend." Perhaps sensing the pain his absence of desire may cause her, he asks a genuine, unrhetorical question: "Can you accept that?" (*M*, p. 221). Still, Truman pursues the past with Meridian. "I want your love the way I had it a long time ago," he tells her and in his turn accepts painfully her declaration that "my love for you changed." She has, she claims, set him *free*, and, therefore, she feels free to issue a warning that implies that true friendship between them should influence his inner voice as well as his actions and speech. "You are *not* free, however, to think I am a fool" (*M*, p. 223). The remark underscores Meridian's determination to be a serious person in every facet of her experience. Her struggle toward a qualified, continually vulnerable wholeness involves benevolence toward the existence of others, a willingness to see them through their eyes as well as hers. Benevolence now seems Meridian's test for those she is intimate with in her work and her life. For his part, Truman first learns to read Anne-Marion's message to Meridian about the Sojourner tree's newly manifested life. Then by "the soft wool of her newly grown hair," he understands that Meridian, too, is, in part, "new, sure and ready, even eager, for the world" (*M*, p. 227).

As always, Meridian and Truman talk, and at first Truman's spoken words continue to be less genuine than his inner voice. "Your ambivalence," he tells her in a language akin to the retrick of the long-head boy in *The Autobiography of Miss Jane Pittman*, "will always be deplored by people who consider themselves revolutionists, and your unorthodox behavior will cause traditionalists to gnash their teeth" (*M*, p. 227). Although Truman's feelings have changed, he still speaks words he has been taught to speak and thinks he is supposed to speak. He fails to distinguish his loneliness from Meridian's solitude. For her, true solitude is a sign of potential community; she and those like her "will one day gather at the river. We will watch the evening sun go down. And in the darkness maybe we will know the truth" (*M*, p. 227). Her words, the last *spoken* in the novel, are at once prophetic and elemental, metaphysical and sensuous. She includes Truman in her company of solitary silent souls; at least she invites him to join these still marching saints. But she does not stay for an answer because she knows his spoken words lag behind the readiness of his inner voice. Instead, she hugs him freely, naturally — "long, lingeringly (her nose and lips rooting about at his neck, *causing him to laugh*" (*M*, p. 228, my italics). Then, she leaves quickly, in the ascent, the prime of her life — "walking as if hurrying to catch up with someone" — herself maybe and maybe the whole revolving world. She leaves keeping faith with the possibility that she will wear the crazy quilt of her world as Hurston's Janie Crawford draped the net of the horizon around her shoulders.

Lovingly, she leaves Truman in her place to do what is now *their* work. She leaves her sleeping bag behind as a nest to shelter him while his evolving self prepares to act differently toward the world. She knows his loneliness is cause for fear, but she also knows that their conversation has gone as far as it can now. So she leaves him to respond to her inner vision, to that interior dialogue to which she contributes even when not physically present. Her words and parting hug call his inner voice. Free to feel and to cry, Truman takes silent, solitary possession of the gifts she has given him. He identifies the house as his, realizes that the people will come to milk his cow, and that they "would wait patiently for him to *perform*, to take them along the next *guideless* step. Perhaps he would" (*M*, p. 228, my italics). In a spirit of moral contingency and integrity reminiscent of Meridian, Truman senses that among these poor people politics follows from personal worthiness and dignity. He senses, too, that political acts are best performed by a self somehow at once in flux and on the way to completion—a revolutionary self.

Truman's thoughts lead to the resumption of his inner dialogue with Meridian. He *hears* the words of her poem, not as she once wrote them down but as if she were speaking to him now. He feels the room turn with the revolving motion of the world. Like Meridian in her time of dissolution, he yields to a spell of dizziness. As a reflex, he fits his body into Meridian's sleeping bag and puts her cap on his head. Located in her former place, Truman imagines the process of self-discovery and restoration extending to others in his generation. "He had a vision of Anne-Marion herself, arriving, lost, someday, at the door, which would remain open"; he makes no pretense of leading her. Rather, his thoughts return to Meridian, and in careful, disciplined, specific, far-reaching words his newly immediate, complex inner voice communicates the spirit of change for which Meridian and now he, Truman, stand. He "wondered if Meridian knew that the sentence of bearing the conflict in her own soul which she had imposed on herself—and lived through—must now be borne in terror by all the rest of them" (*M*, p. 228).

Truman and Walker avoid stitching Meridian's story into a legend. It would be easy for him (and us) to read the images identified with Meridian—her cap, her hair, her frail yet strong stature, her power to lead people—as signs of another African-American woman from the days of the underground railroad and the Civil War. In her struggle Meridian becomes one of those black women she remembers from childhood stories as "always imitating Harriet Tubman—escaping to become something unheard of" (*M*, p. 105). With her contemporaries, Meridian functions as exemplary general on a 1970s underground railroad of politics and personality. But the extrinsic journey is in reverse, from the North to the South, because in Meridian's time the South offers the surest passage from slavery to freedom.[23] Although, unlike Harriet Tubman, Meridian issues no commands, her presence and interior voice call others to become passengers on a journey as terrible and necessary as the escapes led by General Tubman. And in the unlegendary historical present, Truman's words place his dialogue with Meridian on a new plane.

The signs of presence and aura of voice that Meridian leaves all around the house lead Truman to wonder about her from the vantage point of his finally open mind. The *sentence* that he bears in his soul and Walker writes down now in collaboration with *him* testifies to his potential. Already he experiences the conflict Meridian has endured for her own sake, her people's sake, and, especially, her contemporaries' sake. And he begins to be aware that her silent dialogue as well as her speech has given him and the others she touches the time and space they need to rejoin what Michael Harper calls the "dark human struggle to be human."[24] The sentence written and passed by Walker and accepted by Meridian and now Truman calls the rest of us to bear the conflict between restraint and indulgence, pain and pleasure, love and hate, life and death as a condition of personal revolution and a prologue to political action. With its allusion to the intervening years of loss as well as gain, Walker's *sentence* intensifies Invisible Man's 1950s question: "Who knows but that, on the lower frequencies, I speak for you?" For black (*and all*) citizens to know that "the years in America [have] created them One Life" (*M*, p. 204) carries with it the sentence of participation. To discover and create and tell our stories, as Meridian does, using her voice in speech, in silence, in writing, is the essence of the revolutionary task explored in *Meridian*. She and Walker remind us that sometimes the voices of authority we need to overcome are creations of our own diminished hearts.

Of all the words thought and felt, spoken and written in *Meridian*, those Meridian speaks simply, quietly, humbly, to the impoverished black man best embody a loving political voice. "You have to get used to using your voice, you know. You start on simple things and move on" (*M*, p. 210). In her crazy quilt collage of a novel Alice Walker and her characters offer readers a beginning of the restoration of the reciprocal sense of language and experience that is essential if America is to resume a revolutionary course. Walker's call is subtle but not easily ignored, over time, on those "lower frequencies" of consciousness where, heard or unheard, our inner voices live and speak.

NOTES

1. *Interviews with Black Writers*, ed. John T. O'Brien (New York: Liveright, 1973), pp. 194, 192.

2. Black Elk as quoted in *Black Elk Speaks* (1932; rpt., New York: Pocket Books, 1972), p. 230, and in the epigraph to *Meridian* (New York: Harcourt Brace Jovanovich, 1976), p. x. *Meridian* will be cited hereafter as *M*.

3. James Alan McPherson, *Elbow Room* (Boston: Atlantic–Little, Brown, 1977), p. 219. See also McPherson's "Hue and Cry," in *Hue and Cry* (New York: Fawcett, 1959), pp. 216-17, 219, 229.

4. Quoted in *Black Women Writers at Work*, ed. Claudia Tate (New York: Continuum, 1983), p. 184.

5. Alice Walker, *In Search of Our Mothers' Gardens* (San Diego: Harcourt Brace Jovanovich, 1983), p. 5.

6. Quoted in *Black Women Writers at Work*, pp. 184, 176, 178. Walker's mention of Bearden recalls that more than one of his collages are titled "Patchwork Quilt"; in the case of *Meridian*'s form, Walker distinguishes "between a crazy quilt and a patchwork quilt. A patchwork quilt is exactly what the name implies—a quilt made of patches. A crazy quilt, on the other hand, only looks crazy. It is not 'patched'; it is planned" (p. 176).

7. Ralph Ellison, "The Art of Romare Bearden," in *Chant of Saints*, ed. Michael S. Harper and Robert B. Stepto (Urbana: University of Illinois Press, 1979), p. 165.

8. Calvin Tomkins, "Romare Bearden," in ibid., p. 158b.

9. Zora Neale Hurston, *Their Eyes Were Watching God* (1937; rpt., Urbana: University of Illinois Press, 1978), p. 43.

10. Hurston, *Their Eyes Were Watching God*, p. 19.

11. Ibid., p. 133.

12. Robert Hayden, *Angle of Ascent* (New York: Liveright, 1975), p. 131.

13. Barbara Christian, *Black Women Novelists* (Westport: Greenwood Press, 1980), p. 218. See Christian's entire discussion of Walker, pp. 180-238.

14. Michael S. Harper, "American History," *Images of Kin: New and Selected Poems* (Urbana: University of Illinois Press, 1977), p. 196.

15. Quoted in *Interviews with Black Writers*, p. 189. For exposition of the view that slavery was terrible for men and frequently more so for

women, see Linda Brent's *Incidents in the Life of a Slave Girl* (1861; rpt., New York: Harcourt Brace Jovanovich, 1973), and Harriet E. Wilson's *Our Nig; or, Sketches from the Life of a Free Black* (1859; rpt. and ed. with an introduction by Henry Louis Gates, Jr., New York: Random House, 1983).

16. Sojourner Truth quoted in *The Feminist Papers*, ed. Alice S. Rossi (New York: Bantam, 1974), p. 428.

17. The mythic substratum to which Walker appeals in the Sacred Serpent is vital to her. "Another reason I think nobody has been able to deal with *Meridian* as a total work is the whole sublayer of Indian consciousness." Walker also speaks of "vistitations" coming "from what is Indian in me, and I don't necessarily mean Indian blood" (quoted in *Black Women Writers at Work*, pp. 178-79).

18. Walker, *In Search of Our Mothers' Gardens*, p. 5.

19. In "The Self in Bloom: Alice Walker's *Meridian*," *CLA Journal* 24 (Mar. 1981), 272, Deborah E. McDowell argues that it is the *"restored church of her slave ancestors* that Meridian ultimately embraces, the church of Nat Turner, of Denmark Vesey, the church rooted in the soil of protest against oppression, the church of 'communal spirit, togetherness, righteous convergence.' "

20. Watching the television documentary, *Eyes on the Prize*, I am struck by how close the handclapping and singing are to the old way of call-and-response and by how catalytic music was to the actions of the civil rights marchers.

21. For Walker's definition of *womanist*, see *In Search of Our Mothers' Gardens*, pp. xi-xii.

22. On the relationship between intimacy and politics in *Meridian*, see Michael G. Cooke's *Afro-American Literature in the Twentieth Century: The Achievement of Intimacy* (New Haven: Yale University Press, 1984), pp. 157-76.

23. For a discussion of geography in twentieth-century black fiction, see Melvin Dixon's *Ride Out the Wilderness: Geography and Identity in Afro-American Literature* (Urbana: University of Illinois Press, 1987).

24. Harper, "Eve (Rachel)," *Images of Kin*, p. 12. Harper's line calls me back to conversations with Susan Kirschner soon after *Meridian*'s publication in which, ahead of the rest, including me, she argued compellingly for the novel's crucial importance and integrity.

CHAPTER 8

Who We For?: The Extended Call of African-American Fiction

1

In an author's note to her novel, *Dessa Rose*, Sherley Anne Williams observes that "Afro-Americans, having survived by word of mouth—and made of that process a high art—remain at the mercy of literature and writing; often, these have betrayed us."[1] And tracing what he calls the "discourse of distrust" back through literary history, Robert B. Stepto argues that "Afro-American literature has developed as much because of the culture's distrust of literacy as because of its abiding faith in it."[2] African-American writers have long been aware of their vulnerability to distortions of the written word as shaped by the fictions of Joel Chandler Harris and many others. But they also know that distrust poses dangers to storywriting and that the death of fiction is a possibility largely because of estrangement between writer and readers.

Like the narrator of James Alan McPherson's "Elbow Room," black writers recognize that as a narrative principle, distrust could lead to the assumption that "there [are] no new stories in the world." Like him, they recognize that "personal freedom" is bound up with their freedom as citizens and that their identities as writers thrive on "unrestricted access to new stories forming."[3] Many black writers respond to the conflict between trust and distrust with variations on the theme of open narrative form. In their fiction they call readers to take personal responsibility for the still evolving story of American identity and nationhood. For example, even though Richard Wright writes *Native Son* out of an explicit distrust of white American readers, at the end of the novel Bigger Thomas breaks a convention that has shackled him to an ostensibly stereotypical and subservient discourse with white people. "Tell. . . . Tell Mister. . . . Tell Jan hello . . . ,"[4] he calls out in a gesture of equality and friendship despite his imminent execution. Bigger's immediate audience, the character Max, remains Mr. Max and appropriately so, since he responds by closing the conversation. But Wright leaves open the possibility that readers, particularly white Americans, will answer Bigger's challenge outside the novel.

In the 1980s African-American writers continue to favor a narrative discourse of democratic possibility. In their latest novels, Alice Walker, Ernest Gaines, David Bradley, Sherley Anne Williams, and others[5] use elements of call-and-response to overcome distrust and build a readership based on the trust that, however guardedly and complexly, informs the relations between storyteller and audience in oral storytelling. In Walker's *The Color Purple*, the spoken word comes to imaginative life on the pages of Celie's letters just as the letters do in the pages of the novel. To overcome distrust between others in her family and herself and, even more important, to overcome her self-distrust, Celie struggles to find a voice in the only medium open to her: the written word of private letters. Her imagination of an audience—first God, then Nettie, and finally, all that is living or elemental in the universe: "dear everything"[6]—and her gradual mastery of a writer's voice enable her to emerge as a person whose speech has power because those in her world who hear her are moved and changed by her words. The distrust that Celie overcomes both by virtue of letters and speech Walker attempts to overcome with her readers, particularly but not exclusively black readers, and, most daringly, black men. In this connection Celie's husband, Mister, is a figure for those who seek to control what is said and read, and he begins to change his ways as a person and a man only by overcoming his fear of free and open, unpredictable discourse. Unlike the domineering male voices in *Their Eyes Were Watching God*, Mister changes his way of talking and behaving, so much so that, at the end, Celie calls him by his name, Albert, and includes him in her immediate intimate audience.

In *A Gathering of Old Men* Gaines also imagines the coming of a truly integrated, inclusive storytelling (and storywriting and reading) community among black and white, young and old, male and female. His use of call-and-response seems dedicated to the proposition that to be told truthfully, this American story of a remote Louisiana parish needs black and white voices to narrate the story in collaboration, singly and together. Yet Gaines's novel remains a narrative performance rather than a storytelling occasion because its black and white voices have not yet become cultural kin in the manner of the black folks from the quarters in *The Autobiography of Miss Jane Pittman.* In the past, black and white lived side by side but not together. Now, as the old black men speak honestly, stand, and, standing, stand for generations of ancestors who lived and died on this plantation going back to slavery, their voices reveal losses that cannot be calculated or overcome. "You had to be there then to be able to don't see it and don't hear it now,"[7] Johnnie Paul says, as if to acknowledge that there continue to be divergent memories for blacks and whites.

As in so much African-American fiction, there is no final word in *A Gathering of Old Men.* "That's all I'll need to end my story" (*AGOM*, p. 185), one of the white narrators, Louis Alfred Dimoulin, a.k.a. Lou Dimes, a reporter for a Baton Rouge newspaper, tells Candy Marshall, his on-again-off-again fiancée whose family has owned the plantation for generations and whose fierce loyalty to the blacks, "her people," is a contemporary variation on the paternalism of the old South. But Dimes is both premature and presumptuous. The story is nowhere near over; moreover, it belongs to the old black men, its primary voices and agents. Their words and actions free Dimes and Candy to live and tell their story. Like the young black history teacher in *The Autobiography of Miss Jane Pittman*, Dimes learns his trade by learning not to speak for the blacks in the quarters but to listen to them. Because he witnesses and thereby earns the right to participate in the old men's story, Dimes becomes a storyteller able to report on the trial in a trustworthy voice and to close on a note that opens the story of his changed relationship with Candy.

As told by Dimes, the novel's conclusion is a representative anecdote implying that blacks and whites may now be better able to tend their private lives because of what they have come through together. After the trial, old Mathu, a.k.a. the African, whom Candy still seeks to protect, refuses her offer of a lift. Instead, he rides back to the plantation in a truck with the other old black men, newly his equals and, therefore, now his friends. When Candy waves "goodbye to them," she is also saying goodbye to her evasion of a private life, for that has been the effect of her controlling obsession with the black folks in the quarters. Now, because of Mathu's and the other black folks' independence of voice and action, she responds to her own circumstance. "I felt," Dimes says, "her other hand against me, searching for my hand; then I felt her squeezing my fingers" (*AGOM*, p. 214). With one hand Candy waves goodbye; with the other she reaches for and touches the actuality of a new commitment, one thoroughly and immediately hers. In similar acts of contact, many but not all of the disparate storytelling voices in A *Gathering of Old Men* move toward a new relationship with self and the world.[8] Like the story they gather to live and tell, the characters' shared voices are somehow both one and many.

Throughout most of *The Chaneysville Incident* Bradley's narrator, John Washington, lives by distrust. As a black American historian, he distrusts white sources and white readers; as a black man he distrusts his white lover, Judith, though he has lived with her for several years, and she would like to bear his child. Summoned to the deathbed of old Jack Crawley, his father's closest friend and his mentor, John Washington goes home, he thinks alone, to explore the layers of his past. His closed mind ignores but cannot nullify the submerged voices of the living and the dead. He shuts out Judith because she is white and a woman. And because of his deep and nameless fear, he cannot hear in a fully responsive, participatory way the voices of the black folks from the Hill who bury Jack Crawley according to the tradition of call-and-response. Most bitterly, Washington distrusts his own voice and his capacity to tell his story using the black oral tradition. But later, writing down the story, Washington reflects explicitly on call-and-response as a continuing signature of African-American identity. "Those of us who know less about Africa than did the European slavers," he writes, "nevertheless tell tales that echo African tales, and sing songs that call on African patterns; nobody may know that the form is called 'call and response,' but that's the way you sing a song."[9]

As a narrator writing down his story after the action, John Washington testifies to the immanence of call-and-response. Painfully yet needfully, he enacts his theme as he tells the story of old Jack Crawley's funeral. He confesses his failure to participate in the call-and-response of that past occasion when the blacks present grieve through a traditional, improvisatory song and story, and even the hypocritical white eminence, Judge Scott, gets a response after he follows a passage from Tennyson by "giving the age old call: 'Gonna lay down my burden.' " (*CI*, p. 219). But John, as he is willing to tell readers later, "did not sing with them" because he "was trying to think." Even though he has been initiated into the craft of story-telling by old Jack Crawley, when his turn comes, John speaks only others' words, none of his own. Like the audiences who rescue various occasions from Invisible Man's rhetoric, the black mourners fetch the right song, the fitting call at the moment of closure: "Steal away, steal away, steal away to Jesus" (*CI*, p. 221). And they do steal away and so extend the tradition of call-and-response from slavery to the present—a continuum John revivifies in his act of writing.

Bradley's *The Chaneysville Incident* restores the hoop of language essential to storytelling because John Washington finally understands that he cannot reconstruct the story of his great-grandfather, C. K. Washington, a.k.a. Brobdingnag, using only a combination of historical materials and analysis. Neither can he discover the story entirely in his own head or through his efforts alone. He must tell the tale as it occurs to his imagination, and his improvisation requires as a witnessing participant the person he is determined to keep outside the sanctum of his African-American self: Judith, the white woman who loves him. But sometimes history is a happenstance that flows from intimacy, and it is Judith who stumbles over C. K. Washington's grave and makes it possible for John to imagine and create the true end of the story. Moreover, Judith changes her behavior and becomes more responsive to John in defiance of her former values. Up to now she has scorned the toddies, which are the stuff of old Jack Crawley's kinship with John and which have loosened Jack's tongue during a lifetime of storytelling. But now Judith mixes John a toddy from "faith," and because "there *aren't* any more facts," she tells him to "forget the facts" (*CI*, p. 391). Nearly drunk, John embraces his imagination and improvises the story of C. K. and

Harriette Brewer, a tale of love and freedom and, finally, the death chosen by them and the other runaways, men, women, and children, over surrender and capture back in 1859.

In the end Judith asks John to make her a toddy. To solve the story's puzzle he goes against the grain of distrust, and she asks a question impossible for her to ask until now, when she knows John Washington loves her.

> "You're saying the miller—what's his name? Iiames?—you think he took the time to bury them like that, to figure out who loved who?"
> "Yes," I said. "That's what I believe."
> "But he was white," she said.
> "I know," I said.
> "Why would a white man . . . why would you think a white man . . . ?" (*CI*, p. 431)

No more words are spoken in the novel, and Judith's question to John reverberates, to be answered in the experience of their love. Alone to perform his closure, John Washington puts "the books and pamphlets and diaries and maps back where they belonged, ready for the next man who would need them." John protects the paraphernalia of the written word pertaining to this particular episode of history and imagination. But he burns "the tools of [his] trade, the pens and inks and pencils, the pads and the cards" (*CI*, p. 431). He does not forswear history as the pursuit of what happened; rather, his little fire purges him of the false starts and the lies that for a time he accepted even while mocking history as an inevitable succession of *lies*. The past he imagines and reconstructs is a history he both leaves in the cabin and carries with him in his father's folio and, more important, in his (and Judith's) mind, and their lives.

To hear and imagine and speak for the voices of the dead—his father Moses, his great-grandfather C. K. Washington, and the doomed runaways C. K. dies trying futilely to rescue—John has had to come to terms with Judith, whose voice and listening presence he formerly was content to live with in a state of distrust. Now in her absence Judith is present imaginatively as John wonders whether "not just someone" but "Judith" "would understand when she saw the smoke go rising from the far side of the Hill" (*CI*, p. 432). His wonder is a question and a call for further responses first and foremost in his intimate private life and from there in his professional life as a historian.

Essaying this predicament and resolving it *in favor of* the love between John and Judith is a bold fictional act on Bradley's part. Gaining the trust of Judith and white readers, John and Bradley risk the distrust of black readers, especially black women. But in the story John lives and tells, Judith earns everyone's trust because she becomes a genuine participant in a process of call-and-response, which is African-American, simply, universally human, and, in a special way, American. As it did in African tribal communities and African-American communities, slave and free, call-and-response banishes distrust and extends a healing, trusting collaboration to those living, hearing, and reading the story. No one is excluded who is willing to witness and participate, particularly since John's love for Judith is a catalyst for, and intensifies during, his recreation of the love between C. K. Washington and Harriette Brewer, the leader of the group of runaway slaves. Moreover, John hears Harriette's voice distinctly enough so that his voice becomes hers, and, as a black woman, she tells her story as the one remaining agent capable of stirring the slaves to resume their flight. Because Bradley's novel is so centrally about honesty and the need to turn distrust into trust, he tests his theme in relation to a painfully charged subject, and does so in a way that allows seemingly excluded readers—especially black women—to feel included and be responsive on the basis of reciprocal freedom.

The willingness to risk trust as a catalyst and consequence of verbal freedom also informs *Dessa Rose*. Like Bradley in *The Chaneysville Incident*, Williams imagines her characters' experience of slavery and tells another of what Walker calls the "great missing stories." Odessa, a slave who kills for freedom, and Mistress Rufel, her formerly equivocal white benefactress, preserve their freedom (and that of other runaways) by a guileful and reciprocal feminist performance in front of the sheriff and a deranged, driven writer turned slavehunter who has proof of Odessa's past identity. Then the two women declare friendship through intimate acts of naming. First, Odessa calls in the old way: " 'Mis'ess,' I said, 'Miz—.' " Answering, Rufel tears down the verbal convention of race and caste standing between them. " 'My name Ruth,' she say, 'Ruth. I ain't your mistress.' " Unfazed, Odessa accepts Ruth's response in witty good faith and issues her own call to friendship. " 'Well, if it come to that,' I told her, 'my name Dessa, Dessa Rose. Ain't no O to it' " (*DR*, p. 232).

Later, in the epilogue, after the two women have gone their different but no longer separate ways, Dessa tells why she writes down her story. Because she has told it so many times, she *"can't believe it's all in [her] mind."* All the same she knows that others like her past interlocutor and pursuer, Adam Nehemiah, will write down false versions of her personality and her story. *"This why I have it wrote down,"* she says, *"why I has the child say it back"* (*DR*, p. 236). To ward off betrayal by the word, Dessa rescues her story and delivers it into the safekeeping of her voice and the voices of her descendants. As a novelist, Williams pursues freedom and justice through reconstruction of the American narrative imagination. Like Charles Chesnutt at the beginning of the century, Williams relies on her people's tradition of call-and-response and projects for her time a community of readers and citizens occasionally aspired to but not yet achieved in the nation's past or present.

Perhaps because they have had to be alert to the dangers fiction poses to the individual, the race, and the nation, in their stories black writers overcome "some — not much, but some — of the human greed and smallness, yes, and the fear and superstition" which Invisible Man argues have kept others "running."[10] For this reason, too, they demand participatory commitment from their readers. Their work and our work is the work of fiction and citizenship, and from this perspective call-and-response is a name for the evolving dialogic forms of democracy. Writers, readers, and citizens of every background, characteristic, and persuasion: each and every one are called to answer that still reverberating American question: Who we for?

NOTES

1. Sherley Anne Williams, *Dessa Rose* (New York: Morrow, 1986), p. 5. This volume will be cited hereafter as *DR*.

2. Robert B. Stepto, "Distrust of the Reader in Afro-American Narratives," in *Reconstructing American Literary History*, ed. Sacvan Bercovitch

(Cambridge, Mass.: Harvard University Press, 1986), pp. 304, 301. Stepto makes a telling point about the rich interconnections between writer and reader in black American and, for that matter, American fiction when he says that "acts of creative communication are fully initiated not when the text is assaulted but when the reader gets told—or told off—in such a way that he or she finally begins to *hear*" (p. 309).

3. James Alan McPherson, *Elbow Room* (Boston: Atlantic–Little, Brown, 1977), pp. 240, 220.

4. Richard Wright, *Native Son* (New York: Harper & Brothers, 1940), p. 359. In "How Bigger Was Born," an introduction written a month or so after *Native Son* was published, and included in subsequent editions of the novel, Wright explains his quarrel with his readers. "I found that I had written a book," he says of *Uncle Tom's Children*, "which even bankers' daughters could read and weep over and feel good about. I swore to myself that if I ever wrote another book, no one would weep over it; that it would be so hard and deep that they would have to face it without the consolation of tears." See James A. Miller's "Bigger Thomas's Quest for Voice and Audience in Richard Wright's *Native Son*," *Callaloo* 9, no. 3 (Summer 1986), 501-6.

5. Robert B. Stepto's review essay, "After the 1960's: The Boom in Afro-American Fiction," in *Contemporary American Fiction*, ed. Malcolm Bradbury and Sigmund Ro (London: Edward Arnold, 1986), pp. 89-104, touches on other contemporary black writers whose work also involves adaptations of the oral tradition.

6. Alice Walker, *The Color Purple* (San Diego: Harcourt Brace Jovanovich, 1982), p. 249.

7. Ernest J. Gaines, *A Gathering of Old Men* (New York: Knopf, 1983), p. 92. This volume will be cited hereafter as *AGOM*.

8. One of the triumphs of *A Gathering of Old Men* is that Gaines raises some of the racist characters like Tee Jack, Luke Will, Sharp, and even the contemptible Leroy above redneck stereotypes by recognizing that, occasionally, they speak in a richly suggestive, original comic idiom.

9. David Bradley, *The Chaneysville Incident* (New York: Harper and Row, 1981), p. 213. This volume will be cited hereafter as *CI*.

10. Ralph Ellison, *Invisible Man* (1952; rpt. with author's introduction, New York: Random House, 1982), p. 434.

Index

A Note on the Author

John F. Callahan is Morgan S. Odell Professor of Humanities at Lewis and Clark College in Portland, Oregon. He is a graduate of the University of Connecticut and received his M.A. and Ph.D. degrees from the University of Illinois. Mr. Callahan is the author of *The Illusions of a Nation: Myth and History in the Novels of F. Scott Fitzgerald* and numerous articles on American and African American literature. He is also the literary executor of Ralph Ellison's estate and edited Ellison's posthumously published *Juneteenth* and *Flying Home and Other Stories*, as well as the Modern Library editions of *The Collected Essays of Ralph Ellison* and, with Albert Murray, of *Trading Twelves: The Selected Letters of Ralph Ellison and Albert Murray*.

University of Illinois Press
1325 South Oak Street
Champaign, IL 61820-6903
www.press.uillinois.edu